A Vindication
of the Rights of Woman

with Strictures on Political and Moral Subjects

Mary Wollstonecraft

with an introduction
for the Garland edition by
Gina Luria

Garland Publishing, Inc., New York & London

1974

Bibliographical note:

This facsimile has been made from a copy in the
Beinecke Library of Yale University
(Ngk95.G5.792.gbb)

Library of Congress Cataloging in Publication Data

Wollstonecraft, Mary, 1759-1797.
    A vindication of the rights of woman.

    (The Feminist controversy in England, 1788-1810)
    Reprint of the 1792 ed. printed by P. Edes for
Thomas and Andrews, Boston.
    Bibliography: p.
    1. Women--Social and moral questions. 2. Women's
rights. I. Title. II. Series.
HQ1596.W6 1974   301.41'2   74-8287
ISBN 0-8240-0891-X

Introduction

Mary Wollstonecraft (1759-1797) was born in
Yorkshire. The unhappiness of her family life soon
drove her to seek independence. Though she
attended day school in Yorkshire, her husband
William Godwin noted in his *Memoir* of her that
"it was not to any advantage of infant literature,
that she was indebted for her subsequent eminence." Her real education in the teachings of the
Enlightenment *philosophes* probably began during
her informal tutelage with Dr. Richard Price, a
leading radical Dissenter and a member of the
Dissenting colony at Newington Green where
Wollstonecraft and her sisters established a school
in 1783. In her biographical sketch of Wollstonecraft in *Shelley and his Circle* (Volume I, 1961),
Eleanor Nicholes suggests that one of the pivots of
Wollstonecraft's later thought — her belief that
"truth was to be discovered, or validated, by
searching into one's own experiences and thoughts

upon the meaning of those experiences" — derived from her connection with Price and the Rational Dissenters.

Certainly, Mary Wollstonecraft's erudition remains an enigma as much today as when her dazzling *Vindication of the Rights of Woman* was first published in 1792. Her contemporary, student, and close friend, the novelist Mary Hays, expressed the mystery of the genesis of Wollstonecraft's genius in an obituary written several years after her death.

> That something could be added respecting the earlier progress of a mind thus gifted, is to be wished rather than expected; the growth of intellect and the rise of ideas are rarely to be traced. On this subject we have no authority; but are inclined to suspect, that, like the majority of her sex, her studies were desultory and her attainments casual, pursued with little method, under the direction of her taste, or as her feelings took the lead.

Mary Wollstonecraft's personal and creative history continues to be the focus of critical attention. The works reprinted in the present series include three of her least recognized efforts. The first of these, *Thoughts on the Education of Daughters* (1787), is generally regarded as an immature, awkward, and stoic literary attempt. In his biography of Wollstonecraft (1951), Ralph Wardle describes the book as "obviously a pot-boiler scribbled off for the sake of the ten guineas which it would yield," but points to its interest for the student of Wollstonecraft's work in that "in some respects *Thoughts* foreshadowed Mary's later work in *The Rights of Woman*. . . . Her book shows that she was dissatisfied with the status of her sex, but that as yet she had not formulated her objections or traced them to the basic human rights to which women as well as men were entitled." The work is interesting as well for its reflection of Wollstonecraft's responses to contemporary strictures for young women.

Another early work, *Mary; A Fiction* (1788), is reprinted for its interest as Wollstonecraft's youthful attempt at novel writing and for its innovative content. As Wollstonecraft herself writes in the "Preface" to the book, "In delineating the Heroine of this Fiction, the Author attempts to develop a

character different from those generally por-
trayed." Most striking is her specific aim: "in an
artless tale, without episodes, the mind of a woman
who has thinking powers is displayed." As Eleanor
Nicholes suggests, there are several elements in
Mary which anticipated "much of the attitude and
tone of the Romantic period," during which
Shelley and his second wife, Mary Wollstonecraft's
daughter, Mary Wollstonecraft Godwin, flourished.
These elements include the "intensely personal"
style, the striking connection between nature and
conscious man (significantly represented here by
conscious *woman*), and the "portrait" of the
"content of consciousness" of the heroine's mind.

Although available in modern editions, a facsimile of the first edition of *The Rights of Woman*
is included in this series because of its central
and seminal place in the feminist controversy of
the 1790s. Women long before Wollstonecraft had
enunciated much of the content — and the spirit —
of her manifesto, but none had galvanized the
attention and the energies of a generation of
middle-class men and women as she did. No doubt
part of the reason for her success was the prevailing

"spirit of the age": the rights of woman, as Wollstonecraft elucidated them, are simply a logical extension of the eighteenth century's understanding of the Rights of Man. For the first time, the fundamental conceptions of democracy were extended to women by a woman; *A Vindication of the Rights of Woman* is a companion-piece to the *Declaration of Independence*. During a brief period, at least, Wollstonecraft's work — and her life — served as a bill of rights for some of her countrywomen and, for a long time afterwards, as a target for attack for many others.

Finally, Wollstonecraft's *Posthumous Works* (1798) are also reprinted for the light they shed on the directions of her maturer thought. Most interesting among the miscellaneous fragments collected are the "Hints" for a companion volume to *The Rights of Woman*, and an unfinished novel, *The Wrongs of Woman, or Maria*. The central metaphor of the work is, in Wollstonecraft's words, "the world [as] a vast prison, and women born slaves." Margaret George in *One Woman's 'Situation'* (1970) describes the book as "a fictional version of *The Rights of Woman*, a sweeping

INTRODUCTION

artistically designed account of women in the modern world." Eleanor Flexner in her biography of Wollstonecraft (1972) singles out as one of the strengths of the tale the character of Jemima, the heroine's servant in the insane asylum in which she has been legally incarcerated by her husband. Jemima, writes Flexner, "is something new in English fiction, the kind of character who did not really come to life till the advent of Dickens, a woman who has been hunted from hole to hole. . . . [Wollstonecraft] heralded the existence of the Jemimas and demanded that society recognize their plight and its responsibility for them."

It is the hope of the editor that, by making these lesser works of Wollstonecraft's available, a new aspect of her creative endeavors will come under closer scrutiny, a more imaginative, less doctrinal side that has been treated perhaps too casually.

Gina Luria

Select Bibliography

There are numerous studies of Mary Wollstonecraft in addition to the ones mentioned. Charles Hagelman, Jr., provides a partial bibliography in his edition of Wollstonecraft's *Rights of Woman* (1967).

Cameron, Kenneth Neill, ed. *Shelley and His Circle, 1773-1822*. Vols. 1 and 2. Cambridge, Mass.: Harvard University Press, 1961.

Flexner, Eleanor. *Mary Wollstonecraft*. New York: Coward, McCann & Geoghegan, 1972.

Luria, Gina. "Mary Hays: A Critical Biography." Unpub. Ph.D. dissertation, New York University, 1971.

Nixon, Edna. *Mary Wollstonecraft: Her Life and Times*. London: J. M. Dent & Sons Ltd., 1971.

Wardle, Ralph. *Mary Wollstonecraft: A Critical Biography*. A Bison Book, 1966.

VINDICATION

OF THE

RIGHTS OF WOMAN.

Mrs Mary Wollstonecraft,

From an Original Painting by Opie.

Published by Dean & Munday, 35, Threadneedle Street.

A

VINDICATION

OF THE

RIGHTS OF WOMAN:

WITH

STRICTURES

ON

POLITICAL AND MORAL SUBJECTS.

BY MARY WOLLSTONECRAFT.

PRINTED AT *BOSTON*,
BY PETER EDES FOR THOMAS AND ANDREWS,
FAUST'S Statue, No. 45, Newbury-Street.
MDCCXCII.

M. TALLEYRAND-PÉRIGORD,

SIR,

HAVING read with great pleasure a pamphlet, which you have lately published, on National Education, I dedicate this volume to you —the first dedication that I have ever written, to induce you to read it with attention; and, because I think that you will understand me, which I do not suppose many pert witlings will, who may ridicule the arguments they are unable to answer. But, Sir, I carry my respect for your understanding still farther: so far, that I am confident you will not throw my work aside, and hastily conclude that I am in the wrong, because you did not view the subject in the same light yourself. And, pardon my frankness, but I must observe, that you treated it in too cursory a manner, contented to consider it as it had been considered formerly, when the rights of man, not to advert to woman, were trampled on as chimerical—I call upon you, therefore, now

A 3   to

to weigh what I have advanced refpecting the rights of woman, and national education—and I call with the firm tone of humanity. For my arguments, Sir, are dictated by a difinterefted fpirit—I plead for my fex—not for myfelf. Independence I have long confidered as the grand blefling of life, the bafis of every virtue—and independence I will ever fecure by contracting my wants, though I were to live on a barren heath.

It is then an affection for the whole human race that makes my pen dart rapidly along to fupport what I believe to be the caufe of virtue : and the fame motive leads me earneftly to wifh to fee woman placed in a ftation in which fhe would advance, inftead of retarding, the progrefs of thofe glorious principles that give a fubftance to morality. My opinion, indeed, refpecting the rights and duties of woman, feems to flow fo naturally from thefe fimple principles, that I think it fcarcely poffible, but that fome of the enlarged minds who formed your admirable conftitution, will coincide with me.

In France there is undoubtedly a more general diffufion of knowledge than in any part of the European world, and I attribute it, in a great meafure, to the focial intercourfe which has long fubfifted between the fexes. It is true, I utter my fentiments with freedom, that in France the

very

very effence of fenfuality has been extracted to regale the voluptuary, and a kind of fentimental luft has prevailed, which, together with the fyftem of duplicity that the whole tenor of their political and civil government taught, have given a finifter fort of fagacity to the French character, properly termed fineffe, and a polifh of manners that injures the fubftance, by hunting fincerity out of fociety.——And, modefty, the faireft garb of virtue! has been more grofsly infulted in France than even in England, till their women have treated as *prudifh* that attention to decency, which brutes inftinctively obferve.

Manners and morals are fo nearly allied that they have often been confounded; but, though the former fhould only be the natural reflection of the latter, yet, when various caufes have produced factitious and corrupt manners, which are very early caught, morality becomes an empty name. The perfonal referve, and facred refpect for cleanlinefs and delicacy in domeftic life, which French women almoft defpife, are the graceful pillars of modefty; but, far from defpifing them, if the pure flame of patriotifm have reached their bofoms, they fhould labour to improve the morals of their fellow-citizens, by teaching men, not only to refpect modefty in women, but to acquire it themfelves, as the only way to merit their efteem.

A 4 Contending

Contending for the rights of woman, my main argument is built on this simple principle, that if she be not prepared by education to become the companion of man, she will stop the progress of knowledge, for truth must be common to all, or it will be inefficacious with respect to its influence on general practice. And how can woman be expected to co-operate unless she know why she ought to be virtuous? unless freedom strengthen her reason till she comprehend her duty, and see in what manner it is connected with her real good? If children are to be educated to understand the true principle of patriotism, their mother must be a patriot; and the love of mankind, from which an orderly train of virtues spring, can only be produced by considering the moral and civil interest of mankind; but the education and situation of woman, at present, shuts her out from such investigations.

In this work I have prouduced many arguments, which to me were conclusive, to prove that the prevailing notion respecting a sexual character was subversive of morality, and I have contended, that to render the human body and mind more perfect, chastity must more univerfally prevail, and that chastity will never be respected in the male world till the person of a woman is not, as it were, idolized, when little virtue or sense

embellish

embellifh it with the grand traces of mental beauty, or the interefting fimplicity of affection.

Confider, Sir, difpaffionately, thefe obfervations—for a glimpfe of this truth feemed to open before you when you obferved, ' that to fee one ' half of the human race excluded by the other ' from all participation of government, was a ' political phænomenon that, according to ab- ' ftract principles, it was impoffible to explain.' If fo, on what does your conftitution reft ? If the abftract rights of man will bear difcuffion and explanation, thofe of woman, by a parity of reafoning, will not fhrink from the fame teft : though a different opinion prevails in this country, built on the very arguments which you ufe to juftify the oppreffion of woman—prefcription.

Confider, I addrefs you as a legiflator, whether, when men contend for their freedom, and to be allowed to judge for themfelves refpecting their own happinefs, it be not inconfiftent and unjuft to fubjugate women, even though you firmly believe that you are acting in the manner beft calculated to promote their happinefs ? Who made man the exclufive judge, if woman partake with him the gift of reafon ?

In this ftyle, argue tyrants of every denomination, from the weak king to the weak father

of

of a family ; they are all eager to crufh reafon ;
yet always affert that they ufurp its throne only
to be ufeful. Do you not act a fimilar part,
when you *force* all women, by denying them
civil and political rights, to remain immured in
their families groping in the dark ? for furely,
Sir, you will not affert, that a duty can be binding which is not founded on reafon ? If indeed
this be their deftination, arguments may be
drawn from reafon : and thus auguftly fupported, the more underftanding women acquire, the
more they will be attached to their duty—comprehending it—for unlefs they comprehend it,
unlefs their morals be fixed on the fame immutable principle as thofe of man, no authority can
make them difcharge it in a virtuous manner.
They may be convenient flaves, but flavery will
have its conftant effect, degrading the mafter and
the abject dependent.

But, if women are to be excluded, without
having a voice, from a participation of the natural rights of mankind, prove firft, to ward off
the charge of injuftice and inconfiftency, that
they want reafon,—elfe this flaw in your NEW
CONSTITUTION, the firft conftitution founded
on reafon, will ever fhew that man muft, in
fome fhape, act like a tyrant, and tyranny, in
whatever part of fociety it rears its brazen front,
will ever undermine morality.   I

I have repeatedly afferted, and produced what appeared to me irrefragable arguments drawn from matters of fact, to prove my affertion, that women cannot, by force, be confined to domeftic concerns ; for they will, however ignorant, intermeddle with more weighty affairs, neglecting private duties only to difturb, by cunning tricks, the orderly plans of reafon which rife above their comprehenfion.

Befides, whilft they are only made to acquire perfonal accomplifhments, men will feek for pleafure in variety, and faithlefs hufbands will make faithlefs wives ; fuch ignorant beings, indeed, will be very excufable when, not taught to refpect public good, nor allowed any civil rights, they attempt to do themfelves juftice by retaliation.

The box of mifchief thus opened in fociety, what is to preferve private virtue, the only fecurity of public freedom and univerfal happinefs ?

Let there be then no coercion *eftablifhed* in fociety, and the common law of gravity prevailing, the fexes will fall into their proper places. And, now that more equitable laws are forming your citizens, marriage may become more facred : your young men may choofe wives from motives of affection, and your maidens allow love to root out vanity.

The

The father of a family will not then weaken his conftitution and debafe his fentiments, by vifiting the harlot, nor forget, in obeying the call of appetite, the purpofe for which it was implanted.   And, the mother will not neglect her children to practife the arts of coquetry, when fenfe and modefty fecure her the friendfhip of her hufband.

But, till men become attentive to the duty of a father, it is vain to expect women to fpend that time in their nurfery which they, 'wife in their generation,' choofe to fpend at their glafs ; for this exertion of cunning is only an inftinct of nature to enable them to obtain indirectly a little of that power of which they are unjuftly denied a fhare : for, if women are not permitted to enjoy legitimate rights, they will render both men and themfelves vicious, to obtain illicit privileges.

I wifh, Sir, to fet fome inveftigations of this kind afloat in France ; and fhould they lead to a confirmation of my principles, when your conftitution is revifed the Rights of Woman may be refpected, if it be fully proved that reafon calls for this refpect, and loudly demands JUSTICE for one half of the human race.

I am, SIR,

Your's refpectfully,

M. W.

ADVERTISEMENT.

WHEN I began to write this work, I divided it into three parts, suppofing that one volume would contain a full difcuffion of the arguments which feemed to me to rife naturally from a few fimple principles ; but frefh illuftrations occurring as I advanced, I now prefent only the firft part to the public.

Many fubjects, however, which I have curforily alluded to, call for particular inveftigation, efpecially the laws relative to women, and the confideration of their peculiar duties. Thefe will furnifh ample matter for a fecond volume, which in due time will be publifhed, to elucidate fome of the fentiments, and complete many of the fketches begun in the firft.

CONTENTS.

CHAP.

INTRODUCTION.

AFTER considering the historic page, and viewing the living world with anxious solicitude, the most melancholy emotions of sorrowful indignation have depressed my spirits, and I have sighed when obliged to confess, that either nature has made a great difference between man and man, or that the civilization which has hitherto taken place in the world has been very partial. I have turned over various books written on the subject of education, and patiently observed the conduct of parents and the management of schools; but what has been the result?—a profound conviction that the neglected education of my fellow-creatures is the grand source of the misery I deplore; and that women, in particular, are rendered weak and wretched by a variety of concurring causes, originating from one hasty conclusion. The conduct and manners of women, in fact, evidently prove that their minds are not in a healthy state; for, like the flowers which are planted in too rich a soil,

B   strength

ſtrength and uſefulneſs are ſacrificed to beauty ;
and the flaunting leaves, after having pleaſed a
faſtidious eye, fade, diſregarded on the ſtalk,
long before the ſeaſon when they ought to have
arrived at maturity.——One cauſe of this barren
blooming I attribute to a falſe ſyſtem of education, gathered from the books written on this
ſubject by men who, conſidering females rather
as women than human creatures, have been more
anxious to make them alluring miſtreſſes than
rational wives ; and the underſtanding of the
ſex has been ſo bubbled by this ſpecious homage, that the civilized women of the preſent
century, with a few exceptions, are only anxious
to inſpire love, when they ought to cheriſh a
nobler ambition, and by their abilities and virtues exact reſpect.

In a treatiſe, therefore, on female rights and
manners, the works which have been particularly written for their improvement muſt not be
overlooked ; eſpecially when it is aſſerted, in direct terms, that the minds of women are enfee-
bled by falſe refinement ; that the books of inſtruction, written by men of genius, have had
the ſame tendency as more frivolous productions ;
and that, in the true ſtyle of Mahometaniſm,
they are only conſidered as females, and not as a
part of the human ſpecies, when improvable rea-

son

son is allowed to be the dignified diftinction which raifes men above the brute creation, and puts a natural fceptre in a feeble hand.

Yet, becaufe I am a woman, I would not lead my readers to fuppofe that I mean violently to agitate the contefted queftion refpecting the equality or inferiority of the fex ; but as the fubject lies in my way, and I cannot pafs it over without fubjecting the main tendency of my reafoning to mifconftruction, I fhall ftop a moment to deliver, in a few words, my opinion.—In the government of the phyfical world it is obfervable that the female, in general, is inferior to the male. The male purfues, the female yields—this is the law of nature ; and it does not appear to be fufpended or abrogated in favour of woman. This phyfical fuperiority cannot be denied—and it is a noble prerogative ! But not content with this natural pre-eminence, men endeavour to fink us ftill lower, merely to render us alluring objects for a moment ; and women, intoxicated by the adoration which men, under the influence of their fenfes, pay them, do not feek to obtain a durable intereft in their hearts, or to become the friends of the fellow creatures who find amufement in their fociety.

I am aware of an obvious inference :—from every quarter have I heard exclamations againft

masculine

masculine women ; but where are they to be found ? If by this appellation men mean to inveigh against their ardour in hunting, shooting, and gaming, I shall most cordially join in the cry ; but if it be against the imitation of manly virtues, or, more properly speaking, the attainment of those talents and virtues, the exercise of which ennobles the human character, and which raise females in the scale of animal being, when they are comprehensively termed mankind ;— all those who view them with a philosophical eye must, I should think, wish with me, that they may every day grow more and more masculine.

This discussion naturally divides the subject. I shall first consider women in the grand light of human creatures, who, in common with men, are placed on this earth to unfold their faculties ; and afterwards I shall more particularly point out their peculiar designation.

I wish also to steer clear of an error which many respectable writers have fallen into ; for the instruction which has hither been addressed to women, has rather been applicable to *ladies*, if the little indirect advice, that is scattered through Sanford and Merton, be excepted ; but, addressing my sex in a firmer tone, I pay particular attention to those in the middle class, clafs, becaufe they appear to be in the moft natural ftate. Perhaps the feeds of falfe refinement, immorality, and vanity, have ever been fhed by the great. Weak, artificial beings, raifed above the common wants and affections of their race, in a premature unnatural manner, undermine the very foundation of virtue, and fpread corruption through the whole mafs of fociety! As a clafs of mankind they have the ftrongeft claim to pity; the education of the rich tends to render them vain and helplefs, and the unfolding mind is not ftrengthened by the practice of thofe duties which dignify the human character.—They only live to amufe themfelves, and by the fame law which in nature invariably produces certain effects, they foon only afford barren amufement.

But as I purpofe taking a feparate view of the different ranks of fociety, and of the moral character of women, in each, this hint is, for the prefent, fufficient; and I have only alluded to the fubject, becaufe it appears to me to be the very effence of an introduction to give a curfory account of the contents of the work it introduces.

My own fex, I hope, will excufe me, if I treat them like rational creatures, inftead of flat-

tering

tering their *fafcinating* graces, and viewing them
as if they were in a ftate of perpetual childhood,
unable to ftand alone.   I earneftly wifh to point
out in what true dignity and human happinefs
confifts—I wifh to perfuade women to endeavour to acquire ftrength, both of mind and body,
and to convince them that the foft phrafes, fuf-
ceptibility of heart, delicacy of feritiment, and
refinement of tafte, are almoft fynonimous with
epithets of weaknefs, and that thofe beings who
are only the objects of pity and that kind of
love, which has been termed its fifter, will foon
become objects of contempt.

Difmiffing then thofe pretty feminine phrafes,
which the men condefcendingly ufe to foften
our flavifh dependence, and defpifing that weak
elegancy of mind, exquifite fenfibility, and fweet
docility of manners, fuppofed to be the fexual
characteriftics of the weaker veffel, I wifh to
fhew that elegance is inferior to virtue, that the
firft object of laudable ambition is to obtain a
character as a human being, regardlefs of the
diftinction of fex ; and that fecondary views
fhould be brought to this fimple touchftone.

This is a rough fketch of my plan ; and
fhould I exprefs my conviction with the energetic emotions that I feel whenever I think of
the fubject, the dictates of experience and reflection

flection will be felt by some of my readers. Animated by this important object, I shall disdain to cull my phrases or polish my style ;—I aim at being useful, and sincerity will render me unaffected ; for, wishing rather to persuade by the force of my arguments, than dazzle by the elegance of my language, I shall not waste my time in rounding periods, nor in fabricating the turgid bombast of artificial feelings, which, coming from the head, never reach the heart.— I shall be employed about things, not words ! —and, anxious to render my sex more respectable members of society, I shall try to avoid that flowery diction which has slided from essays into novels, and from novels into familiar letters and conversation.

These pretty nothings—these caricatures of the real beauty of sensibility, dropping glibly from the tongue, vitiate the taste, and create a kind of sickly delicacy that turns away from simple unadorned truth ; and a deluge of false sentiments and overstretched feelings, stifling the natural emotions of the heart, render the domestic pleasures insipid, that ought to sweeten the exercise of those severe duties, which educate a rational and immortal being for a nobler field of action.

The

The education of women has, of late, been more attended to than formerly ; yet they are ftill reckoned a frivolous fex, and ridiculed or pitied by the writers who endeavor by fatire or inftruction to improve them. It is acknowledged that they fpend many of the firft years of their lives in acquiring a fmattering of accomplifhments : meanwhile ftrength of body and mind are facrificed to libertine notions of beauty, to the defire of eftablifhing themfelves,—the only way women can rife in the world,—by marriage. And this defire making mere animals of them, when they marry they act as fuch children may be expected to act :—they drefs ; they paint, and nickname God's creatures.—Surely thefe weak beings are only fit for a feraglio !—Can they govern a family, or take care of the poor babes whom they bring into the world ?

If then it can be fairly deduced from the prefent conduct of the fex, from the prevalent fondnefs for pleafure which takes place of ambition and thofe nobler paffions that open and enlarge the foul ; that the inftruction which women have received has only tended, with the conftitution of civil fociety, to render them infignificant objects of defire—mere propagators of fools !—if it can be proved that in aiming to accomplifh

accomplifh them, without cultivating their underftandings, they are taken out of their fphere
of duties, and made ridiculous and ufelefs when
the fhort-lived bloom of beauty is over*, I prefume that *rational* men will excufe me for endeavouring to perfuade them to become more
mafculine and refpectable.

Indeed the word mafculine is only a bugbear:
there is little reafon to fear that women will acquire too much courage or fortitude; for their
apparent inferiority with refpect to bodily
ftrength, muft render them, in fome degree, dependent on men in the various relations of life;
but why fhould it be increafed by prejudices
that give a fex to virtue, and confound fimple
truths with fenfual reveries?

Women are, in fact, fo much degraded by
miftaken notions of female excellence, that I do
not mean to add a paradox when I affert, that
this artificial weaknefs produces a propenfity to
tyrannize, and gives birth to cunning, the natural opponent of ftrength, which leads them
to play off thofe contemptible infantile airs that
undermine efteem even whilft they excite defire. Do not fofter thefe prejudices, and they
will

---

* A lively writer, I cannot recollect his name, afks what bufinefs
women turned of forty have to do in the world?

will naturally fall into their fubordinate, yet refpectable ftation, in life.

It feems fcarcely neceffary to fay, that I now fpeak of the fex in general. Many individuals have more fenfe than their male relatives ; and, as nothing preponderates where there is a con-ftant ftruggle for an equilibrium, without it has naturally more gravity, fome women gov-ern their hufbands without degrading them-felves, becaufe intellect will always govern.

VINDICATION

RIGHTS OF WOMAN.

PART I.

CHAP. I.

THE RIGHTS AND INVOLVED DUTIES OF MANKIND CONSIDERED.

IN the prefent ftate of fociety it appears neceffary to go back to firft principles in fearch of the
moft fimple truths, and to difpute with fome
prevailing prejudice every inch of ground. To
clear my way, I muft be allowed to afk fome
plain queftions, and the anfwers will probably
appear as unequivocal as the axioms on which
reafoning is built; though, when entangled with
various motives of action, they are formally contradicted, either by the words or conduct of men.

In what does man's pre-eminence over the
brute creation confift? The anfwer is as clear as
that a half is lefs than the whole; in Reafon.

What

What acquirement exalts one being above another ? Virtue ; we spontaneously reply.

For what purpose were the passions implanted ? That man by struggling with them might attain a degree of knowledge denied to the brutes ; whispers Experience.

Consequently the perfection of our nature and capability of happiness, must be estimated by the degree of reason, virtue, and knowledge, that distinguish the individual, and direct the laws which bind society : and that from the exercise of reason, knowledge and virtue naturally flow, is equally undeniable, if mankind be viewed collectively.

The rights and duties of man thus simplified, it seems almost impertinent to attempt to illustrate truths that appear so incontrovertible ; yet such deeply rooted prejudices have clouded reason, and such spurious qualities have assumed the name of virtues, that it is necessary to pursue the course of reason as it has been perplexed and involved in error, by various adventitious circumstances, comparing the simple axiom with casual deviations.

Men, in general, seem to employ their reason to justify prejudices, which they have imbibed, they cannot trace how, rather than to root them out. The mind must be strong that resolutely forms its own principles ; for a kind of intellectual cowardice prevails which makes many men shrink from the task, or only do it by halves. Yet the imperfect conclusions thus drawn, are frequently very plausible, because they are built on partial experience, on just, though narrow, views.

Going

Going back to firſt principles, vice ſkulks, with all its native deformity, from cloſe inveſtigation ; but a ſet of ſhallow reaſoners are always exclaiming that theſe arguments prove too much, and that a meaſure rotten at the core may be expedient. Thus expediency is continually contraſted with ſimple principles, till truth is loſt in a miſt of words, virtue, in forms, and knowledge rendered a ſounding nothing, by the ſpecious prejudices that aſſume its name.

That the ſociety is formed in the wiſeſt manner, whoſe conſtitution is founded on the nature of man, ſtrikes, in the abſtract, every thinking being ſo forcibly, that it looks like preſumption to endeavour to bring forward proofs ; though proof muſt be brought, or the ſtrong hold of preſcription will never be forced by reaſon ; yet to urge preſcription as an argument to juſtify the depriving men (or women) of their natural rights, is one of the abſurd ſophiſms which daily inſult common ſenſe.

The civilization of the bulk of the people of Europe is very partial ; nay, it may be made a queſtion, whether they have acquired any virtues in exchange for innocence, equivalent to the miſery produced by the vices that have been plaſtered over unſightly ignorance, and the freedom which has been bartered for ſplendid ſlavery. The deſire of dazzling by riches, the moſt certain pre-eminence that man can obtain, the pleaſure of commanding flattering ſycophants, and many other complicated low calculations of doting ſelf-love, have all contributed to overwhelm the maſs of mankind, and make liberty a convenient

venient handle for mock patriotifm. For whilſt
rank and titles are held of the utmoſt importance, before which Genius " muſt hide its diminiſhed head," it is, with a few exceptions, very
unfortunate for a nation when a man of abilities,
without rank or property, puſhes himſelf forward to notice.—Alas ! what unheard of miſery
have thouſands ſuffered to purchaſe a cardinal's
hat for an intriguing obſcure adventurer, who
longed to be ranked with princes, or lord it over
them by ſeizing the triple crown !

Such, indeed, has been the wretchedneſs that
has flowed from hereditary honours, riches, and
monarchy, that men of lively ſenſibility have almoſt uttered blaſphemy in order to juſtify the
diſpenſations of providence. Man has been held
out as independent of his power who made him,
or as a lawleſs planet darting from its orbit to
ſteal the celeſtial fire of reaſon ; and the vengeance of heaven, lurking in the ſubtile flame, ſufficiently puniſhed his temerity, by introducing
evil into the world.

Impreſſed by this view of the miſery and diſorder which pervaded ſociety, and fatigued with
joſtling againſt artificial fools, Rouſſeau became
enamoured of ſolitude, and, being at the ſame
time an optimiſt, he labours with uncommon
eloquence to prove that man was naturally a ſolitary animal. Miſled by his reſpect for the goodneſs of God, who certainly—for what man of
ſenſe and feeling can doubt it !—gave life only
to communicate happineſs, he conſiders evil as
poſitive, and the work of man ; not aware that
he

he was exalting one attribute at the expense of another, equally necessary to divine perfection.

Reared on a false hypothesis his arguments in favour of a state of nature are plausible, but unfound. I say unfound; for to assert that a state of nature is preferable to civilization, in all its possible perfection, is, in other words, to arraign supreme wisdom; and the paradoxical exclamation, that God has made all things right, and that evil has been introduced by the creature, whom he formed, knowing what he formed, is as unphilosophical as impious.

When that wise Being who created us and placed us here, saw the fair idea, he willed, by allowing it to be so, that the passions should unfold our reason, because he could see that present evil would produce future good. Could the helpless creature whom he called from nothing break loose from his providence, and boldly learn to know good by practising evil, without his permission? No.—How could that energetic advocate for immortality argue so inconsistently? Had mankind remained for ever in the brutal state of nature, which even his magic pen cannot paint as a state in which a single virtue took root, it would have been clear, though not to the sensitive unreflecting wanderer, that man was born to run the circle of life and death, and adorn God's garden for some purpose which could not easily be reconciled with his attributes.

But, if, to crown the whole, there were to be rational creatures produced, allowed to rise in excellence by the exercise of powers implanted for that purpose; if benignity itself thought fit to call

call

call into existence a creature above the brutes*, who could think and improve himself, why should that inestimable gift, for a gift it was, if man was so created as to have a capacity to rise above the state in which sensation produced brutal ease, be called, in direct terms, a curse? A curse it might be reckoned, if all our existence was bounded by our continuance in this world; for why should the gracious fountain of life give us passions, and the power of reflecting, only to imbitter our days and inspire us with mistaken notions of dignity? Why should he lead us from love of ourselves to the sublime emotions which the discovery of his wisdom and goodness excites, if these feelings were not set in motion to improve our nature, of which they make a part†, and render us capable of enjoying a more godlike portion of happiness? Firmly persuaded that no evil exists in the world that God did not design to take place, I build my belief on the perfection of God.

Rousseau exerts himself to prove that all *was* right originally: a crowd of authors that all *is* now right: and I, that all will *be* right.

But,

---

* Contrary to the opinion of anatomists, who argue by analogy from the formation of the teeth, stomach, and intestines, Rousseau will not allow a man to be a carnivorous animal. And, carried away from nature by a love of system, he disputes whether man be a gregarious animal, though the long and helpless state of infancy seems to point him out as particularly impelled to pair.

† What would you say to a mechanic whom you had desired to make a watch to point out the hour of the day, if, to shew his ingenuity, he added wheels to make it a repeater, &c. that perplexed the simple mechanism; should he urge, to excuse himself—had you not touched a certain spring, you would have known nothing of the matter, and that he should have amused himself by making *an experiment* without doing you any harm: would you not retort fairly upon him, by insisting that if he had not added those needless wheels and springs, the accident could not have happened?

But, true to his first position, next to a state of nature, Rousseau celebrates barbarism, and, apostrophizing the shade of Fabricius, he forgets that, in conquering the world, the Romans never dreamed of establishing their own liberty on a firm basis, or of extending the reign of virtue. Eager to support his system, he stigmatizes, as vicious, every effort of genius; and, uttering the apotheosis of savage virtues, he exalts those to demi-gods, who were scarcely human—the brutal Spartans, who, in defiance of justice and gratitude, sacrificed, in cold blood, the slaves who had shewn themselves men to rescue their oppressors.

Disgusted with artificial manners and virtues, the citizen of Geneva, instead of properly sifting the subject, threw away the wheat with the chaff, without waiting to inquire whether the evils which his ardent soul turned from indignantly, were the consequence of civilization or the vestiges of barbarism. He saw vice trampling on virtue, and the semblance of goodness taking place of the reality; he saw talents bent by power to sinister purposes, and never thought of tracing the gigantic mischief up to arbitrary power, up to the hereditary distinctions that clash with the mental superiority that naturally raises a man above his fellows. He did not perceive that regal power, in a few generations, introduces idiotism into the noble stem, and holds out baits to render thousands idle and vicious.

Nothing can set the regal character in a more contemptible point of view, than the various crimes that have elevated men to the supreme dignity.—Vile intrigues, unnatural crimes, and every vice that degrades our nature, have been the steps to this distinguished eminence ; yet millions of men have supinely allowed the nerveless limbs of the posterity of such rapacious prowlers to rest quietly on their ensanguined thrones*.

What but a pestilential vapour can hover over society when its chief director is only instructed in the invention of crimes, or the stupid routine of childish ceremonies ? Will men never be wise ?—will they never cease to expect corn from tares, and figs from thistles ?

It is impossible for any man, when the most favourable circumstances concur, to acquire sufficient knowledge and strength of mind to discharge the duties of a king, entrusted with uncontrouled power ; how then must they be violated when his very elevation is an insuperable bar to the attainment of either wisdom or virtue ; when all the feelings of a man are stifled by flattery, and reflection shut out by pleasure ! Surely it is madness to make the fate of thousands depend on the caprice of a weak fellow creature, whose very station sinks him *necessarily* below the meanest of his subjects ! But one power should not be thrown down to exalt another— for all power intoxicates weak man ; and its abuse proves, that the more equality there is established among men, the more virtue and happiness will reign in society. But this, and any similar maximum

im

---

* Could there be a greater insult offered to the rights of man than the beds of justice in France, when an infant was made the organ of the detestable Dubois !

im deduced from fimple reafon, raifes an outcry—the church or the ftate is in danger, if faith in the wifdom of antiquity is not implicit ; and they who, roufed by the fight of human calamity, dare to attack human authority, are reviled as defpifers of God, and enemies of man. Thefe are bitter calumnies, yet they reached one of the beft of men*, whofe afhes ftill preach peace, and whofe memory demands a refpectful paufe, when fubjects are difcuffed that lay fo near his heart.

After attacking the facred majefty of Kings, I fhall fcarcely excite furprife by adding my firm perfuafion that every profeffion, in which great fubordination of rank conftitutes its power, is highly injurious to morality.

A ftanding army, for inftance, is incompatible with freedom ; becaufe fubordination and rigour are the very finews of military difcipline ; and defpotifm is neceffary to give vigour to enterprizes that one will directs. A fpirit infpired by romantic notions of honour, a kind of morality founded on the fafhion of the age, can only be felt by a few officers, whilft the main body muft be moved by command, like the waves of the fea ; for the ftrong wind of authority pufhes the crowd of fubalterns forward, they fcarcely know or care why, with headlong fury.

Befides, nothing can be fo prejudicial to the morals of the inhabitants of country towns as the occafional refidence of a fet of idle fuperficial young men, whofe only occupation is gallantry, and whofe polifhed manners render vice more dangerous, by concealing its deformity under gay ornamental

C 2   drapery.

* Dr. Price.

drapery. An air of fashion, which is but a badge of slavery, and proves that the soul has not a strong individual character, awes simple country people into an imitation of the vices, when they cannot catch the slippery graces, of politeness. Every corps is a chain of despots, who, submitting and tyrannizing without exercising their reason, become dead weights of vice and folly on the community. A man of rank or fortune, sure of rising by interest, has nothing to do but to pursue some extravagant freak ; whilst the needy *gentleman*, who is to rise, as the phrase turns, by his merit, becomes a servile parasite or vile pander.

Sailors, the naval gentlemen, come under the same description, only their vices assume a different and a grosser cast. They are more positively indolent, when not discharging the ceremonials of their station ; whilst the insignificant fluttering of soldiers may be termed active idleness. More confined to the society of men, the former acquire a fondness for humour and mischievous tricks ; whilst the latter, mixing frequently with well-bred women, catch a sentimental cant.—But mind is equally out of the question, whether they indulge the horse-laugh, or polite simper.

May I be allowed to extend the comparison to a profession where more mind is certainly to be found ; for the clergy have superior opportunities of improvement, tho' subordination almost equally cramps their faculties ? The blind submission imposed at college to forms of belief serves as a novitiate to the curate, who must obsequiously respect the opinion of his rector or patron, if he

means

means to rife in his profeſſion. Perhaps there cannot be a more forcible contraſt than between the ſervile dependent gait of a poor curate and the courtly mien of a biſhop. And the reſpect and contempt they inſpire render the diſcharge of their ſeparate functions equally uſeleſs.

It is of great importance to obſerve that the character of every man is, in ſome degree, formed by his profeſſion. A man of ſenſe may only have a caſt of countenance that wears off as you trace his individuality, whilſt the weak, common man has ſcarcely ever any character, but what belongs to the body ; at leaſt, all his opinions have been ſo ſteeped in the vat conſecrated by authority, that the faint ſpirit which the grape of his own vine yields cannot be diſtinguiſhed.

Society, therefore, as it becomes more enlightened, ſhould be very careful not to eſtabliſh bodies of men who muſt neceſſarily be made fooliſh or vicious by the very conſtitution of their profeſſion.

In the infancy of ſociety, when men were juſt emerging out of barbariſm, chiefs and prieſts, touching the moſt powerful ſprings of ſavage conduct, hope and fear, muſt have had unbounded ſway. An ariſtocracy, of courſe, is naturally the firſt form of government. But, claſhing intereſts ſoon loſing their equipoiſe, a monarchy and hierarchy break out of the confuſion of ambitious ſtruggles, and the foundation of both is ſecured by feudal tenures. This appears to be the origin of monarchical and prieſtly power, and the dawn of civilization. But ſuch combuſtible materials cannot long be pent up ; and, getting

vent

vent in foreign wars and inteſtine inſurrections the people acquire ſome power in the tumult, which obliges their rulers to gloſs over their oppreſſion with a ſhew of right. Thus, as wars, agriculture, commerce, and literature, expand the mind, deſpots are compelled, to make covert corruption hold faſt the power which was formerly ſnatched by open force*. And this baneful lurking gangrene is moſt quickly ſpread by luxury and ſuperſtition, the ſure dregs of ambition. The indolent puppet of a court firſt becomes a luxurious monſter, or faſtidious ſenſualiſt, and then makes the contagion which his unnatural ſtate ſpread, the inſtrument of tyranny.

It is the peſtiferous purple which renders the progreſs of civilization a curſe, and warps the underſtanding, till men of ſenſibility doubt whether the expanſion of intellect produces a greater portion of happineſs or miſery. But the nature of the poiſon points out the antidote; and had Rouſſeau mounted one ſtep higher in his inveſtigation, or could his eye have pierced through the foggy atmoſphere, which he almoſt diſdained to breathe, his active mind would have darted forward to contemplate the perfection of man in the eſtabliſhment of true civilization, inſtead of taking his ferocious flight back to the night of ſenſual ignorance.

---

* Men of abilities ſcatter ſeeds that grow up and have a great influence on the forming opinion; and when once the public opinion preponderates, through the exertion of reaſon, the overthrow of arbitrary power is not very diſtant.

CHAP.

C H A P. II.

THE PREVAILING OPINION OF A SEXUAL
CHARACTER DISCUSSED.

To account for, and excuse the tyranny of man, many ingenious arguments have been brought forward to prove, that the two sexes, in the acquirement of virtue, ought to aim at attaining a very different character : or, to speak explicitly, women are not allowed to have sufficient strength of mind to acquire what really deserves the name of virtue. Yet it should seem, allowing them to have souls, that there is but one way appointed by Providence to lead *mankind* to either virtue or happiness.

If then women are not a swarm of ephemeron triflers, why should they be kept in ignorance under the specious name of innocence ? Men complain, and with reason, of the follies and caprices of our sex, when they do not keenly satirize our headstrong passions and groveling vices. Behold, I should answer, the natural effect of ignorance ! The mind will ever be unstable that has only prejudices to rest on, and the current will run with destructive fury when there are no barriers to break its force. Women are told from their infancy, and taught by the example of their mothers, that a little knowledge of human weakness, justly termed cunning, softness of temper, *outward* obedience, and a scrupulous attention

C 4 to

to a puerile kind of propriety, will obtain for them the protection of man ; and fhould they be beautiful, every thing elfe is needlefs, for, at leaft, twenty years of their lives.

Thus Milton defcribes our firft frail mother ; though when he tells us that women are formed for foftnefs and fweet attractive grace, I cannot comprehend his meaning, unlefs, in the true Mahometan ftrain, he meant to deprive us of fouls, and infinuate that we were beings only defigned by fweet attractive grace, and docile blind obedience, to gratify the fenfes of man when he can no longer foar on the wing of contemplation.

How grofsly do they infult us who thus advife us only to render ourfelves gentle, domeftic brutes ! For inftance, the winning foftnefs fo warmly, and frequently, recommended, that governs by obeying. What childifh expreffions, and how infignificant is the being—can it be an immortal one ? who will condefcend to govern by fuch finifter methods ! 'Certainly, fays Lord Bacon, 'man is of kin to the beafts by his body ; 'and if he be not of kin to God by his fpirit, he 'is a bafe and ignoble creature !' Men, indeed, appear to me to act in a very unphilofophical manner when they try to fecure the good conduct of women by attempting to keep them always in a ftate of childhood. Rouffeau was more confiftent when he wifhed to ftop the progrefs of reafon in both fexes, for if men eat of the tree of knowledge, women will come in for a tafte ; but, from the imperfect cultivation which their underftandings now receive, they only attain a knowledge of evil.

Children,

Children, I grant, should be innocent; but when the epithet is applied to men, or women, it is but a civil term for weakness. For if it be allowed that women were destined by Providence to acquire human virtues, and by the exercise of their understanding, that stability of character which is the firmest ground to rest our future hopes upon, they must be permitted to turn to the fountain of light, and not forced to shape their course by the twinkling of a mere satellite. Milton, I grant, was of a very different opinion; for he only bends to the indefeasible right of beauty, though it would be difficult to render two passages which I now mean to contrast, consistent. But into similar inconsistencies are great men often led by their senses.

> ' To whom thus Eve with *perfect beauty* adorn'd,
> ' My Author and Disposer, what thou bidst
> ' *Unargued* I obey; so God ordains;
> ' God is *thy law, thou mine* : to know no more
> ' Is Woman's *happiest* knowledge and her *praise*.'

These are exactly the arguments that I have used to children; but I have added, your reason is now gaining strength, and, till it arrives at some degree of maturity, you must look up to me for advice—then you ought to *think*, and only rely on God.

Yet in the following lines Milton seems to coincide with me; when he makes Adam thus expostulate with his Maker.

> ' Hast thou not made me here thy substitute,
> ' And these inferior far beneath me set?
> ' Among *unequals* what society

' Can

    ‘ Can fort, what harmony or true delight ?
    ‘ Which muſt be mutual, in proportion due
    ‘ Giv’n and receiv’d ; but in *diſparity*
    ‘ The one intenſe, the other ſtill remiſs
    ‘ Cannot well ſuit with either, but ſoon prove
    ‘ Tedious alike : of *fellowſhip* I ſpeak
    ‘ Such as I ſeek, fit to participate
    ‘ All rational delight—

In treating, therefore, of the manners of women, let us, diſregarding ſenſual arguments, trace what we ſhould endeavour to make them in order to co-operate, if the expreſſion be not too bold, with the ſupreme Being.

By individual education, I mean, for the ſenſe of the word is not preciſely defined, ſuch an attention to a child as will ſlowly ſharpen the ſenſes, form the temper, regulate the paſſions, as they begin to ferment, and ſet the underſtanding to work before the body arrives at maturity ; ſo that the man may only have to proceed, not to begin, the important taſk of learning to think and reaſon.

To prevent any miſconſtruction, I muſt add, that I do not believe that a private education can work the wonders which ſome ſanguine writers have attributed to it. Men and women muſt be educated, in a great degree, by the opinions and manners of the ſociety they live in. In every age there has been a ſtream of popular opinion that has carried all before it, and given a family character, as it were, to the century. It may then fairly be inferred, that, till ſociety be differently conſtituted, much cannot be expected from education. It is, however, ſufficient for

my

my prefent purpofe to affert, that whatever effect circumftances have on the abilities, every being may become virtuous by the exercife of its
own reafon ; for if but one being was created
with vicious inclinations, that is pofitively bad,
what can fave us from atheifm ? or if we worfhip a God, is not that God a devil ?

Confequently, the moft perfect education, in
my opinion, is fuch an exercife of the underftanding as is beft calculated to ftrengthen the
body and form the heart. Or, in other words,
to enable the individual to attain fuch habits of
virtue as will render it independent. In fact, it
is a farce to call any being virtuous whofe virtues do not refult from the exercife of its own
reafon. This was Rouffeau's opinion refpecting
men I extend it to women, and confidently affert that they have been drawn out of their
fphere by falfe refinement, and not by an endeavour to acquire mafculine qualities. Still the
regal homage which they receive is fo intoxicating, that till the manners of the times are changed, and formed on more reafonable principles, it
may be impoffible to convince them that the il-
legitimate power which they obtain, by degrading themfelves, is a curfe, and that they muft
return to nature and equality, if they wifh to fecure the placid fatisfaction that unfophifticated
affections impart. But for this epoch we muft
wait—wait, perhaps, till kings and nobles, enlightened by reafon, and, preferring the real dignity of man to childifh ftate, throw off their
gaudy hereditary trappings : and if then women
do not refign the arbitrary power of beauty—

they

they will prove that they have *lefs* mind than man.

I may be accufed of arrogance; ftill I muft declare, what I firmly believe, that all the writ-ers who have written on the fubject of female education and manners, from Rouffeau to Dr. Gregory, have contributed to render women more artificial, weak characters, than they would otherwife have been; and, confequently, more ufelefs members of fociety, I might have expref-fed this conviction in a lower key; but I am afraid it would have been the whine of affecta-tion, and not the faithful expreffion of my feel-ings; of the clear refult, which experience and reflection have led me to draw. When I come to that divifion of the fubject, I fhall advert to the paffages that I more particularly difapprove of, in the works of the authors I have juft allud-ed to; but it is firft neceffary to obferve, that my objection extends to the whole purport of thofe books, which tend, in my opinion, to dé-grade one half of the human fpecies, and render women pleafing at the expenfe of every folid virtue.

Though, to reafon on Rouffeau's ground, if man did attain a degree of perfection of mind when his body arrived at maturity, it might be proper, in order to make a man and his wife *one*, that fhe fhould rely entirely on his underftand-ing; and the graceful ivy, clafping the oak that fupported it, would form a whole in which ftrength and beauty would be equally confpicu-ous. But, alas! hufbands, as well as their help-mates, are often only overgrown children; nay,

thanks

thanks to early debauchery, scarcely men in their outward form—and if the blind lead the blind, one need not come from heaven to tell us the consequence.

Many are the causes that, in the present corrupt state of society, contribute to enslave women by cramping their underftandings and sharpening their senses. One, perhaps, that silently does more mischief than all the rest, is their disregard of order.

To do every thing in an orderly manner, is a most important precept, which women, who, generally speaking, receive only a disorderly kind of education, seldom attend to with that degree of exactness, that men, who from their infancy are broken into method, obferve. This negligent kind of guefs-work, for what other epithet can be used to point out the random exertions of a fort of inftinctive common sense, never brought to the teft of reason? prevents their generalizing matters of fact—so they do to-day, what they did yesterday, merely because they did it yesterday.

This contempt of the underftanding in early life has more baneful confequences than is commonly fuppofed; for the little knowledge which women of ftrong minds attain, is, from various circumftances, of a more defultory kind than the knowledge of men, and it is acquired more by fheer obfervations on real life, than from comparing what has been individually obferved with the refults of experience generalized by fpeculation. Led by their dependent fituation and domeftic employments more into fociety, what they

learn

learn is rather by fnatches; and as learning is with them, in general, only a fecondary thing, they do not purfue any one branch with that perfevering ardour neceffary to give vigour to the faculties, and clearnefs to the judgment. In the prefent ftate of fociety, a little learning is re-quired to fupport the character of a gentleman; and boys are obliged to fubmit to a few years of difcipline. But in the education of women, the cultivation of the underftanding is always fubor-dinate to the acquirement of fome corporeal ac-complifhment; even while enervated by confine-ment and falfe notions of modefty, the body is prevented from attaining that grace and beauty which relaxed half-formed limbs never exhibit. Befides, in youth their faculties are not brought forward by emulation; and having no ferious fcientific ftudy, if they have natural fagacity it is turned too foon on life and manners. They dwell on effects, and modifications, without tracing them back to caufes; and complicated rules to adjuft behaviour, are a weak fubftitute for fim-ple principles.

As a proof that education gives this appear-ance of weaknefs to females, we may inftance the example of military men, who are, like them, fent into the world before their minds have been ftored with knowledge or fortified by principles. The confequences are fimilar; foldiers acquire a little fuperficial knowledge, fnatched from the muddy current of converfation, and, from conti-nually mixing with fociety, they gain, what is termed a knowledge of the world; and this ac-quaintance with manners and cuftoms has fre-

quently

quently been confounded with a knowledge of the human heart. But can the crude fruit of casual observation, never brought to the test of judgment, formed by comparing speculation and experience, deserve such a distinction? Soldiers, as well as women, practise the minor virtues with punctilious politeness. Where is then the sexual difference, when the education has been the same? All the difference that I can discern, arises from the superior advantage of liberty, which enables the former to see more of life.

It is wandering from my present subject, perhaps, to make a political remark; but, as it was produced naturally by the train of my reflections, I shall not pass it silently over.

Standing armies can never consist of resolute, robust men; they may be well disciplined machines, but they will seldom contain men under the influence of strong passions, or with very vigorous faculties. And as for any depth of understanding, I will venture to affirm, that it is as rarely to be found in the army as amongst women; and the cause, I maintain, is the same. It may be further observed, that officers are also particularly attentive to their persons, fond of dancing, crowded rooms, adventures, and ridicule*. Like the *fair* sex, the business of their lives is gallantry —— They were taught to please, and they only live to please. Yet they do not lose their rank in the distinction of sexes, for they are still reckoned superior to women, though in what their superi-

riority

---

* Why should women be censured with petulent acrimony, because they seem to have a passion for a scarlet coat? Has not education placed them more on a level with soldiers than any other class of men?

riority confifts, beyond what I have juft mentioned, it is difficult to difcover.

The great misfortune is this, that they both
acquire manners before morals, and a knowledge
of life before they have, from reflection, any acquaintance with the grand ideal outline of human nature. The confequence is natural; fatif-
fied with common nature, they become a prey
to prejudices, and taking all their opinions on
credit, they blindly fubmit to authority. So
that, if they have any fenfe, it is a kind of inftinctive glance, that catches proportions, and decides with refpect to manners ; but fails when
arguments are to be purfued below the furface,
or opinions analyzed.

May not the fame remark be applied to women ? Nay, the argument may be carried ftill
further, for they are both thrown out of a ufeful ftation by the unnatural diftinctions eftablifhed in civilized life. Riches and hereditary
honours have made cyphers of women to give
confequence to the numerical figure ; and idlenefs has produced a mixture of gallantry and defpotifm into fociety, which leads the very men
who are the flaves of their miftreffes to tyrannize
over their fifters, wives, and daughters. This
is only keeping them in rank and file, it is true.
Strengthen the female mind by enlarging it, and
there will be an end to blind obedience ; but, as
blind obedience is ever fought for by power, tyrants and fenfualifts are in the right when they
endeavour to keep women in the dark, becaufe
the former only want flaves, and the latter a
play-thing. The fenfualift, indeed, has been the

most

most dangerous of tyrants, and women have been duped by their lovers, as princes by their minifters, whilft dreaming that they reigned over them.

I now principally allude to Roufſeau, for his character of Sophia is, undoubtedly, a captivating one, though it appears to me groſsly unnatural ; however, it is not the ſuperſtructure, but the foundation of her character, the principles on which her education was built, that I mean to attack ; nay, warmly as I admire the genius of that able writer, whoſe opinions I ſhall often have occaſion to cite, indignation always takes place of admiration, and the rigid frown of inſulted virtue effaces the ſmile of complacency, which his eloquent periods are wont to raiſe, when I read his voluptuous reveries. Is this the man, who, in his ardour for virtue, would baniſh all the ſoft arts of peace, and almoſt carry us back to Spartan diſcipline ? Is this the man who delights to paint the uſeful ſtruggles of paſſion, the triumphs of good diſpoſition, and the heroic flights which carry the glowing ſoul out of itſelf ?—How are theſe mighty ſentiments lowered when he deſcribes the pretty foot and enticing airs of his little favourite ! But, for the preſent I wave the ſubject, and, inſtead of ſeverely reprehending the tranſient effuſions of overweening ſenſibility, I ſhall only obſerve, that whoever has caſt a benevolent eye on ſociety, muſt often have been gratified by the ſight of humble mutual love, not dignified by ſentiment, nor ſtrengthened by a union in intellectual purſuits. The domeſtic trifles of the day have afforded mat-

D   ter

ter for cheerful converse, and innocent caresses have softened toils which did not require great exercise of mind or stretch of thought : yet, has not the sight of this moderate felicity excited more tenderness than respect ? An emotion similar to what we feel when children are playing, or animals sporting*, whilst the contemplation of the noble struggles of suffering merit has raised admiration, and carried our thoughts to that world where sensation will give place to reason.

Women are, therefore, to be considered either as moral beings, or so weak that they must be entirely subjected to the superior faculties of men.

Let us examine this question. Rousseau declares that a woman should never, for a moment, feel herself independent, that she should be governed by fear to exercise her *natural* cunning, and made a coquetish slave in order to render her a more alluring object of desire, a *sweeter* companion to man, whenever he chooses to relax himself. He carries the arguments, which he pretends to draw from the indications of nature, still further, and insinuates that truth and fortitude, the corner stones of all human virtue, should be cultivated with certain restrictions, because, with respect to the female character, obedience is the grand lesson which ought to be impressed with unrelenting rigour.   What

* Similar feelings has Milton's pleasing picture of paradisiacal happiness ever raised in my mind ; yet, instead of envying the lovely pair, I have, with conscious dignity, or Satanic pride, turned to hell for sublimer objects. In the same style, when viewing some noble monument of human art, I have traced the emanation of the Deity in the order I admired, till, descending from that giddy height, I have caught myself contemplating the grandest of all human sights ;—for fancy quickly placed, in some solitary recess, an outcast of fortune, rising superior to passion and discontent.

What nonsense! when will a great man arise with sufficient strength of mind to puff away the fumes which pride and sensuality have thus spread over the subject! If women are by nature inferior to men, their virtues must be the same in quality, if not in degree, or virtue is a relative idea; consequently, their conduct should be founded on the same principles, and have the same aim.

Connected with man as daughters, wives, and mothers, their moral character may be estimated by their manner of fulfilling those simple duties; but the end, the grand end of their exertions should be to unfold their own faculties and acquire the dignity of conscious virtue. They may try to render their road pleasant; but ought never to forget, in common with man, that life yields not the felicity which can satisfy an immortal soul. I do not mean to insinuate, that either sex should be so lost in abstract reflections or distant views, as to forget the affections and duties that lie before them, and are, in truth, the means appointed to produce the fruit of life; on the contrary, I would warmly recommend them, even while I assert, that they afford most satisfaction when they are considered in their true subordinate light.

Probably the prevailing opinion, that woman was created for man, may have taken its rise from Moses's poetical story; yet, as very few, it is presumed, who have bestowed any serious thought on the subject, ever supposed that Eve was, literally speaking, one of Adam's ribs, the deduction must be allowed to fall to the ground;

or,

or, only be so far admitted as it proves that man, from the remotest antiquity, found it convenient to exert his strength to subjugate his companion, and his invention to shew that she ought to have her neck bent under the yoke; because she, as well as the brute creation, was created to do his pleasure.

Let it not be concluded that I wish to invert the order of things; I have already granted, that, from the constitution of their bodies, men seem to be designed by Providence to attain a greater degree of virtue. I speak collectively of the whole sex; but I see not the shadow of a reason to conclude that their virtues should differ in respect to their nature. In fact, how can they, if virtue has only one eternal standard? I must therefore, if I reason consequentially, as strenuously maintain that they have the same simple direction, as that there is a God.

It follows then that cunning should not be opposed to wisdom, little cares to great exertions, nor insipid softness, varnished over with the name of gentleness, to that fortitude which grand views alone can inspire.

I shall be told that woman would then lose many of her peculiar graces, and the opinion of a well known poet might be quoted to refute my unqualified assertion. For Pope has said, in the name of the whole male sex,

'   Yet ne'er so sure our passion to create,
'   As when she touch'd the brink of all we hate.'

In what light this sally places men and women, I shall leave to the judicious to determine; meanwhile

meanwhile I ſhall content myſelf with obſerving, that I cannot diſcover why, unleſs they are mortal, females ſhould always be degraded by being made ſubſervient to love or luſt.

To ſpeak diſreſpectfully of love is, I know, high treaſon againſt ſentiment and fine feelings ; but I wiſh to ſpeak the ſimple language of truth, and rather to addreſs the head than the heart. To endeavour to reaſon love out of the world, would be to out Quixote Cervantes, and equally offend againſt common ſenſe ; but an endeavour to reſtrain this tumultuous paſſion, and to prove that it ſhould not be allowed to dethrone ſuperior powers, or to uſurp the ſceptre which the underſtanding ſhould ever coolly wield, appears leſs wild.

Youth is the ſeaſon for love in both ſexes ; but in thoſe days of thoughtleſs enjoyment proviſion ſhould be made for the more important years of life, when reflection takes place of ſenſation. But Rouſſeau, and moſt of the male writers who have followed his ſteps, have warmly inculcated that the whole tendency of female education ought to be directed to one point :— to render them pleaſing.

Let me reaſon with the ſupporters of this opinion who have any knowledge of human nature, do they imagine that marriage can eradicate the habitude of life? The woman who has only been taught to pleaſe will ſoon find that her charms are oblique ſunbeams, and that they cannot have much effect on her huſband's heart when they are ſeen every day, when the ſummer is paſſed and gone. Will ſhe then have ſufficient native energy to

look

look to herself for comfort, and cultivate h
dormant faculties? or, is it not more rational to
expect that she will try to please other men; and,
in the emotions raised by the expectation of new
conquests, endeavour to forget the mortification
her love or pride has received? When the hufband ceases to be a lover—and the time will inevitably come, her defire of pleafing will then
grow languid, or become a spring of bitterness;
and love, perhaps, the moft evanescent of all paffions, gives place to jealoufy or vanity.

I now fpeak of women who are reftrained by
principle or prejudice; fuch women, though they
would fhrink from an intrigue with real abhorrence, yet, neverthelefs, wifh to be convinced by
the homage of gallantry that they are cruelly
neglected by their hufbands; or, days and weeks
are fpent in dreaming of the happinefs enjoyed
by congenial fouls, till the health is undermined
and the fpirits broken by difcontent. How
then can the great art of pleafing be fuch a neceffary ftudy; it is only ufeful to a miftrefs; the
chafte wife, and ferious mother, fhould only confider her power to pleafe as the polifh of her virtues, and the affection of her hufband as one of
the comforts that render her tafk lefs difficult and
her life happier.—But, whether fhe be loved or
neglected, her firft wifh fhould be to make herfelf refpectable, and not to rely for all her happinefs on a being fubject to like infirmities with
herfelf.

The amiable Dr. Gregory fell into a fimilar
error. I refpect his heart; but entirely difapprove of his celebrated Legacy to his Daughters.   He

He advises them to cultivate a fondness for dress, because a fondness for dress, he asserts, is natural to them. I am unable to comprehend what either he or Rousseau mean, when they frequently use this indefinite term. If they told us that in a pre-existent state the soul was fond of dress, and brought this inclination with it into a new body, I should listen to them with a half smile, as I often do when I hear a rant about innate elegance.—But if he only meant to say that the exercise of the faculties will produce this fondness—I deny it.—It is not natural; but arises, like false ambition in men, from a love of power.

Dr. Gregory goes much further; he actually recommends dissimulation, and advises an innocent girl to give the lie to her feelings, and not dance with spirit, when gaiety of heart would make her feet eloquent without making her gestures immodest. In the name of truth and common sense, why should not one woman acknowledge that she can take more exercise than another? or, in other words, that she has a sound constitution; and why, to damp innocent vivacity, is she darkly to be told that men will draw conclusions which she little thinks of? Let the libertine draw what inference he pleases; but, I hope, that no sensible mother will restrain the natural frankness of youth by instilling such indecent cautions. Out of the abundance of the heart the mouth speaketh; and a wiser than Solomon hath said, that the heart should be made clean, and not trivial ceremonies observed, which

it

it is not very difficult to fulfil with scrupulous exactness when vice reigns in the heart.

Women ought to endeavour to purify their heart ; but can they do so when their uncultivated understandings make them entirely dependent on their senses for employment and amusement, when no noble pursuit sets them above the little vanities of the day, or enables them to curb the wild emotions that agitate a reed over which every passing breeze has power ? To gain the affections of a virtuous man is affectation necessary ? Nature has given woman a weaker frame than man ; but, to ensure her husband's affections, must a wife, who by the exercise of her mind and body whilst she was discharging the duties of a daughter, wife, and mother, has allowed her constitution to retain its natural strength, and her nerves a healthy tone, is she, I say, to condescend to use art and feign a sickly delicacy in order to secure her husband's affection ? Weakness may excite tenderness, and gratify the arrogant pride of man ; but the lordly caresses of a protector will not gratify a noble mind that pants for, and deserves to be respected. Fondness is a poor substitute for friendship !

In a seraglio, I grant, that all these arts are necessary ; the epicure must have his palate tickled, or he will sink into apathy ; but have women so little ambition as to be satisfied with such a condition ? Can they supinely dream life away in the lap of pleasure, or the languor of weariness, rather than assert their claim to pursue reasonable pleasures and render themselves conspicuous by practising the virtues which dignify mankind ? Surely
she

she has not an immortal soul who can loiter life away merely employed to adorn her person, that she may amuse the languid hours, and soften the cares of a fellow-creature who is willing to be enlivened by her smiles and tricks, when the serious business of life is over.

Besides, the woman who strengthens her body and exercises her mind will, by managing her family and practising various virtues, become the friend, and not the humble dependent of her husband, and if she deserves his regard by possessing such substantial qualities, she will not find it necessary to conceal her affection, nor to pretend to an unnatural coldness of constitution to excite her husband's passions. In fact, if we revert to history, we shall find that the women who have distinguished themselves have neither been the most beautiful nor the most gentle of their sex.

Nature, or, to speak with strict propriety, God, has made all things right; but man has sought him out many inventions to mar the work. I now allude to that part of Dr. Gregory's treatise, where he advises a wife never to let her husband know the extent of her sensibility or affection. Voluptuous precaution, and as ineffectual as absurd.—Love, from its very nature, must be transitory. To seek for a secret that would render it constant, would be as wild a search as for the philosopher's stone, or the grand panacea : and the discovery would be equally useless, or rather pernicious, to mankind. The most holy band of society is friendship. It has been well said, by a shrewd satirist, " that rare as true love is, true friendship is still rarer."

This

This is an obvious truth, and the cause not lying deep, will not elude a slight glance of inquiry.

Love, the common passion, in which chance and sensation take place of choice and reason, is, in some degree, felt by the mass of mankind; for it is not necessary to speak, at present, of the emotions that rise above or sink below love. This passion, naturally increased by suspense and difficulties, draws the mind out of its accustomed state, and exalts the affections; but the security of marriage, allowing the fever of love to subside, a healthy temperature is thought insipid, only by those who have not sufficient intellect to substitute the calm tenderness of friendship, the confidence of respect, instead of blind admiration, and the sensual emotions of fondness.

This is, must be, the course of nature :—friendship or indifference inevitably succeeds love. —And this constitution seems perfectly to harmonize with the system of government which prevails in the moral world. Passions are spurs to action, and open the mind; but they sink into mere appetites, become a personal and momentary gratification, when the object is gained, and the satisfied mind rests in enjoyment. The man who had some virtue whilst he was struggling for a crown, often becomes a voluptuous tyrant when it graces his brow; and, when the lover is not lost in the husband, the dotard, a prey to childish caprices, and fond jealousies, neglects the serious duties of life, and the caresses which should excite confidence in his children are lavished on the overgrown child, his wife.

In

In order to fulfil the duties of life, and to be able to purfue with vigour the various employments which form the moral character, a mafter and miftrefs of a family ought not to continue to love each other with paffion. I mean to fay, that they ought not to indulge thofe emotions which difturb the order of fociety, and engrofs the thoughts that fhould be otherwife employed. The mind that has never been engroffed by one object wants vigour—if it can long be fo, it is weak.

A miftaken education, a narrow, uncultivated mind, and many fexual prejudices, tend to make women more conftant than men ; but, for the prefent, I fhall not touch on this branch of the fubject. I will go ftill further, and advance, without dreaming of a paradox, that an unhappy marriage is often very advantageous to a family, and that the neglected wife is, in general, the beft mother. And this would almoft always be the confequence if the female mind was more enlarged : for, it feems to be the common difpenfation of Providence, that what we gain in prefent enjoyment fhould be deducted from the treafure of life, experience ; and that when we are gathering the flowers of the day and revelling in pleafure, the folid fruit of toil and wifdom fhould not be caught at the fame time. The way lies before us, we muft turn to the right or left ; and he who will pafs life away in bounding from one pleafure to another, muft not complain if he neither acquires wifdom nor refpectability of character.

Suppofing,

Suppofing, for a moment, that the foul is not immortal, and that man was only created for the prefent fcene,—I think we fhould have reafon to complain that love, infantile fondnefs, ever grew infipid and pallid upon the fenfe. Let us eat, drink, and love, for to-morrow we die, would be, in fact, the language of reafon, the morality of life ; and who but a fool would part with a reality for a fleeting fhadow ? But, if awed by ob-ferving the improvable powers of the mind, we difdain to confine our wifhes or thoughts to fuch a comparatively mean field of action ; that only appears grand and important, as it is connected with a boundlefs profpect and fublime hopes, what neceffity is there for falfehood in conduct, and why muft the facred majefty of truth be vio-lated to detain a deceitful good that faps the very foundation of virtue ? Why muft the female mind be tainted by coquetifh arts to gratify the fenfu-alift, and prevent love from fubfiding into friend-fhip, or compaffionate tendernefs, when there are not qualities on which friendfhip can be built ? Let the honeft heart fhew itfelf, and *reafon* teach paffion to fubmit to neceffity ; or, let the dig-nified purfuit of virtue and knowledge raife the mind above thofe emotions which rather imbit-ter than fweeten the cup of life, when they are not reftrained within due bounds.

I do not mean to allude to the romantic paf-fion, which is the concomitant of genius.—Who can clip its wing ? But that grand paffion not proportioned to the puny enjoyments of life, is only true to the fentiment, and feeds on itfelf. The paffions which have been celebrated for
their

their durability have always been unfortunate. They have acquired strength by absence and constitutional melancholy.—The fancy has hovered round a form of beauty dimly seen—but familiarity might have turned admiration into disgust; or, at least, into indifference, and allowed the imagination leisure to start fresh game. With perfect propriety, according to this view of things, does Rousseau make the mistress of his soul, Eloisa, love St. Preux, when life was fading before her; but this is no proof of the immortality of the passion.

Of the same complexion is Dr. Gregory's advice respecting delicacy of sentiment, which he advises a woman not to acquire, if she has determined to marry. This determination, however, perfectly consistent with his former advice, he calls *indelicate*, and earnestly persuades his daughters to conceal it, though it may govern their conduct: as if it were indelicate to have the common appetites of human nature.

Noble morality! and consistent with the cautious prudence of a little soul that cannot extend its views beyond the present minute division of existence. If all the faculties of woman's mind are only to be cultivated as they respect her dependence on man; if, when she obtains a husband she has arrived at her goal, and meanly proud is satisfied with such a paltry crown, let her grovel contentedly, scarcely raised by her employments above the animal kingdom; but, if she is struggling for the prize of her high calling, let her cultivate her understanding without stopping to consider what character the husband

may

may have whom she is deftined to marry. Let her only determine, without being too anxious about prefent happinefs, to acquire the qualities that ennoble a rational being, and a rough inelegant hufband may fhock her tafte without deftroying her peace of mind. She will not model her foul to fuit the frailties of her companion, but to bear with them : his character may be a trial, but not an impediment to virtue.

If Dr. Gregory confined his remark to romantic expectations of conftant love and congenial feelings, he fhould have recollected that experience will banifh what advice can never make us ceafe to wifh for, when the imagination is kept alive at the expenfe of reafon.

I own it frequently happens that women who have foftered a romantic unnatural delicacy of feeling, wafte their * lives in *imagining* how happy they fhould have been with a hufband who could love them with a fervid increafing affection every day, and all day. But they might as well pine married as fingle—and would not be a jot more unhappy with a bad hufband than longing for a good one. That a proper education ; or, to fpeak with more precifion, a well ftored mind, would enable a woman to fupport a fingle life with dignity, I grant ; but that fhe fhould avoid cultivating her tafte, left her hufband fhould occafionally fhock it, is quitting a fubftance for a fhadow. To fay the truth, I do not know of what ufe is an improved tafte, if the individual is not rendered more independent of the cafualties of life ; if new fources of enjoyment, only dependent on the folitary operations of the mind, are not

* For example, the kind of novelifts.

not opened. People of taſte, married or ſingle, without diſtinction, will ever be diſguſted by various things that touch not leſs obſerving minds. On this concluſion the argument muſt not be allowed to hinge; but in the whole ſum of enjoyment is taſte to be denominated a bleſſing?

The queſtion is, whether it procures moſt pain or pleaſure? The anſwer will decide the propriety of Dr. Gregory's advice, and ſhew how abſurd and tyrannic it is thus to lay down a ſyſtem of ſlavery; or to attempt to educate moral beings by any other rules than thoſe deduced from pure reaſon, which apply to the whole ſpecies.

Gentleneſs of manners, forbearance and long-ſuffering, are ſuch amiable Godlike qualities, that in ſublime poetic ſtrains the Deity has been inveſted with them; and, perhaps no repreſentation of his goodneſs ſo ſtrongly faſtens on the human affections as thoſe that repreſent him abundant in mercy and willing to pardon. Gentleneſs, conſidered in this point of view, bears on its front all the characteriſtics of grandeur, combined with the winning graces of condeſcenſion; but what a different aſpect it aſſumes when it is the ſubmiſſive demeanour of dependence, the ſupport of weakneſs that loves, becauſe it wants protection; and is forbearing, becauſe it muſt ſilently endure injuries; ſmiling under the laſh at which it dare not ſnarl. Abject as this picture appears, it is the portrait of an accompliſhed woman, according to the received opinion of female excellence, ſeparated by ſpecious reaſoners from human excellence. Or, they * kindly reſtore the rib,

* Vide Rouſſeau, and Swedenborg.

rib, and make one moral being of a man and woman; not forgetting to give her all the ' submiffive charms.'

How women are to exift in that ftate where there is to be neither marrying nor giving in marriage, we are not told.—For though moralifts have agreed that the tenor of life feems to prove that *man* is prepared by various circumftances for a future ftate, they conftantly concur in advifing *woman* only to provide for the prefent. Gentlenefs, docility, and a fpaniel-like affection are, on this ground, confiftently recommended as the cardinal virtues of the fex; and, difregarding the arbitrary economy of nature, one writer has declared that it is mafculine for a woman to be melancholy. She was created to be the toy of man, his rattle, and it muft jingle in his ears whenever, difmiffing reafon, he choofes to be amufed.

To recommend gentlenefs, indeed, on a broad bafis is ftrictly philofophical. A frail being fhould labour to be gentle. But when forbearance confounds right and wrong, it ceafes to be a virtue; and, however convenient it may be found in a companion—that companion will ever be confidered as an inferior, and only infpire a vapid tendernefs, which eafily degenerates into contempt. Still, if advice could really make a being gentle, whofe natural difpofition admitted not of fuch a fine polifh, fomething towards the advancement of order would be attained; but if, as might quickly be demonftrated, only affectation be produced by this indifcriminate counfel, which throws a ftumbling-block in the way of

gradual

gradual improvement, and true melioration of temper, the sex is not much benefited by sacrificing solid virtues to the attainment of superficial graces, though for a few years they may procure the individuals regal sway.

As a philosopher, I read with indignation the plausible epithets which men use to soften their insults; and, as a moralist, I ask what is meant by such heterogeneous associations, as fair defects, amiable weaknesses, &c.? If there is but one criterion of morals, but one archetype for man, women appear to be suspended by destiny, according to the vulgar tale of Mahomet's coffin; they have neither the unerring instinct of brutes, nor are allowed to fix the eye of reason on a perfect model. They were made to be loved, and must not aim at respect, lest they should be hunted out of society as masculine.

But to view the subject in another point of view. Do passive indolent women make the best wives? Confining our discussion to the present moment of existence, let us see how such weak creatures perform their part? Do the women, who, by the attainment of a few superficial accomplishments, have strengthened the prevailing prejudice, merely contribute to the happiness of their husbands? Do they display their charms merely to amuse them? And have women, who have early imbibed notions of passive obedience, sufficient character to manage a family or educate children? So far from it, that, after surveying the history of woman, I cannot help agreeing with the severest satirist, considering the sex as the weakest as well as the most oppressed half of the species. What does history disclose but marks

of inferiority, and how few women have emancipated themfelves from the galling yoke of fovereign man ?—So few, that the exceptions remind
me of an ingenious conjecture refpecting Newton : that he was probably a being of a fuperior
order, accidentally caged in a human body.   In
the fame ftyle I have been led to imagine that the
few extraordinary women who have rufhed in ec-
centrical directions out of the orbit prefcribed to
their fex, were *male* fpirited, confined by miftake
in a female frame.   But if it be not philofophical to think of fex when the foul is mentioned,
the inferiority muft depend on the organs ; or
the heavenly fire, which is to ferment the clay,
is not given in equal portions.

But avoiding, as I have hitherto done, any direct comparifon of the two fexes collectively, or
frankly acknowledging the inferiority of woman,
according to the prefent appearance of things, I
fhall only infift that men have increafed that inferiority till women are almoft funk below the
ftandard of rational creatures.   Let their faculties
have room to unfold, and their virtues to gain
ftrength, and then determine where the whole
fex muft ftand in the intellectual fcale.   Yet let
it be remembered, that for a fmall number of
diftinguifhed women I do not afk a place.

It is difficult for us purblind mortals to fay to
what height human difcoveries and improvements
may arrive when the gloom of defpotifm fub-
fides, which makes us ftumble at every ftep ; but,
when morality fhall be fettled on a more folid bafis, then, without being gifted with a prophetic
fpirit, I will venture to predict that woman will
be

be either the friend or slave of man. We shall not, as at present, doubt whether she is a moral agent, or the link which unites man with brutes. But, should it then appear, that like the brutes they were principally created for the use of man, he will let them patiently bite the bridle, and not mock them with empty praise; or, should their rationality be proved, he will not impede their improvement merely to gratify his sensual appetites. He will not, with all the graces of rhetoric, advise them to submit implicitly their understanding to the guidance of man. He will not, when he treats of the education of women, assert that they ought never to have the free use of reason, nor would he recommend cunning and dissimulation to beings who are acquiring, in like manner as himself, the virtues of humanity.

Surely there can be but one rule of right, if morality has an eternal foundation, and whoever sacrifices virtue, strictly so called, to present convenience, or whose *duty* it is to act in such a manner, lives only for the passing day, and cannot be an accountable creature.

The poet then should have dropped his sneer when he says,

> " If weak women go astray,
> " The stars are more in fault than they."

For that they are bound by the adamantine chain of destiny is most certain, if it be proved that they are never to exercise their own reason, never to be independent, never to rise above opinion, or to feel the dignity of a rational will that only bows to God, and often forgets that the universe contains

E 2   tains

tains any being but itself and the model of perfection to which its ardent gaze is turned, to adore
attributes that, softened into virtues, may be im-
itated in kind, though the degree overwhelms the
enraptured mind.

If, I say, for I would not imprefs by declamation when Reason offers her sober light, if they
are really capable of acting like rational creatures,
let them not be treated like slaves ; or, like the
brutes who are dependent on the reason of man,
when they affociate with him ; but cultivate their
minds, give them the falutary, fublime curb of
principle, and let them attain, confcious dignity
by feeling themselves only dependent on God.
Teach them, in common with man, to fubmit
to neceffity, inftead of giving, to render them
more pleafing, a fex to morals.

Further, fhould experience prove that they
cannot attain the fame degree of ftrength of mind,
perfeverence, and fortitude, let their virtues be
the fame in kind, though they may vainly ftruggle for the fame degree ; and the fuperiority of
man will be equally clear, if not clearer ; and
truth, as it is a fimple principle, which admits
of no modification, would be common to both.
Nay, the order of fociety as it is at prefent regulated would not be inverted, for woman would
then only have the rank that reafon affigned her,
and arts could not be practifed to bring the balance even, much lefs to turn it.

These may be termed Utopian dreams.——
Thanks to that Being who impreffed them on
my foul, and gave me fufficient ftrength of mind
to dare to exert my own reafon, till, becoming
                                        dependent

dependent only on him for the support of my virtue, I view, with indignation, the miftaken notions that enflave my fex.

I love man as my fellow ; but his fcepter, real, or ufurped, extends not to me, unlefs the reafon of an individual demands my homage ; and even then the fubmiffion is to reafon, and not to man. In fact, the conduct of an accountable being muft be regulated by the operations of its own reafon ; or on what foundation refts the throne of God ?

It appears to me neceffary to dwell on thefe obvious truths, becaufe females have been infulated, as it were ; and, while they have been ftripped of the virtues that fhould clothe humanity, they have been decked with artificial graces that enable them to exercife a fhort-lived tyranny. Love, in their bofoms, taking place of every nobler paffion, their fole ambition is to be fair, to raife emotion inftead of infpiring refpect ; and this ignoble defire, like the fervility in abfolute monarchies, deftroys all ftrength of character. Liberty is the mother of virtue, and if women are, by their very conftitution, flaves, and not allowed to breathe the fharp invigorating air of freedom, they muft ever languifh like exotics and be reckoned beautiful flaws in nature ;—let it alfo be remembered, that they are the only flaw.

As to the argument refpecting the fubjection in which the fex has ever been held, it retorts on man. The many have always been enthralled by the few ; and monfters, who fcarcely have fhewn any difcernment of human excellence, have tyrannized over thoufands of their fellow creatures.

Why

Why have men of superior endowments submitted to such degration? For, is it not universally acknowledged that kings, viewed collectively, have ever been inferior, in abilities and virtue, to the same number of men taken from the common mass of mankind—yet, have they not, and are they not still treated with a degree of reverence that is an insult to reason; China is not the only country where a living man has been made a God. *Men* have submitted to superior strength to enjoy with impunity the pleasure of the moment—*women* have only done the same, and therefore till it is proved that the courtier, who servilely resigns the birthright of a man, is not a moral agent, it cannot be demonstrated that woman is essentially inferior to man because she has always been subjugated.

Brutal force has hitherto governed the world, and that the science of politics is in its infancy, is evident from philosophers scrupling to give the knowledge most useful to man that determinate distinction.

I shall not pursue this argument any further than to establish an obvious inference, that as sound politics diffuse liberty, mankind, including woman, will become more wise and virtuous.

CHAP

C H A P. III.

THE SAME SUBJECT CONTINUED.

BODILY ſtrength from being the diſtinction of heroes is now ſunk into ſuch unmerited contempt, that men, as well as women, ſeem to think it unneceſſary : the latter, as it takes from their feminine graces, and from that lovely weakneſs, the ſource of their undue power ; and the former, becauſe it appears inimical with the character of a gentleman.

That they have both by departing from one extreme run into another, may eaſily be proved ; but firſt it may be proper to obſerve, that a vulgar error has obtained a degree of credit, which has given force to a falſe concluſion, in which an effect has been miſtaken for a cauſe.

People of genius have, very frequently, impaired their conſtitutions by ſtudy or careleſs inattention to their health, and the violence of their paſſions bearing a proportion to the vigour of their intellects, the ſword's deſtroying the ſcabbard has become almoſt proverbial, and ſuperficial obſervers have inferred from thence, that men of genius have commonly weak, or, to uſe a more faſhionable phraſe, delicate conſtitutions. Yet the contrary, I believe, will appear to be the fact ; for, on diligent inquiry, I find that ſtrength of mind has, in moſt caſes, been accompanied by ſuperior ſtrength of body,—natural ſoundneſs of conſtitution,—not that robuſt tone

of

of nerves and vigour of mufcles, which arife from bodily labour, when the mind is quiefcent, or only directs the hands.

Dr. Prieftley has remarked, in the preface to his biographical chart, that the majority of great men have lived beyond forty-five. And, confidering the thoughtlefs manner in which they have lavifhed their ftrength, when inveftigating a favourite fcience they have wafted the lamp of life, forgetful of the midnight hour ; or, when loft in poetic dreams, fancy has peopled the fcene, and the foul has been difturbed, till it fhook the conftitution, by the paffions that meditation had raifed ; whofe objects, the bafelefs fabric of a vifion, faded before the exhaufted eye, they muft have had iron frames. Shakefpeare never grafped the airy dagger with a nervelefs hand, nor did Milton tremble when he led Satan far from the confines of his dreary prifon.—Thefe were not the ravings of imbecility, the fickly effufions of diftempered brains ; but the exuberance of fancy, that ' in a fine phrenzy' wandering, was not continually reminded of its material fhackles.

I am aware that this argument would carry me further than it may be fuppofed I wifh to go ; but I follow truth, and, ftill adhering to my firft pofition, I will allow that bodily ftrength feems to give man a natural fuperiority over woman ; and this is the only folid bafis on which the fuperiority of the fex can be built. But I ftill infift, that not only the virtue, but the *knowledge* of the two fexes fhould be the fame in nature, if not in degree, and that women, confidered not only as moral, but rational creatures,

ought

ought to endeavour to acquire human virtues (or perfections) by the *same* means as men, instead of being educated like a fanciful kind of *half* being—one of Rousseau's wild chimeras*.

But,

* ' Researches into abstract and speculative truths, the principles and axioms of sciences, in short, every thing which tends to generalize our ideas, is not the proper province of women ; their studies should be relative to point of practice ; it belongs to them to apply those principles which men have discovered ; and it is their part to make observations, which direct men to the establishment of general principles. All the ideas of women, which have not the immediate tendency to points of duty, should be directed to the study of men, and to the attainment of those agreeable accomplishments which have taste for their object ; for as to works of genius, they are beyond their capacity ; neither have they sufficient precision or power of attention to succeed in sciences which require accuracy : and as to physical knowledge, it belongs to those only who are most active, most inquisitive ; who comprehend the greatest variety of objects : in short, it belongs to those who have the strongest powers, and who exercise them most, to judge of the relations between sensible beings and the laws of nature. A woman who is naturally weak, and does not carry her ideas to any great extent, knows how to judge and make a proper estimate of those movements which she sets to work, in order to aid her weakness ; and these movements are the passions of men. The mechanism she employs is much more powerful than ours ; for all her levers move the human heart. She must have the skill to incline us to do every thing which her sex will not enable her to do of herself, and which is necessary or agreeable to her ; therefore she ought to study the mind of man thoroughly, not the mind of man in general, abstracted, but the dispositions of those men to whom she is subject, either by the laws of her country or by the force of opinion. She should learn to penetrate into their real sentiments from their conversation, their actions, their looks, and gestures. She should also have the art, by her own conversation, actions, looks, and gestures, to communicate those sentiments which are agreeable to them, without seeming to intend it. Men will argue more philosophically about the human heart ; but women will read the heart of man better than they. It belongs to women, if I may be allowed the expression, to form an experimental morality, and to reduce the study of man to a system. Women have most wit, men have most genius ; women observe, men reason : from the concurrence of both we derive the clearest light and the most perfect knowledge, which the human mind is, of itself, capable of attaining. In one word, from hence we acquire the most intimate acquaintance, both with ourselves and others, of which our nature is capable ; and it is thus that art has a constant tendency to perfect those endowments which nature has bestowed.—The world is the book of women.' *Rousseau's Emilius.* I hope my readers still remember the comparison, which I have brought forward, between women and officers.

But, if ſtrength of body be, with ſome ſhew of reaſon, the boaſt of men, why are women ſo infatuated as to be proud of a defect ? Rouſſeau has furniſhed them with a plauſible excuſe, which could only have occurred to a man, whoſe imagination had been allowed to run wild, and refine on the impreſſions made by exquiſite ſenſes ;—that they might, forſooth, have a pre- text for yielding to a natural appetite without vi- olating a romantic ſpecies of modeſty, which gratifies the pride and libertiniſm of man.

Women, deluded by theſe ſentiments, ſometimes boaſt of their weakneſs, cunningly obtaining pow- er by playing on the *weakneſs* of men ; and they may well glory in their illicit ſway, for, like Tur- kiſh baſhaws, they have more real power than their maſters : but virtue is ſacrificed to tempo- rary gratifications, and the reſpectability of life to the triumph of an hour.

Women, as well as deſpots have now, perhaps, more power than they would have if the world, divided and ſubdivided into kingdoms and fami- lies, was governed by laws deduced from the ex- erciſe of reaſon ; but in obtaining it, to carry on the compariſon, their character is degraded, and licentiouſneſs ſpread through the whole aggregate of ſociety. The many become pedeſtal to the few. I, therefore, will venture to aſſert, that till women are more rationally educated, the progreſs of human virtue and improvement in knowledge muſt receive continual checks. And if it be granted that woman was not created merely to gratify the appetite of man, nor to be the upper ſervant, who provides his meals and takes care of

his

his linen, it muſt follow, that the firſt care of thoſe mothers or fathers, who really attend to the education of females, ſhould be, if not to ſtrengthen the body, at leaſt, not to deſtroy the conſtitution by miſtaken notions of beauty and female excellence ; nor ſhould girls ever be allowed to imbibe the pernicious notion that a defect can, by any chemical proceſs of reaſoning, become an excellence. In this reſpect, I am happy to find, that the author of one of the moſt inſtructive books, that our country has produced for children, coincides with me in opinion ; I ſhall quote his pertinent remarks to give the force of his reſpectable authority to reaſon*. But

* A reſpectable old man gives the following ſenſible account of the method he purſued when educating his daughter. ‘ I endeavoured to ‘ give both to her mind and body a degree of vigour, which is ſeldom ‘ found in the female ſex. As ſoon as ſhe was ſufficiently advanced ‘ in ſtrength to be capable of the lighter labours of huſbandry and gar- ‘ dening, I employed her as my conſtant companion. Selene, for that ‘ was her name, ſoon acquired a dexterity in all theſe ruſtic employ- ‘ ments, which I conſidered with equal pleaſure and admiration. If ‘ women are in general feeble both in body and mind, it ariſes leſs from ‘ nature than from education. We encourage a vicious indolence and ‘ inactivity, which we falſely call delicacy ; inſtead of hardening their ‘ minds by the ſeverer principles of reaſon and philoſophy, we breed ‘ them to uſeleſs arts, which terminate in vanity and ſenſuality. In ‘ moſt of the countries which I had viſited, they are taught nothing of ‘ an higher nature than a few modulations of the voice, or uſeleſs poſ- ‘ tures of the body ; their time is conſumed in ſloth or trifles, and tri- ‘ fles become the only purſuits capable of intereſting them. We ſeem ‘ to forget, that it is upon the qualities of the female ſex that our own ‘ domeſtic comforts and the education of our children muſt depend. ‘ And what are the comforts or the education which a race of beings, ‘ corrupted from their infancy, and unacquainted with all the duties of ‘ life, are fitted to beſtow? To touch a muſical inſtrument with uſeleſs ‘ ſkill, to exhibit their natural or affected graces to the eyes of indolent ‘ and debauched young men, to diſſipate their huſband's patrimony in ‘ riotous and unneceſſary expenſes, theſe are the only arts cultivated by ‘ women in moſt of the poliſhed nations I had ſeen. And the conſe- ‘ quences are uniformly ſuch as may be expected to proceed from ſuch ‘ poluted ſources, private miſery and public ſervitude.

‘ But Selene's education was regulated by different views, and con- ‘ ducted upon ſeverer principles ; if that can be called ſeverity which ‘ opens the mind to a ſenſe of moral and religious duties, and moſt ef- fectually arms it againſt the inevitable evils of life.'

Mr. Day's Sanford and Merton, Vol. III.

But fhould it be proved that woman is naturally weaker than man, from whence does it follow that it is natural for her to labour to become ftill weaker than nature intended her to be? Arguments of this caft are an infult to common fenfe, and favour paffion. The *divine right* of hufbands, like the divine right of kings, may, it is to be hoped, in this enlightened age, be contefted without danger, and, though conviction may not filence many boifterous difputants, yet when any prevailing prejudice is attacked, the wife will confider, and leave the narrow-minded to rail with thoughtlefs vehemence at innovation.

The mother, who wifhes to give true dignity of character to her daughter, muft, regardlefs of the fneers of ignorance, proceed on a plan diametrically oppofite to that which Roufſeau has recommended with all the deluding charms of eloquence and philofophical fophiftry : for his eloquence renders abfurdities plaufible, and his dogmatic conclufions puzzle, without convincing, thofe who have not ability to refute them.

Throughout the whole animal kingdom every young creature requires almoft continual exercife, and the infancy of children, conformable to this intimation, fhould be paffed in harmlefs gambols, that exercife the feet and hands, without requiring very minute direction from the head, or the conftant attention of a nurfe. In fact, the care neceffary for felf-prefervation is the firft natural exercife of the underftanding, as little inventions to amufe the prefent moment unfold the imagination. But thefe wife defigns of nature are counteracted by miftaken fondnefs or blind

blind zeal. The child is not left a moment to its own direction, particularly a girl, and thus rendered dependent—dependence is called natural.

To preserve personal beauty, woman's glory! the limbs and faculties are cramped with worse than Chinese bands, and the sedentary life which they are condemned to live, whilst boys frolic in the open air, weakens the muscles and relaxes the nerves.—As for Rousseau's remarks, which have since been echoed by several writers, that they have naturally, that is from their birth, independent of education, a fondness for dolls, dressing, and talking—they are so puerile as not to merit a serious refutation. That a girl, condemned to sit for hours together listening to the idle chat of weak nurses, or to attend at her mother's toilet, will endeavour to join the conversation, is, indeed, very natural; and that she will imitate her mother or aunts, and amuse herself by adorning her lifeless doll, as they do in dressing her, poor innocent babe! is undoubtedly a most natural consequence. For men of the greatest abilities have seldom had sufficient strength to rise above the surrounding atmosphere; and, if the page of genius has always been blurred by the prejudices of the age, some allowance should be made for a sex, who like kings, always see things through a false medium.

In this manner may the fondness for dress, conspicuous in women, be easily accounted for, without supposing it the result of a desire to please the sex on which they are dependent. The absurdity, in short, of supposing that a girl is naturally a coquette, and that a desire connected with

the

the impulfe of nature to propagate the fpecies, fhould appear even before an improper education has, by heating the imagination, called it forth prematurely, is fo unphilofophical, that fuch a fagacious obferver as Rouffeau would not have adopted it, if he had not been accuftomed to make reafon give way to his defire of fingularity, and truth to a favourite paradox.

Yet thus to give a fex to mind was not very confiftent with the principles of a man who argued fo warmly, and fo well, for the immortality of the foul.—But what a weak barrier is truth when it ftands in the way of an hypothefis ! Rouffeau refpected—almoft adored virtue—and yet he allowed himfelf to love with fenfual fondnefs. His imagination conftantly prepared inflammable fewel for his inflammable fenfes ; but, in order to reconcile his refpect for felfdenial, fortitude, and thofe heroic virtues, which a mind like his could not coolly admire, he labours to invert the law of nature, and broaches a doctrine pregnant with mifchief and derogatory to the character of fupreme wifdom.

His ridiculous ftories, which tend to prove that girls are *naturally* attentive to their perfons, without laying any ftrefs on daily example, are below contempt.—And that a little mifs fhould have fuch a correct tafte as to neglect the pleafing amufement of making O's, merely becaufe fhe perceived that it was an ungraceful attitude, fhould be felected with the anecdotes of the learned pig*.   I

* ‘ I once knew a young perfon who learned to write before fhe learn-
‘ ed to read, and began to write with her needle before fhe could ufe
‘ a pen. At firft, indeed, fhe took it into her head to make no other
‘ letter than the O : this letter fhe was conftantly making of all fizes,
                                                        ‘ and

I have, probably, had an opportunity of obferving more girls in their infancy than J. J. Roufleau—I can recollect my own feelings, and I have looked fteadily around me ; yet, fo far from coinciding with him in opinion refpecting the firft dawn of the female character, I will venture to affirm, that a girl, whofe fpirits have not been damped by inactivity, or innocence tainted by falfe fhame, will always be a romp, and the doll will never excite attention unlefs confinement allows her no alternative. Girls and boys, in fhort, would play harmlefsly together, if the diftinction of fex was not inculcated long before nature makes any difference.—I will go further, and affirm, as an indifputable fact, that moft of the women, in the circle of my obfervation, who have acted like rational creatures, or fhewn any vigour of intellect, have accidentally been allowed to run wild—as fome of the elegant formers of the fair fex would infinuate.

The baneful confequences which flow from inattention to health during infancy, and youth, extend further than is fuppofed—dependence of body naturally produces dependence of mind ; and how can fhe be a good wife or mother, the greater part of whofe time is employed to guard againft or endure ficknefs ? Nor can it be expected that a woman will refolutely endeavour to
ftrengthen

‘ and always the wrong way. Unluckily, one day, as fhe was intent on
‘ this employment, fhe happened to fee herfelf in the looking-glafs; when,
‘ taking a difike to the conftrained attitude in which fhe fat while writing,
‘ fhe threw away her pen, like another Pallas, and determined againft mak-
‘ ing the O any more. Her brother was alfo equally averfe to writing : it
‘ was the confinement, however, and not the conftrained attitude, that
‘ moft difgufted him .’ *Roufeau's Emilius.*

strengthen her conftitution and abftain from enervating indulgencies, if artificial notions of beauty, and falfe defcriptions of fenfibility, have been
early entangled with her motives of action. Moft
men are fometimes obliged to bear with bodily
inconveniencies, and to endure, occafionally, the
inclemency of the elements ; but genteel women
are, literally fpeaking, flaves to their bodies, and
glory in their fubjection.

I once knew a weak woman of fashion, who
was more than commonly proud of her delicacy
and fenfibility. She thought a diftinguishing
tafte and puny appetite the height of all human
perfection, and acted accordingly.—I have feen
this weak fophifticated being neglect all the duties of life, yet recline with felf-complacency
on a fofa, and boaft of her want of appetite as a
proof of delicacy that extended to, or, perhaps,
arofe from, her exquifite fenfibility : for it is difficult to render intelligible fuch ridiculous jargon.
—Yet, at the moment, I have feen her infult a
worthy old gentlewoman, whom unexpected
misfortunes had made dependent on her oftenta-
tious bounty, and who, in better days, had claims
on her gratitude. Is it poffible that a human
creature could have become fuch a weak and depraved being, if, like the Sybarites, diffolved in
luxury, every thing like virtue had not been worn
away, or never impreffed by precept, a poor fubftitute, it is true, for cultivation of mind, though
it ferves as a fence againft vice ?

Such a woman is not a more irrational monfter than fome of the Roman emperors, who
were depraved by lawlefs power. Yet, fince

kings

kings have been more under the restraint of law,
and the curb, however weak, of honour, the re-
cords of history are not filled with such unnatural instances of folly and cruelty, nor does the
despotism that kills virtue and genius in the bud,
hover over Europe with that destructive blast
which desolates Turky, and renders the men, as
well as the soil, unfruitful.

Women are every where in this deplorable
state; for, in order to preserve their innocence, as
ignorance is courteously termed, truth is hidden
from them, and they are made to assume an artificial character before their faculties have acquired
any strength. Taught from their infancy that
beauty is woman's sceptre, the mind shapes itself
to the body, and, roaming round its gilt cage,
only seeks to adorn its prison. Men have various
employments and pursuits which engage their attention, and give a character to the opening
mind; but women, confined to one, and having
their thoughts constantly directed to the most insignificant part of themselves, seldom extend their
views beyond the triumph of the hour. But was
their understanding once emancipated from the
slavery to which the pride and sensuality of man and
their short-sighted desire, like that of dominion
in tyrants, of present sway, has subjected them,
we should probably read of their weaknesses with
surprise. I must be allowed to pursue the argument a little farther.

Perhaps, if the existence of an evil being was
allowed, who, in the allegorical language of scrip-
ture, went about seeking whom he should devour,
he could not more effectually degrade the human

F character

character than by giving a man abfolute power.

This argument branches into various ramifications.—Birth, riches, and every extrinfic advantage that exalt a man above his fellows, without any mental exertion, fink him in reality below them. In proportion to his weaknefs, he is played upon by defigning men, till the bloated monfter has loft all traces of humanity. And that tribes of men, like flocks of fheep, fhould quietly follow fuch a leader, is a folecifm that only a defire of prefent enjoyment and narrownefs of underftanding can folve. Educated in flavifh dependence, and enervated by luxury and floth, where fhall we find men who will ftand forth to affert the rights of man ;—or claim the privilege of moral beings, who fhould have but one road to excellence ? Slavery to monarchs and minifters, which the world will be long in freeing itfelf from, and whofe deadly grafp ftop the progrefs of the human mind, is not yet abolifhed.

Let not men then in the pride of power, ufe the fame arguments that tyrannic kings and venal minifters have ufed, and fallacioufly affert that woman ought to be fubjected becaufe fhe has always been fo.—But, when man, governed by reafonable laws, enjoys his natural freedom, let him defpife woman, if fhe do not fhare it with him ; and till that glorious period arrives, in defcanting on the folly of the fex, let him not overlook his own.

Women, it is true, obtaining power by unjuft means, by practifing or foftering vice, evidently lofe the rank which reafon would affign them, and they

become

become either abject flaves or capricious tyrants. They lofe all fimplicity, all dignity of mind, in acquiring power, and act as men are obferved to act when they have been exalted by the fame means.

It is time to effect a revolution in female manners—time to reftore to them their loft dignity—and make them, as a part of the human fpecies, labour by reforming themfelves to reform the world. It is time to feparate unchangeable morals from local manners.—If men be demi-gods—why let us ferve them ! And if the dignity of the female foul be as difputable as that of animals—if their reafon does not afford fufficient light to direct their conduct whilft unerring inftinct is denied—they are furely of all creatures the moft miferable ! and, bent beneath the iron hand of deftiny, muft fubmit to be a *fair defect* in creation. But to juftify the ways of Providence refpecting them, by pointing out fome irrefragable reafon for thus making fuch a large portion of mankind accountable and not accountable, would puzzle the fubtileft cafuift.

The only folid foundation for morality appears to be the character of the fupreme Being ; the harmony of which arifes from a balance of attributes ;—and, to fpeak with reverence, one attribute feems to imply the *neceffity* of another. He muft be juft, becaufe he is wife, he muft be good, becaufe he is omnipotent. For to exalt one attribute at the expenfe of another equally noble and neceffary, bears the ftamp of the warped reafon of man—the homage of paffion. Man, accuftomed to bow down to power in his favage state, can seldom divest himself of this barbarous prejudice, even when civilization determines how much superior mental is to bodily strength ; and his reason is clouded by these crude opinions, even when he thinks of the Deity. His omnipotence is made to swallow up, or preside over his other attributes, and those mortals are supposed to limit his power irreverently, who think that it must be regulated by his wisdom.

I disclaim that specious humility which, after investigating nature, stops at the author.—The High and Lofty One, who inhabiteth eternity, doubtless possesses many attributes of which we can form no conception ; but reason tells me that they cannot clash with those I adore—and I am compelled to listen to her voice.

It seems natural for man to search for excellence, and either to trace it in the object that he worships, or blindly to invest it with perfection, as a garment. But what good effect can the latter mode of worship have on the moral conduct of a rational being ? He bends to power ; he adores a dark cloud, which may open a bright prospect to him, or burst in angry, lawless fury, on his devoted head—he knows not why. And, supposing that the Deity acts from the vague impulse of an undirected will, man must also follow his own, or act according to rules, deduced from principles which he disclaims as irreverent. Into this dilemma have both enthusiasts and cooler thinkers fallen, when they laboured to free men from the wholesome restraints which a just conception of the character of God imposes.

It

It is not impious thus to scan the attributes of the Almighty : in fact, who can avoid it that exercises his faculties ? For to love God as the fountain of wisdom, goodness, and power, appears to be the only worship useful to a being who wishes to acquire either virtue or knowledge. A blind unsettled affection may, like human passions, occupy the mind and warm the heart, whilst, to do justice, love mercy, and walk humbly with our God, is forgotten. I shall pursue this subject still further, when I consider religion in a light opposite to that recommended by Dr. Gregory, who treats it as a matter of sentiment or taste.

To return from this apparent digression. It were to be wished that women would cherish an affection for their husbands, founded on the same principle that devotion ought to rest upon. No other firm base is there under heaven—for let them beware of the fallacious light of sentiment ; too often used as a softer phrase for sensuality. It follows then, I think, that from their infancy women should either be shut up like eastern princes, or educated in such a manner as to be able to think and act for themselves.

Why do men halt between two opinions, and expect impossibilities ? Why do they expect virtue from a slave, from a being whom the constitution of civil society has rendered weak, if not vicious ?

Still I know that it will require a considerable length of time to eradicate the firmly rooted prejudices which sensualists have planted ; it will also require some time to convince women that

they

they act contrary to their real intereſt on an enlarged ſcale, when they cheriſh or affect weakneſs under the name of delicacy, and to convince
the world that the poiſoned ſource of female vices
and follies, if it be neceſſary, in compliance with
cuſtom, to uſe ſynonymous terms in a lax ſenſe,
has been the ſenſual homage paid to beauty :—to
beauty of features ; for it has been ſhrewdly obſerved by a German writer, that a pretty woman,
as an object of deſire, is generally allowed to be
ſo by men of all deſcriptions ; whilſt a fine woman, who inſpires more ſublime emotions by diſ-
playing intellectual beauty, may be overlooked
or obſerved with indifference, by thoſe men who
find their happineſs in the gratification of their
appetites. I foreſee an obvious retort—whilſt
man remains ſuch an imperfect being as he appears hitherto to have been, he will, more or leſs,
be the ſlave of his appetites ; and thoſe women
obtaining moſt power who gratify a predominant
one, the ſex is degraded by a phyſical, if not by
a moral neceſſity,

This objection has, I grant, ſome force ; but
while ſuch a ſublime precept exiſts, as, ‘ be pure
as your heavenly Father is pure ;’ it would ſeem
that the virtues of man are not limited by the Being who alone could limit them ; and that he
may preſs forward without conſidering whether
he ſteps out of his ſphere by indulging ſuch a
noble ambition. To the wild billows it has been
ſaid, ‘ thus far ſhalt thou go, and no further ;
‘ and here ſhall thy proud waves be ſtayed.’
Vainly then do they beat and foam, reſtrained by
the power that confines the ſtruggling planets in
their

their orbits, matter yields to the great governing Spirit.——But an immortal foul, not reftrained by mechanical laws and ftruggling to free itfelf from the fhackles of matter, contributes to, inftead of difturbing, the order of creation, when, co-operating with the Father of fpirits, it tries to govern itfelf by the invariable rule that, in a degree, before which our imagination faints, the univerfe is regulated.

Befides, if women are educated for dependence; that is, to act according to the will of another fallible being, and fubmit, right or wrong, to power, where are we to ftop? Are they to be confidered as vicegerents allowed to reign over a fmall domain, and anfwerable for their conduct to a higher tribunal, liable to error?

It will not be difficult to prove that fuch delegates will act like men fubjected by fear, and make their children and fervants endure their tyrannical oppreffion. As they fubmit without reafon, they will, having no fixed rules to fquare their conduct by, be kind, or cruel, juft as the whim of the moment directs; and we ought not to wonder if fometimes, galled by their heavy yoke, they take a malignant pleafure in refting it on weaker fhoulders.

But, fuppofing a woman, trained up to obedience, be married to a fenfible man, who directs her judgment without making her feel the fervility of her fubjection, to act with as much propriety by this reflected light as can be expected when reafon is taken at fecond hand, yet fhe cannot enfure the life of her protector; he may die and leave her with a large family.

A double duty devolves on her ; to educate them in the character of both father and mother ; to form their principles and secure their property. But, alas ! she has never thought, much less acted for herself. She has only learned to please * men, to depend gracefully on them ; yet, encumbered with children, how is she to obtain another protector—a husband to supply the place of reason ? A rational man, for we are not treading on romantic ground, though he may think her a pleasing docile creature, will not choose to marry a *family* for love, when the world contains many more pretty creatures. What is then to become of her ? She either falls an easy prey to some mean fortune-hunter, who defrauds her children of their paternal inheritance, and renders her miserable ; or becomes the victim of discontent

tent

* ' In the union of the sexes, both pursue one common object, but ' not in the same manner. From their diversity in this particular, arises the ' first determinate difference between the moral relations of each. The one ' should be active and strong, the other passive and weak : it is necessary ' the one should have both the power and the will, and that the other ' should make little resistance.

' This principle being established, it follows that woman is expressly ' formed to please the man : if the obligation be reciprocal also, and the man ' ought to please in his turn, it is not so immediately necessary : his great ' merit is in his power, and he pleases merely because he is strong. ' This, I must confess, is not one of the refined maxims of love ; it is, ' however, one of the laws of nature, prior to love itself.

' If woman be formed to please and be subjected to man it is her place, ' doubtless, to render herself agreeable to him, instead of challenging his ' passion. The violence of his desires depends on her charms ; it is by ' means of these she should urge him to the exertion of those powers which ' nature hath giving him. The most successful method of exciting them, ' is, to render such exertion necessary by their resistance ; as, in that case, ' self-love is added to desire, and the one triumphs in the victory which ' the other obliged to acquire. Hence arise the various modes of attack ' and defence between the sexes ; the boldness of one sex and the timidity of ' the other ; and, in a word, that bashfulness and modesty with which nature ' hath armed the weak, in order to subdue the strong.' *Rousseau's Emilius.*

I shall make no other comment on this ingenius passage, than just to observe, that it is the philosophy of lasciviousness.

tent and blind indulgence. Unable to educate her sons, or imprefs them with refpect; for it is not a play on words to affert, that people are never refpected, though filling an important ftation, who are not refpectable; fhe pines under the anguifh of unavailing impotent regret. The ferpent's tooth enters into her very foul, and the vices of licentious youth bring her with forrow, if not with poverty alfo, to the grave.

This is not an overcharged picture; on the contrary, it is a very poffible cafe, and fomething fimilar muft have fallen under every attentive eye.

I have, however, taken it for granted, that fhe was well-difpofed, though experience fhews, that the blind may as eafily be led into a ditch as along the beaten road. But fuppofing no very improbable conjecture, that a being only taught to pleafe muft ftill find her happinefs in pleafing;—what an example of folly, not to fay vice, will fhe be to her innocent daughters! The mother will be loft in the coquette, and inftead of making friends of her daughters, view them with eyes afkance, for they are rivals—rivals more cruel than any other, becaufe they invite a comparifon, and drive her from the throne of beauty, who has never thought of a feat on the bench of reafon.

It does not require a lively pencil, or the difcriminating outline of a caricature, to fketch the domeftic miferies and petty vices which fuch a miftrefs of a family diffufes. Still fhe only acts as a woman ought to act, brought up according to Rouffeau's fyftem. She can never be reproached

proached for being mafculine, or turning out of
her fphere; nay, fhe may obferve another of his
grand rules, and cautioufly preferving her reputation free from fpot, be reckoned a good kind of
woman. Yet in what refpect can fhe be termed
good? She abftains, it is true, without any great
ftruggle, from committing grofs crimes; but
how does fhe fulfil her duties? Duties!—in
truth fhe has enough to think of to adorn her
body and nurfe a weak conftitution.

With refpect to religion, fhe never prefumed
to judge for herfelf; but conformed, as a dependent creature fhould, to the ceremonies of the
church which fhe was brought up in, pioufly
believing that wifer heads than her own have fettled that bufinefs:—and not to doubt is her point
of perfection. She therefore pays her tythe of
mint and cummin—and thanks her God that fhe
is not as other women are. Thefe are the blef-
fed effects of a good education! Thefe the virtues
of man's help-mate*!

I muft relieve myfelf by drawing a different
picture.

Let fancy now prefent a woman with a tolerable underftanding, for I do not wifh to leave the
line of mediocrity, whofe conftitution, ftrengthened by exercife, has allowed her body to acquire
its full vigour; her mind, at the fame time, gradually

---

* ' O how lovely,' exclaims Rouffeau, fpeaking of Sophia, ' is her igno-
' rance! Happy is he who is deftined to inftruct her! She will never pre-
' tend to be the tutor of her hufband, but will be content to be his pupil.
' Far from attempting to fubject him to her tafte, fhe will accommodate
' herfelf to his. She will be more eftimable to him, than if fhe was learn-
' ed: he will have a pleafure in inftructing her.' *Rouffeau's Emilius.*

I fhall content myfelf with fimply afking, how friendfhip can fubfift,
when love expires, between the mafter and his pupil?

dually expanding itself to comprehend the moral duties of life, and in what human virtue and dignity confift.

Formed thus by the difcharge of the relative duties of her ftation, fhe marries from affection, without lofing fight of prudence, and looking beyond matrimonial felicity, fhe fecures her hufband's refpect before it is neceffary to exert mean arts to pleafe him and feed a dying flame, which nature doomed to expire when the object became familiar, when friendfhip and forbearance take place of a more ardent affection.—This is the natural death of love, and domeftic peace is not deftroyed by ftruggles to prevent its extinction. I alfo fuppofe the hufband to be virtuous; or fhe is ftill more in want of independent principles.

Fate, however, breaks this tie.—She is left a widow, perhaps, without a fufficient provifion; but fhe is not defolate! The pang of nature is felt; but after time has foftened forrow into melancholy refignation, her heart turns to her children with redoubled fondnefs, and anxious to provide for them, affection gives a facred heroic caft to her maternal duties. She thinks that not only the eye fees her virtuous efforts from whom all her comfort now muft flow, and whofe approbation is life; but her imagination, a little abftracted and exalted by grief, dwells on the fond hope that the eyes which her trembling hand clofed, may ftill fee how fhe fubdues every wayward paffion to fulfil the double duty of being the father as well as the mother of her children. Raifed to heroifm by misfortunes, fhe reprefies the firft faint dawning of a natural inclination,

before

before it ripens into love, and in the bloom of life forgets her sex—forgets the pleasure of an awakening passion, which might again have been inspired and returned. She no longer thinks of pleasing, and conscious dignity prevents her from priding herself on account of the praise which her conduct demands. Her children have her love, and her brightest hopes are beyond the grave, where her imagination often strays.

I think I see her surrounded by her children, reaping the reward of her care. The intelligent eye meets hers, whilst health and innocence smile on their chubby cheeks, and as they grow up the cares of life are lessened by their grateful attention. She lives to see the virtues which she endeavoured to plant on principles fixed into habits, to see her children attain a strength of character sufficient to enable them to endure adversity without forgetting their mother's example.

The task of life thus fulfilled, she calmly waits for the sleep of death, and rising from the grave, may say—Behold, thou gavest me a talent—and here are five talents.

I wish to sum up what I have said in a few words, for I here throw down my gauntlet, and deny the existence of sexual virtues, not excepting modesty. For man and woman, truth, if I understand the meaning of the word, must be the same; yet the fanciful female character, so prettily drawn by poets and novelists, demanding the sacrifice of truth and sincerity, virtue becomes a relative idea, having no other foundation than utility, and of that utility men pretend arbitrarily to judge, shaping it to their own convenience.

Women,

Women, I allow, may have different duties to fulfil; but they are *human* duties, and the principles that should regulate the discharge of them, I sturdily maintain, must be the same.

To become respectable, the exercise of their understanding is necessary, there is no other foundation for independence of character; I mean explicitly to say that they must only bow to the authority of reason, instead of being the *modest* slaves of opinion.

In the superiour ranks of life how seldom do we meet with a man of superior abilities, or even common acquirements? The reason appears to me clear, the state they are born in was an unnatural one. The human character has ever been formed by the employments the individual, or class, pursues; and if the faculties are not sharpened by necessity, they must remain obtuse. The argument may fairly be extended to women; for, seldom occupied by serious business, the pursuit of pleasure gives that insignificancy to their character which renders the society of the *great* so insipid. The same want of firmness, produced by a similar cause, forces them both to fly from themselves to noisy pleasures, and artificial passions, till vanity takes place of every social affection, and the characteristics of humanity can scarcely be discerned. Such are the blessings of civil governments, as they are at present organized, that wealth and female softness equally tend to debase mankind, and are produced by the same cause; but allowing women to be rational creatures, they should be incited to acquire virtues which they may call their own, for how can a rational being be ennobled by any thing that is not obtained by its *own* exertions?

CHAP.

C H A P. IV.

OBSERVATIONS ON THE STATE OF DEGRA-
DATION TO WHICH WOMAN IS REDUCED
BY VARIOUS CAUSES.

THAT woman is naturally weak, or degraded by a concurrence of circumstances, is, I
think, clear. But this position I shall simply con-
traft with a conclusion, which I have frequen-
ly heard fall from sensible men in favour of an
aristocracy: that the mass of mankind cannot be
any thing, or the obsequious slaves, who patiently allow themselves to be penned up, would feel
their own consequence, and spurn their chains.
Men, they further observe, submit every where
to oppression, when they have only to lift up
their heads to throw off the yoke; yet, instead
of asserting their birthright, they quietly lick the
dust, and say, let us eat and drink, for to-morrow
we die. Women, I argue from analogy, are degraded by the same propensity to enjoy the present moment; and, at last, despise the freedom
which they have not sufficient virtue to struggle
to attain. But I must be more explicit.

With respect to the culture of the heart, it is
unanimously allowed that sex is out of the question; but the line of subordination in the mental
powers is never to be passed over*. Only ' ab-
                                        solute

* Into what inconsistencies do men fall when they argue without the
compass of principles. Women, weak women, are compared with angels;
yet, a superiour order of beings should be supposed to possess more intellect
                                                              than

folute in lovelinefs,' the portion of rationality granted to woman, is indeed very fcanty ; for, denying her genius and judgment, it is fcarcely pofsible to divine what remains to characterize intellect.

The ftamina of immortality, if I may be allowed the phrafe, is the perfectibility of human reafon : for, was man created perfect, or did a flood of knowledge break in upon him, when he arrived at maturity, that precluded error, I fhould doubt whether his exiftence would be continued after the diffolution of the body. But, in the prefent ftate of things, every difficulty in morals that efcapes from human difcuffion, and equally baffles the inveftigation of profound thinking, and the lightning glance of genius, is an argument on which I build my belief of the immortality of the foul. Reafon is, confequentially, the fimple power of improvement ; or, more properly fpeaking, of difcerning truth. Every individual is in this refpect a world in itfelf. More or lefs may be confpicuous in one being than another ; but the nature of reafon muft be the fame in all, if it be an emanation of divinity, the tie that connects the creature with the Creator ; for, can that foul be ftamped with the heavenly image, that is not perfected by the exercife of its

own

than man ; or, in what does their fuperiority confift ? In the fame ftyle, to drop the fneer, they are allowed to poffefs more goodnefs of heart, piety, and benevolence.—I doubt the fact, though it be courteoufly brought forward, unlefs ignorance be allowed to be the mother of devotion ; for I am firmly perfuaded that, on an average, the proportion between virtue and knowledge, is more upon a par than is commonly granted.

own reafon * ? Yet outwardly ornamented with elaborate care, and fo adorned to delight man, ' that with honour he may love †,' the foul of woman is not allowed to have this diftinction, and man, ever placed between her and reafon, fhe is always reprefented as only created to fee through a grofs medium, and to take things on truft. But, difmiffing thefe fanciful theories, and confidering woman as a whole, let it be what it will, inftead of a part of man, the inquiry is whether fhe has reafon or not. If fhe has, which, for a moment, I will take for granted, fhe was not created merely to be the folace of man, and the fexual fhould not deftroy the human character.

Into this error men have, probably, been led by viewing education in a falfe light; not confidering it as the firft ftep to form a being advancing gradually towards perfection ‡; but only as a preparation for life. On this fenfual error, for I muft call it fo, has the falfe fyftem of female manners been reared, which robs the whole fex of its dignity, and claffes the brown and fair with the fmiling flowers that only adorns the land. This has ever been the language of men, and the fear of departing from a fuppofed fexual character, has made even women of fuperiour

fenfe

---

* ' The brutes,' fays Lord Monboddo, ' remain in the ftate in which ' nature has placed them, except in fo far as their natural inftinct is im- ' proved by the culture we beftow upon them.'

† Vide Milton.

‡ This word is not ftrictly juft, but I cannot find a better.

ſenſe adopt the ſame ſentiments*. Thus underſtanding, ſtrictly ſpeaking, has been denied to
woman; and inſtinct, ſublimated into wit and
cunning, for the purpoſes of life, has been ſub-
ſtituted in its ſtead.

The power of generalizing ideas, of drawing
comprehenſive concluſions from individual obſervations, is the only acquirement, for an immortal being, that really deſerves the name of
knowledge. Merely to obſerve, without endeavouring to account for any thing, may (in a very
incomplete manner) ſerve as the common ſenſe of
life; but where is the ſtore laid up that is to
clothe the ſoul when it leaves the body?

This power has not only been denied to women; but writers have inſiſted that it is inconſiſtent,

---

* ' Pleaſure's the portion of th' *inferiour* kind;
  ' But glory, virtue, Heaven for *man* deſign'd.'

After writing theſe lines, how could Mrs. Barbauld write the following
ignoble compariſon?

> ' *To a Lady, with ſome painted flowers.*'
> ' Flowers to the fair: to you theſe flowers I bring,
> ' And ſtrive to greet you with an earlier ſpring.
> ' *Flowers* SWEET, *and gay, and* DELICATE LIKE YOU;
> ' *Emblems of innocence, and beauty too.*
> ' With flowers the Graces bind their yellow hair,
> ' And flowery wreaths conſenting lovers wear.
> ' *Flowers, the ſole luxury which nature knew;*
> ' *In Eden's pure and guiltleſs garden grew.*
> ' *To loftier forms are rougher taſks aſſign'd;*
> ' *The ſheltering oak reſiſts the ſtormy wind,*
> ' *The tougher yew repels invading foes,*
> ' *And the tall pine for future navies grows;*
> ' *But this ſoft family, to cares unknown,*
> ' *Were born for pleaſure and delight* ALONE.
> ' Gay without toil, and lovely without art,
> ' *They ſpring to* CHEER *the ſenſe, and* GLAD *the heart,*
> ' Nor bluſh, my fair, to own you copy theſe;
> ' *Your* BEST, *your* SWEETEST *empire is—to* PLEASE.'

So the men tell us; but virtue muſt be acquired by *rough* toils, and uſeful ſtruggles with worldly *cares*.

G

fiftent, with a few exceptions, with their fexual character. Let men prove this, and I fhall grant that woman only exifts for man. I muft, however, previoufly remark, that the power of generalizing ideas, to any great extent, is not very common amongft men or women. But this exercife is the true cultivation of the underftanding ; and every thing confpires to render the cultivation of the underftanding more difficult in the female than the male world.

I am naturally led by this affertion to the main fubject of the prefent chapter, and fhall now attempt to point out fome of the caufes that degrade the fex, and prevent women from generalizing their obfervations.

I fhall not go back to the remote annals of antiquity to trace the hiftory of woman ; it is fufficient to allow that fhe has always been either a flave, or a defpot, and to remark, that each of thefe fituations equally retards the progrefs of reafon. The grand fource of female folly and vice has ever appeared to me to arife from narrownefs of mind ; and the very conftitution of civil governments has put almoft infuperable obftacles in the way to prevent the cultivation of the female underftanding :—yet virtue can be built on no other foundation ! The fame obftacles are thrown in the way of the rich, and the fame confequences enfue.

Neceffity has been proverbially termed the mother of invention—the aphorifm may be extended to virtue. It is an acquirement, and an acquirement to which pleafure muft be facrificed —and who facrifices pleafure when it is within the

the grafp, whofe mind has not been opened and ftrengthened by adverfity, or the purfuit of knowledge goaded on by neceffity ?—Happy is it when people have the cares of life to ftruggle with ; for thefe ftruggles prevent their becoming a prey to enervating vices, merely from idlenefs ! But, if from their birth men and women are placed in a torrid zone, with the meridian fun of pleafure darting directly upon them, how can they fufficiently brace their minds to difcharge the duties of life, or even to relifh the affections that carry them out of themfelves ?

Pleafure is the bufinefs of woman's life, according to the prefent modification of fociety, and while it continues to be fo, little can be expected from fuch weak beings. Inheriting, in a lineal defcent from the firft fair defect in nature, the fovereignty of beauty, they have, to maintain their power, refigned the natural rights, which the exercife of reafon might have procured them, and chofen rather to be fhort-lived queens than labour to obtain the fober pleafures that arife from equality. Exalted by their inferiority (this founds like a contradiction) they conftantly demand homage as women, though experience fhould teach them that the men who pride themfelves upon paying this arbitrary infolent refpect to the fex, with the moft fcrupulous exactnefs, are moft inclined to tyrannize over, and defpife, the very weaknefs they cherifh. Often do they repeat Mr. Hume's fentiments ; when, comparing the French and Athenian character, he alludes to women. ' But what is more fingular ' in this whimfical nation, fay I to the Athenians,

G 2   ' is,

' is, that a frolick of yours during the Saturnalia,
' when the flaves are ferved by their mafters, is,
' ferioufly, continued by them through the whole
' year, and through the whole courfe of their
' lives ; accompanied too with fome circum-
' ftances, which ftill further augment the abfur-
' dity and ridicule.   Your fport only elevates for
' a few days thofe whom fortune has thrown
' down, and whom fhe too, in fport, may really
' elevate for ever above you.   But this nation
' gravely exalts thofe, whom nature has fubjected
' to them, and whofe inferiority and infirmities
' are abfolutely incurable.   The women, though
' without virtue, are their mafters and fovereigns.'

Ah ! why do women, I write with affectionate folicitude, condefcend to receive a degree of
attention and refpect from ftrangers, different
from that reciprocation of civility which the dictates of humanity and the politenefs of civilization authorife between man and man ? And, why
do they not difcover, when ' in the noon of beauty's power,' that they are treated like queens only to be deluded by hollow refpect, till they are
led to refign, or not affume, their natural prerogatives ? Confined then in cages like the fea-
thered race, they have nothing to do but to plume
themfelves, and ftalk with mock majefty from
perch to perch.   It is true they are provided
with food and raiment, for which they neither
toil nor fpin ; but health, liberty, and virtue, are
given in exchange.   But, where, amongft mankind has been found fufficient ftrength of mind
to enable a being to refign thefe adventitious prerogatives ; one who, rifing with the calm digni-

ty

ty of reason above opinion, dared to be proud of the privileges inherent in man? And it is vain to expect it whilst hereditary power chokes the affections and nips reason in the bud.

The passions of men have thus placed women on thrones, and, till mankind become more reasonable, it is to be feared that women will avail themselves of the power which they attain with the least exertion, and which is the most indisputable. They will smile,—yes, they will smile, though told that—

> ‘ In beauty's empire is no mean,
> ‘ And woman, either slave or queen,
> ‘ Is quickly scorn'd when not ador'd.’

But the adoration comes first, and the scorn is not anticipated.

Lewis the XIVth, in particular, spread factitious manners, and caught, in a specious way, the whole nation in his toils; for, establishing an artful chain of despotism, he made it the interest of the people at large, individually to respect his station and support his power. And women, whom he flattered by a puerile attention to the whole sex, obtained in his reign that prince-like distinction so fatal to reason and virtue.

A king is always a king—and a woman always a woman*: his authority and her sex, ever stand between them and rational converse. With a lover, I grant, she should be so, and her sensibility will naturally lead her to endeavour to excite emotion, not to gratify her vanity, but her

heart.

---

* And a wit, always a wit, might be added; for the vain fooleries of wits and beauties to obtain attention, and make conquests, are much upon a par.

heart. This I do not allow to be coquetry, it is the artless impulse of nature, I only exclaim against the sexual desire of conquest when the heart is out of the question.

This desire is not confined to women ; ' I ' have endeavoured,' says Lord Chesterfield, ' to ' gain the hearts of twenty women, whose per- ' sons I would not have given a fig for.' The libertine, who, in a gust of passion, takes advantage of unsuspecting tenderness, is a faint when compared with this cold-hearted rascal ; for I like to use significant words. Yet only taught to please, women are always on the watch to please, and with true heroic ardour endeavour to gain hearts merely to resign, or spurn them, when the victory is decided, and conspicuous.

I must descend to the minutiæ of the sub-ject.

I lament that women are systematically degrad-ed by receiving the trivial attentions, which men think it manly to pay to the sex, when, in fact, they are insultingly supporting their own superiority. It is not condescension to bow to an inferiour. So ludicrous, in fact, do these ceremonies appear to me, that I scarcely am able to govern my mus-cles, when I see a man start with eager, and seri-ous solicitude to lift a handkerchief, or shut a door, when the *lady* could have done it herself, had she only moved a pace or two.

A wild wish has just flown from my heart to my head, and I will not stifle it though it may excite a horse-laugh.—I do earnestly wish to see the distinction of sex confounded in society, un-less where love animates the behaviour. For this
distinction

diſtinction is, I am firmly perſuaded, the foundation of the weakneſs of character aſcribed to woman ; is the cauſe why the underſtanding is neglected, whilſt accompliſhments are acquired
with ſedulous care: and the ſame cauſe accounts
for their preferring the graceful before the heroic
virtues.

Mankind, including every deſcription, wiſh to
be loved and reſpected for *ſomething*; and the common herd will always take the neareſt road to the
completion of their wiſhes. The reſpect paid to
wealth and beauty is the moſt certain, and unequivocal ; and, of courſe, will always attract the
vulgar eye of common minds. Abilities and virtues are abſolutely neceſſary to raiſe men from the
middle rank of life into notice ; and the natural
conſequence is notorious, the middle rank contains moſt virtue and abilities. Men have thus,
in one ſtation, at leaſt, an opportunity of exerting
themſelves with dignity, and of riſing by the exertions which really improve a rational creature ;
but the whole female ſex are, till their character
is formed, in the ſame condition as the rich : for
they are born, I now ſpeak of a ſtate of civilization, with certain ſexual privileges, and whilſt
they are gratuitouſly granted them, few will ever
think of works of ſupererogation, to obtain the
eſteem of a ſmall number of ſuperiour people.

When do we hear of women who, ſtarting out
of obſcurity, boldly claim reſpect on account of
their great abilities or daring virtues ? Where are
they to be found ?—‘ To be obſerved, to be at-
‘ tended to, to be taken notice of with ſympathy,
‘ complacency, and approbation, are all the advan-

‘ tages

' tages which they feek.'—True ! my male readers will probably exclaim ; but let them, before
they draw any conclufion, recollect that this was
not written originally as defcriptive of women,
but of the rich. In Dr. Smith's Theory of Moral Sentiments, I have found a general character of
people of rank and fortune, that, in my opinion,
might with the greateft propriety be applied to
the female fex. I refer the fagacious reader to the
whole comparifon ; but muft be allowed to quote
a paffage to enforce an argument that I mean to
infift on, as the one moft conclufive againft a fexual character. For if, excepting warriors, no great
men, of any denomination, have ever appeared
amongft the nobility, may it not be fairly inferred
that their local fituation fwallowed up the man,
and produced a character fimilar to that of women,
who are *localized*, if I may be allowed the word,
by the rank they are placed in, by *courtefy ?* Women, commonly called Ladies, are not to be contradicted in company, are not allowed to exert any
manual ftrength ; and from them the negative virtues only are expected, when any virtues are expected, patience, docility, good-humour, and flex-
ibility ; virtues incompatible with any vigorous
exertion of intellect. Befides, by living more
with each other, and being feldom abfolutely alone,
they are more under the influence of fentiments
than paffions. Solitude and reflection are neceffary to give to wifhes the force of paffions, and to
enable the imagination to enlarge the object, and
make it the moft defirable. The fame may be
faid of the rich ; they do not fufficiently deal in
general ideas, collected by impaffioned thinking,

or

or calm investigation, to acquire that strength of character on which great resolves are built. But hear what an acute observer says of the great.

' Do the great seem insensible of the easy price
' at which they may acquire the publick admira-
' tion; or do they seem to imagine that to them,
' as to other men, it must be the purchase either
' of sweat or of blood? By what important ac-
' complishments is the young nobleman instruct-
' ed to support the dignity of his rank, and to ren-
' der himself worthy of that superiority over his
' fellow-citizens, to which the virtue of his an-
' cestors had raised them? Is it by knowledge, by
' industry, by patience, by self-denial, or by virtue
' of any kind? As all his words, as all his motions
' are attended to, he learns an habitual regard to
' every circumstance of ordinary behaviour, and
' studies to perform all those small duties with
' the most exact propriety. As he is conscious
' how much he is observed, and how much man-
' kind are disposed to favour all his inclinations,
' he acts, upon the most indifferent occasions with
' that freedom and elevation which the thought
' of this naturally inspires. His air, his manner,
' his deportment, all mark that elegant and grace-
' ful sense of his own superiority, which those
' who are born to inferiour station can hardly ever
' arrive at. These are the arts by which he pro-
' poses to make mankind more easily submit to
' his authority, and to govern their inclinations
' according to his own pleasure: and in this he
' is seldom disappointed. These arts, supported
' by rank and pre-eminence, are, upon ordinary
' occasions, sufficient to govern the world. Lew-

' is

' is XIV. during the greater part of his reign,
' was regarded, not only in France, but over all
' Europe, as the moſt perfect model of a great
' prince. But what were the talents and virtues
' by which he acquired this great reputation ?
' Was it by the ſcrupulous and inflexible juſtice
' of all his undertakings, by the immenſe dangers
' and difficulties with which they were attended,
' or by the unwearied and unrelenting applica-
' tion with which he purſued them ? Was it by
' his extenſive knowledge, by his exquiſite judg-
' ment, or by his heroic valour ? It was by none
' of theſe qualities. But he was, firſt of all, the
' moſt powerful prince in Europe, and conſe-
' quently held the higheſt rank among kings ;
' and then, ſays his hiſtorian, " he ſurpaſſed all
" his courtiers in the gracefulneſs of his ſhape,
" and the majeſtic beauty of his features. The
" ſound of his voice, noble and affecting, gained
" thoſe hearts which his preſence intimidated.
" He had a ſtep and a deportment which could
" ſuit only him and his rank, and which would
" have been ridiculous in any other perſon. The
" embarraſſment which he occaſioned to thoſe
" who ſpoke to him, flattered that ſecret ſatiſ-
" faction with which he felt his own ſuperiori-
" ty." ' Theſe frivolous accompliſhments, ſup-
' ported by his rank, and, no doubt too, by a de-
' gree of other talents and virtues, which ſeems,
' however, not to have been much above medi-
' ocrity, eſtabliſhed this prince in the eſteem of
' his own age, and have drawn, even from poſ-
' terity, a good deal of reſpect for his memory.
' Compared with theſe, in his own times, and in
his

' his own prefence, no other virtue, it feems, ap-
' peared to have any merit. Knowledge, induf-
' try, valour, and beneficence, trembled, were
' abafhed, and loft all dignity before them.'

Woman alfo thus ' in herfelf complete,' by
poffeffing all thefe *frivolous* accomplifhments, fo
changes the nature of things

> ———— ' That what fhe wills to do or fay
> ' Seems wifeft, virtuoufeft, difcreeteft, beft ;
> ' All higher knowledge in *her prefence* falls
> ' Degraded. Wifdom in difcourfe with her
> ' Lofes difcountenanc'd, and, like Folly, fhows ;
> ' Authority and Reafon on her wait.'——

And all this is built on her lovelinefs !

In the middle rank of life, to continue the
comparifon, men, in their youth, are prepared for
profeffions, and marriage is not confidered as the
grand feature in their lives ; whilft women, on
the contrary, have no other fcheme to fharpen
their faculties. It is not bufinefs, extenfive
plans, or any of the excurfive flights of ambition,
that engrofs their attention ; no, their thoughts
are not employed in rearing fuch noble ftructures.
To rife in the world, and have the liberty of running from pleafure to pleafure, they muft marry
advantageoufly, and to this object their time is
facrificed, and their perfons often legally profti-
tuted. A man when he enters any profeffion has
his eye fteadily fixed on fome future advantage
(and the mind gains great ftrength by having all
its efforts directed to one point) and, full of his
bufinefs, pleafure is confidered as mere relaxation ;
whilft women feek for pleafure as the main purpofe of exiftence. In fact, from the education,

which

which they receive from society, the love of pleasure may be said to govern them all; but does this prove that there is a sex in souls? It would be just as rational to declare that the courtiers in France, when a destructive system of despotism had formed their character, were not men, because liberty, virtue, and humanity, were sacrificed to pleasure and vanity.—Fatal passions, which have ever domineered over the *whole* race!

The same love of pleasure, fostered by the whole tendency of their education, gives a trifling turn to the conduct of women in most circumstances: for instance, they are ever anxious about secondary things; and on the watch for adventures, instead of being occupied by duties.

A man, when he undertakes a journey, has, in general, the end in view; a woman thinks more of the incidental occurrences, the strange things that may possibly occur on the road; the impression that she may make on her fellow-travellers; and, above all, she is anxiously intent on the care of the finery that she carries with her, which is more than ever a part of herself, when going to figure on a new scene; when, to use an apt French turn of expression, she is going to produce a sensation.—Can dignity of mind exist with such trivial cares?

In short, women, in general, as well as the rich of both sexes, have acquired all the follies and vices of civilization, and missed the useful fruit. It is not necessary for me always to premise, that I speak of the condition of the whole sex, leaving exceptions out of the question. Their senses are inflamed, and their understandings neglected, consequently

consequently they become the prey of their senses, delicately termed sensibility, and are blown about by every momentary gust of feeling. They are, therefore, in a much worse condition than they would be in were they in a state nearer to nature. Ever restless and anxious, their over exercised sensibility not only renders them uncomfortable themselves, but troublesome, to use a soft phrase, to others. All their thoughts turn on things calculated to excite emotion; and feeling, when they should reason, their conduct is unstable, and their opinions are wavering—not the wavering produced by deliberation or progressive views, but by contradictory emotions. By fits and starts they are warm in many pursuits; yet this warmth, never concentrated into perseverance, soon exhausts itself; exhaled by its own heat, or meeting with some other fleeting passion, to which reason has never given any specific gravity, neutrality ensues. Miserable, indeed, must be that being whose cultivation of mind has only tended to inflame its passions! A distinction should be made between inflaming and strengthening them. The passions thus pampered, whilst the judgment is left unformed, what can be expected to ensue?—Undoubtedly, a mixture of madness and folly!

This observation should not be confined to the *fair* sex; however, at present, I only mean to apply it to them.

Novels, music, poetry, and gallantry, all tend to make women the creatures of sensation, and their character is thus formed during the time they are acquiring accomplishments, the only improvement

provement they are excited, by their station in society, to acquire. This overstretched sensibility naturally relaxes the other powers of the mind, and prevents intellect from attaining that sovereignty which it ought to attain to render a rational creature useful to others, and content with its own station : for the exercise of the understanding, as life advances, is the only method pointed out by nature to calm the passions.

Satiety has a very different effect, and I have often been forcibly struck by an emphatical description of damnation :—when the spirit is represented as continually hovering with abortive eagerness round the defiled body, unable to enjoy any thing without the organs of sense. Yet, to their senses, are women made slaves, because it is by their sensibility that they obtain present power.

And will moralists pretend to assert, that this is the condition in which one half of the human race should be encouraged to remain with listless inactivity and stupid acquiescence ? Kind instructors ! what were we created for ? To remain, it may be said, innocent ; they mean in a state of childhood.—We might as well never have been born, unless it were necessary that we should be created to enable man to acquire the noble privilege of reason, the power of discerning good from evil, whilst we lie down in the dust from whence we were taken, never to rise again.—

It would be an endless task to trace the variety of meannesses, cares, and sorrows, into which women are plunged by the prevailing opinion, that they were created rather to feel than reason,

and

and that all the power they obtain, muſt be obtained by their charms and weakneſs :

‘ Fine by defect, and amiably weak !’

And, made by this amiable weakneſs entirely dependent, excepting what they gain by illicit ſway, on man, not only for protection, but advice, is it ſurpriſing that, neglecting the duties that reaſon alone points out, and ſhrinking from trials calculated to ſtrengthen their minds, they only exert themſelves to give their defects a graceful covering, which may ſerve to heighten their charms in the eye of the voluptuary, though it ſink them below the ſcale of moral excellence ?

Fragile in every ſenſe of the word, they are obliged to look up to man for every comfort. In the moſt trifling dangers they cling to their ſupport, with paraſitical tenacity, piteouſly demanding ſuccour ; and their *natural* protector extends his arm, or lifts up his voice, to guard the lovely trembler—from what ? Perhaps the frown of an old cow, or the jump of a mouſe ; a rat, would be a ſerious danger. In the name of reaſon, and even common ſenſe, what can ſave ſuch beings from contempt ; even though they be ſoft and fair ?

Theſe fears, when not affected, may be very pretty ; but they ſhew a degree of imbecility that degrades a rational creature in a way women are not aware of—for love and eſteem are very diſtinct things.

I am fully perſuaded that we ſhould hear of none of theſe infantile airs, if girls were allowed to take ſufficient exerciſe, and not confined in cloſe

rooms

rooms till their mufcles are relaxed, and their
powers of digeftion deftroyed. To carry the remark ftill further, if fear in girls, inftead of being cherifhed, perhaps, created, was treated in
the fame manner as cowardice in boys, we fhould
quickly fee women with more dignified afpects.
It is true, they could not then with equal propriety be termed the fweet flowers that fmile in
the walk of man; but they would be more refpectable members of fociety, and difcharge the
important duties of life by the light of their own
reafon. 'Educate women like men,' fays Rouffeau, 'and the more they refemble our fex the
'lefs power will they have over us.' This is
the very point I aim at. I do not wifh them to
have power over men; but over themfelves.

In the fame ftrain have I heard men argue
againft inftructing the poor; for many are the
forms that ariftocracy affumes. 'Teach them
'to read and write,' fay they, 'and you take them
'out of the ftation affigned them by nature.'
An eloquent Frenchman has anfwered them, I
will borrow his fentiments. But they know
not, when they make man a brute, that they
may expect every inftant to fee him transformed
into a ferocious beaft. Without knowledge there
can be no morality!

Ignorance is a frail bafe for virtue! Yet, that
it is the condition for which woman was organized, has been infifted upon by the writers who
have moft vehemently argued in favour of the fuperiority of man; a fuperiority not in degree,
but effence; though, to foften the argument,
they have laboured to prove, with chivalrous
generofity,

generofity, that the fexes ought not to be compared ; man was made to reafon, woman to feel ; and that together, flefh and fpirit, they make the moft perfect whole, by blending happily reafon and fenfibility into one character.

And what is fenfibility ? ' Quicknefs of fen-' fation ; quicknefs of perception ; delicacy.' Thus is it defined by Dr. Johnfon ; and the definition gives me no other idea than of the moft exquifitely polifhed inftinct. I difcern not a trace of the image of God in either fenfation or matter. Refined feventy times feven, they are ftill material ; intellect dwells not there ; nor will fire ever make lead gold !

I come round to my old argument ; if woman be allowed to have an immortal foul, fhe muft have, as the employment of life, an underftanding to improve. And when, to render the prefent ftate more complete, though every thing proves it to be but a fraction of a mighty fum, fhe is incited by prefent gratification to forget her grand deftination, Nature is counteracted, or fhe was born only to procreate and die. Or, granting brutes, of every defcription, a foul, though not a reafonable one, the exercife of inftinct and fenfibility may be the ftep, which they are to take, in this life, towards the attainment of reafon in the next ; fo that through all eternity they will lag behind man, who, why we cannot tell, had the power given him of attaining reafon in his firft mode of exiftence.

When I treat of the peculiar duties of women, as I fhould treat of the peculiar duties of a citizen or father, it will be found that I do not mean to

H   infinuate

infinuate that they fhould be taken out of their families, fpeaking of the majority. 'He that hath 'wife and children,' fays Lord Bacon, 'hath giv-'en hoftages to fortune ; for they are impedi-'ments to great enterprifes, either of virtue or 'mifchief. Certainly the beft works, and of '.greateft merit for the public, have proceeded 'from the unmarried or childlefs men.' I fay the fame of women. But, the welfare of fociety is not built on extraordinary exertions ; and were it more reafonably organized, there would be ftill lefs need of great abilities, or heroic vir-tues.

In the regulation of a family, in the education of children, underftanding, in an unfophifticated fenfe, is particularly required : ftrength both of body and mind ; yet the men who, by their writings, have moft earneftly laboured to domef-ticate women, have endeavoured, by arguments dictated by a grofs appetite, that fatiety had ren-dered faftidious, to weaken their bodies and cramp their minds. But, if even by thefe finifter me-thods they really *perfuaded* women, by working on their feelings, to ftay at home, and fulfil the duties of a mother and miftrefs of a family, I fhould cautioufly oppofe opinions that led wo-men to right conduct, by prevailing on them to make the difcharge of a duty the bufinefs of life, though reafon were infulted. Yet, and I appeal to experience, if by neglecting the underftanding they are as much, nay, more detached from thefe domeftic duties, than they could be by the moft ferious intellectual purfuit, though it may be ob-ferved that the mafs of mankind will never vigor-

oufly

oufly purfue an intellectual object*, I may be allowed to infer that reafon is abfolutely neceffary to enable a woman to perform any duty properly, and I muft again repeat, that fenfibility is not reafon.

The comparifon with the rich ftill occurs to me, for, when men neglect the duties of humanity, women will do the fame; a common ftream hurries them both along with thoughtlefs celerity. Riches and honours prevent a man from enlarging his underftanding, and enervate all his powers by reverfing the order of nature, which has ever made true pleafure the reward of labour. Pleafure—enervating pleafure is, likewife, within women's reach without earning it. But, till hereditary poffeffions are fpread abroad, how can we expect men to be proud of virtue? And, till they are, women will govern them by the moft direct means, neglecting their dull domeftic duties to catch the pleafure that is on the wing of time.

' The power of the woman,' fays fome author, ' is her fenfibility;' and men, not aware of the confequence, do all they can to make this power fwallow up every other. Thofe who conftantly employ their fenfibility will have moft; for example; poets, painters, and compofers†. Yet, when the fenfibility is thus increafed at the expenfe of reafon, and even the imagination, why

do

---

* The mafs of mankind are rather the flaves of their appetites than of their paffions.

† Men of thefe defcriptions pour it into their compofitions, to amalgamate the grofs materials; and, moulding them with paffion, give to the inert body a foul; but, in woman's imagination, love alone concentrates thefe etherial beams.

do philosophical men complain of their fickleness? The sexual attention of man particularly acts on female sensibility, and this sympathy has been exercised from their youth up. A husband cannot long pay those attentions with the passion necessary to excite lively emotions, and the heart, accustomed to lively emotions, turns to a new lover, or pines in secret, the prey of virtue or prudence. I mean when the heart has really been rendered susceptible, and the taste formed; for I am apt to conclude, from what I have seen in fashionable life, that vanity is oftener fostered than sensibility by the mode of education, and the intercourse between the sexes, which I have reprobated; and that coquetry more frequently proceeds from vanity than from that inconstancy, which overstrained sensibility naturally produces.

Another argument that has had a great weight with me, must, I think, have some force with every considerate, benevolent heart. Girls who have been thus weakly educated, are often cruelly left by their parents without any provision; and, of course, are dependent on, not only the reason, but the bounty of their brothers. These brothers are, to view the fairest side of the question, good sort of men, and give as a favour, what children of the same parents had an equal right to. In this equivocal humiliating situation, a docile female may remain some time, with a tolerable degree of comfort. But, when the brother marries, a probable circumstance, from being considered as the mistress of the family, she is viewed with averted looks as an intruder, an unnecessary

burden

burden on the benevolence of the master of the house, and his new partner.

Who can recount the misery, which many unfortunate beings, whose minds and bodies are equally weak, suffer in such situations—unable to work, and ashamed to beg? The wife, a coldhearted, narrow-minded, woman, and this is not an unfair supposition; for the present mode of education does not tend to enlarge the heart any more than the understanding, is jealous of the little kindness which her husband shews to his relations; and her sensibility not rising to humanity, she is displeased at seeing the property of *her* children lavished on an helpless sister.

These are matters of fact, which have come under my eye, again and again. The consequence is obvious; the wife has recourse to cunning to undermine the habitual affection, which she is afraid openly to oppose; and neither tears nor caresses are spared till the spy is worked out of her home, and thrown on the world, unprepared for its difficulties; or sent, as a great effort of generosity, or from some regard to propriety, with a small stipend, and an uncultivated mind, into joyless solitude.

These two women may be much upon a par, with respect to reason and humanity; and changing situations might have acted just the same selfish part; but had they been differently educated, the case would also have been very different. The wife would not have had that sensibility, of which self is the centre, and reason might have taught her not to expect, and not even to be flattered, by the affection of her husband, if it led him to violate prior duties. She would wish not to love him merely because he loved her, but on account of his virtues ; and the sister might have been able to struggle for herself instead of eating the bitter bread of dependence.

I am, indeed, persuaded that the heart, as well as the understanding, is opened by cultivation ; and by, which may not appear so clear, strengthening the organs ; I am not now talking of momentary flashes of sensibility, but of affections. And, perhaps, in the education of both sexes, the most difficult task is so to adjust instruction as not to narrow the understanding, whilst the heart is warmed by the generous juices of spring, just raised by the electric fermentation of the season ; nor to dry up the feelings by employing the mind in investigations remote from life.

With respect to women, when they receive a careful education, they are either made fine ladies, brimful of sensibility, and teeming with capricious fancies ; or mere notable women. The latter are often friendly, honest creatures, and have a shrewd kind of good sense joined with worldly prudence, that often render them more useful members of society than the fine sentimental lady, though they possess neither greatness of mind nor taste. The intellectual world is shut against them ; take them out of their family or neighbourhood, and they stand still ; the mind finding no employment, for literature affords a fund of amusement which they have never sought to relish, but frequently to despise. The sentiments and taste of more cultivated minds appear ridiculous, even in those whom chance and

family

family connections have led them to love; but in mere acquaintance they think it all affectation.

A man of sense can only love such a woman, on account of her sex, and respect her, because she is a trusty servant. He lets her, to preserve his own peace, scold the servants, and go to church in clothes made of the very best materials. A man of her own size of understanding would, probably, not agree so well with her; for he might wish to encroach on her prerogative, and manage some domestic concerns himself. Yet women, whose minds are not enlarged by cultivation, or the natural selfishness of sensibility expanded by reflection, are very unfit to manage a family; for, by an undue stretch of power, they are always tyrannizing to support a superiority that only rests on the arbitrary distinction of fortune. The evil is sometimes more serious, and domestics are deprived of innocent indulgences, and made to work beyond their strength, in order to enable the notable woman to keep a better table, and outshine her neighbours in finery and parade. If she attend to her children, it is, in general, to dress them in a costly manner—and, whether this attention arises from vanity or fondness, it is equally pernicious.

Besides, how many women of this description pass their days; or, at least, their evenings, discontentedly. Their husbands acknowledge that they are good managers, and chaste wives; but leave home to seek for more agreeable, may I be allowed to use a significant French word, *piquant* society; and the patient drudge, who fulfils her task, like a blind horse in a mill, is defrauded of

her

her juſt reward ; for the wages due to her are the careſſes of her huſband ; and women who have ſo few reſources in themſelves, do not very patiently bear this privation of a natural right.

A fine lady, on the contrary, has been taught to look down with contempt on the vulgar employments of life ; though ſhe has only been incited to acquire accompliſhments that riſe a degree above ſenſe ; for even corporeal accompliſhments cannot be acquired with any degree of preciſion unleſs the underſtanding has been ſtrengthened by exerciſe. Without a foundation of principles taſte is ſuperficial ; and grace muſt ariſe from ſomething deeper than imitation. The imagination, however, is heated, and the feelings rendered faſtidious, if not ſophiſticated ; or, a counterpoiſe of judgment is not acquired, when the heart ſtill remains artleſs, though it becomes too tender.

Theſe women are often amiable ; and their hearts are really more ſenſible to general benevolence, more alive to the ſentiments that civilize life, than the ſquare-elbowed family drudge ; but, wanting a due proportion of reflection and ſelf-government, they only inſpire love ; and are the miſtreſſes of their huſbands, whilſt they have any hold on their affections ; and the platonic friends of his male acquaintance. Theſe are the fair defects in nature ; the women who appear to be created not to enjoy the fellowſhip of man, but to ſave him from ſinking into abſolute brutality, by rubbing off the rough angles of his character ; and by playful dalliance to give ſome dignity to the appetite that draws him to them.

Gracious

Gracious Creator of the whole human race! haft thou created such a being as woman, who can trace thy wisdom in thy works, and feel that thou alone art by thy nature, exalted above her,—for no better purpose?—Can she believe that she was only made to submit to man, her equal; a being, who, like her, was sent into the world to acquire virtue?—Can she consent to be occupied merely to please him; merely to adorn the earth, when her soul is capable of rising to thee?—And can she reft supinely dependent on man, for reason, when she ought to mount with him the arduous steeps of knowledge?—

Yet, if love be the supreme good, let women be only educated to inspire it, and let every charm be polished to intoxicate the senses; but, if they are moral beings, let them have a chance to become intelligent; and let love to man be only a part of that glowing flame of universal love, which, after encircling humanity, mounts in grateful incense to God.

To fulfil domestic duties much resolution is necessary, and a serious kind of perseverance that requires a more firm support than emotions, however lively and true to nature. To give an example of order, the soul of virtue, some austerity of behaviour muft be adopted, scarcely to be expected from a being who, from its infancy, has been made the weathercock of its own sensations. Whoever rationally means to be useful must have a plan of conduct; and, in the difcharge of the simplest duty, we are often obliged to act contrary to the present impulfe of tenderness or compassion. Severity is frequently the most certain,

as

as well as the moſt ſublime proof of affection ; and the want of this power over the feelings, and of that lofty, dignified affection, which makes a perſon prefer the future good of the beloved object to a preſent gratification, is the reaſon why ſo many fond mothers ſpoil their children; and has made it queſtionable whether negligence or indulgence is moſt hurtful : but I am inclined to think, that the latter has done moſt harm.

Mankind ſeem to agree that children ſhould be left under the management of women during their childhood.   Now, from all the obſervation that I have been able to make, women of ſenſibility are the moſt unfit for this taſk, becauſe they will infallibly, carried away by their feelings, ſpoil a child's temper.   The management of the temper, the firſt, and moſt important branch of education, requires the ſober ſteady eye of reaſon ; a plan of conduct equally diſtant from tyranny and indulgence : yet theſe are the extremes that people of ſenſibility alternately fall into ; always ſhooting beyond the mark.   I have followed this train of reaſoning much further, till I have concluded, that a perſon of genius is the moſt improper perſon to be employed in education, public or private.   Minds of this rare ſpecies ſee things too much in maſſes, and ſeldom, if ever, have a good temper.   That habitual cheerfulneſs, termed good-humour, is, perhaps, as ſeldom united with great mental powers, as with ſtrong feelings.   And thoſe people who follow, with intereſt and admiration, the flights of genius ; or, with cooler approbation ſuck in the inſtruction which has been elaborately prepared for

for them by the profound thinker, ought not to be difgufted, if they find the former choleric, and the latter morofe; becaufe livelinefs of fancy, and a tenacious comprehenfion of mind, are fcarcely compatible with that pliant urbanity which leads a man, at leaft, to bend to the opinions and prejudices of others, inftead of roughly confronting them.

But, treating of education or manners, minds of a fuperior clafs are not to be confidered, they may be left to chance; it is the multitude, with moderate abilities, who call for inftruction, and catch the colour of the atmofphere they breathe. This refpectable concourfe, I contend, men and women, fhould not have their fenfations heightened in the hot-bed of luxurious indolence, at the expenfe of their underftanding; for, unlefs there be a ballaft of underftanding, they will never become either virtuous or free: an ariftocracy, founded on property, or fterling talents, will ever fweep before it, the alternately timid, and ferocious, flaves of feeling.

Numberlefs are the arguments, to take another view of the fubject, brought forward with a fhew of reafon: becaufe fuppofed to be deduced from nature, that men have ufed morally and phyfically, to degrade the fex. I muft notice a few.

The female underftanding has often been fpoken of with contempt, as arriving fooner at maturity than the male. I fhall not anfwer this argument by alluding to the early proofs of reafon, as well as genius, in Cowley, Milton, and Pope[*], but only appeal to experience to decide whether young men, who are early introduced

into

---

[*] Many other names might be added.

into company (and examples now abound) do
not acquire the same precocity. So notorious is
this fact, that the bare mentioning of it must
bring before people, who at all mix in the world,
the idea of a number of swaggering apes of men,
whose understandings are narrowed by being
brought into the society of men when they ought
to have been spinning a top or twirling a hoop.

It has also been asserted, by some naturalists,
that men do not attain their full growth and
strength till thirty; but that women arrive at
maturity by twenty. I apprehend that they reason on false ground, led astray by the male prejudice, which deems beauty the perfection of
woman—mere beauty of features and complexion, the vulgar acceptation of the word, whilst
male beauty is allowed to have some connection
with the mind. Strength of body, and that
character of countenance, which the French
term a *physionomie*, women do not acquire before
thirty, any more than men. The little artless
tricks of children, it is true, are particularly
pleasing and attractive; yet, when the pretty
freshness of youth is worn off, these artless graces
become studied airs, and disgust every person of
taste. In the countenance of girls we only look
for vivacity and bashful modesty; but, the spring-
tide of life over, we look for soberer sense in the
face, and for traces of passion, instead of the dimples of animal spirits; expecting to see individuality of character, the only fastener of the affections *. We then wish to converse, not to
fondle;

---

* The strength of an affection is, generally, in the same proportion as
the character of the species in the object beloved, is lost in that of the individual.

fondle ; to give scope to our imaginations as well as to the sensations of our hearts.

At twenty the beauty of both sexes is equal ; but the libertinism of man leads him to make the distinction, and superannuated coquettes are commonly of the same opinion ; for, when they can no longer inspire love, they pay for the vigour and vivacity of youth. The French, who admit more of mind into their notions of beauty, give the preference to women of thirty. I mean to say that they allow women to be in their most perfect state, when vivacity gives place to reason, and to that majestic seriousness of character, which marks maturity ;—or, the resting point. In youth, till twenty, the body shoots out, till thirty the solids are attaining a degree of density ; and the flexible muscles, growing daily more rigid, give character to the countenance ; that is, they trace the operations of the mind with the iron pen of fate, and tell us not only what powers are within, but how they have been employed.

It is proper to observe, that animals who arrive slowly at maturity, are the longest lived, and of the noblest species. Men cannot, however, claim any natural superiority from the grandeur of longevity ; for in this respect nature has not distinguished the male.

Polygamy is another physical degradation ; and a plausible argument for a custom, that blasts every domestic virtue, is drawn from the well-attested fact, that in the countries where it is established, more females are born than males. This appears to be an indication of nature, and to nature, apparently reasonable speculations must yield. A further conclusion obviously presented itself ; if polygamy be necessary, woman must be inferiour to man, and made for him.

With respect to the formation of the fœtus in the womb, we are very ignorant ; but it appears to me probable, that an accidental physical cause may account for this phenomenon, and prove it not to be a law of nature. I have met with some pertinent observations on the subject in Forster's Account of the Isles of the South-Sea, that will explain my meaning. After observing that of the two sexes amongst animals, the most vigorous and fiery constitution always prevails, and produces its kind ; he adds,—' If this be applied to ' the inhabitants of Africa, it is evident that the ' men there, accustomed to polygamy, are ener- ' vated by the use of so many women, and there- ' fore less vigorous ; the women, on the contra- ' ry, are of a warmer constitution, not only on ' account of their more irritable nerves, more sen- ' sible organization, and more lively fancy ; but ' likewise because they are deprived in their ma- ' trimony of that share of physical love which, in ' a monogamous condition, would all be theirs ; ' and thus, for the above reasons, the generality ' of children are born females.'

' In the greater part of Europe it has been ' proved by the most accurate lists of mortality, ' that the proportion of men to women is nearly ' equal, or, if any difference takes place, the males ' born are more numerous, in the proportion of ' 105 to 100.'

The

The neceffity of polygamy, therefore, does not appear ; yet when a man feduces a woman, it fhould, I think, be termed a *left-handed* marriage, and the man fhould be *legally* obliged to maintain the woman and her children, unlefs adultery, a natural divorcement, abrogated the law. And this law fhould remain in force as long as the weaknefs of women caufed the word feduction to be ufed as an excufe for their frailty and want of principle ; nay, while they depend on man for a fubfiftence, inftead of earning it by the exertion of their own hands or heads. But thefe women fhould not, in the full meaning of their relation-fhip, be termed wives, or the very purpofe of marriage would be fubverted, and all thofe endearing charities that flow from perfonal fidelity, and give a fanctity to the tie, when neither love nor friendfhip unites the hearts, would melt into felfifhnefs. The woman who is faithful to the father of her children demands refpect, and fhould not be treated like a proftitute ; though I readily grant that if it be neceffary for a man and woman to live together in order to bring up their offspring, nature never intended that a man fhould have more than one wife.

Still, highly as I refpect marriage, as the foundation of almoft every focial virtue, I cannot avoid feeling the moft lively compaffion for thofe unfortunate females who are broken off from fociety, and by one error torn from all thofe affections and relationfhips that improve the heart and mind. It does not frequently even deferve the name of error ; for many innocent girls become the dupes of a fincere affectionate heart, and ftill

more

more are, as it may emphatically be termed, *ru-ined* before they know the difference between virtue and vice :—and thus prepared by their education for infamy, they become infamous. Asylums and Magdalens are not the proper remedies for these abuses. It is justice, not charity, that is wanting in the world !

A woman who has lost her honour, imagines that she cannot fall lower, and as for recovering her former station, it is impossible ; no exertion can wash this stain away. Losing thus every spur, and having no other means of support, prostitution becomes her only refuge, and the character is quickly depraved by circumstances over which the poor wretch has little power, unless she possesses an uncommon portion of sense and loftiness of spirit. Necessity never makes prostitution the business of men's lives ; though numberless are the women who are thus rendered systematically vicious. This, however, arises, in a great degree, from the state of idleness in which women are educated, who are always taught to look up to man for a maintenance, and to consider their persons as the proper return for his exertions to support them. Meretricious airs, and the whole science of wantonness, has then a more powerful stimulous than either appetite or vanity ; and this remark gives force to the prevailing opinion, that with chastity all is lost that is respectable in woman. Her character depends on the observance of one virtue, though the only passion fostered in her heart—is love. Nay, the honour of a woman is not made even to depend on her will.

When

When Richardson * makes Clariffa tell Love-lace that he had robbed her of her honour, he muft have had ftrange notions of honour and vir-tue. For, miferable beyond all names of mifery is the condition of a being, who could be de-graded without its own confent! This excefs of ftrictnefs I have heard vindicated as a falutary er-ror. I fhall anfwer in the words of Leibnitz— ' Errors are often ufeful ; but it is commonly to remedy other errors.'

Moft of the evils of life arife from a defire of prefent enjoyment that outruns itfelf. The obedience required of women in the marriage ftate comes under this defcription ; the mind naturally weakened by depending on authority, never exerts its own powers, and the obedient wife is thus rendered a weak indolent mother. Or, fuppofing that this is not always the confequence, a future ftate of exiftence is fcarcely taken into the reckoning when only negative virtues are cul-tivated. For, in treating of morals, particularly when women are alluded to, writers have too oft-en confidered virtue in a very limited fenfe, and made the foundation of it *folely* worldly utility ; nay, a ftill more fragile bafe has been given to this ftupendous fabric, and the wayward fluctuating feelings of men have been made the ftandard of virtue. Yes, virtue as well as religion, has been fubjected to the decifions of tafte.

It would almoft provoke a fmile of contempt, if the vain abfurdities of man did not ftrike us on all fides, to obferve, how eager men are to degrade

I   the

---

* Dr. Young fupports the fame opinion, in his plays, when he talks of the misfortune that fhunned the light of day.

the fex from whom they pretend to receive the chief pleafure of life ; and I have frequently with full conviction retorted Pope's farcafm on them ; or, to fpeak explicitly, it has appeared to me ap- plicable to the whole human race. A love of pleafure or fway feems to divide mankind, and the hufband who lords it in his little haram thinks only of his pleafure or his convenience. To fuch lengths, indeed, does an intemperate love of pleafure carry fome prudent men, or worn out libertines, who marry to have a fafe bed-fellow, that they feduce their own wives.——Hymen ban- ifhes modefty, and chafte love takes its flight.

Love, confidered as an animal appetite, cannot long feed on itfelf without expiring. And this extinction, in its own flame, may be termed the violent death of love. But the wife who has thus been rendered licentious, will probably en- deavour to fill the void left by the lofs of her hufband's attentions ; for fhe cannot contented- ly become merely an upper fervant after having been treated like a goddefs. She is ftill hand- fome, and, inftead of transferring her fondnefs to her children, fhe only dreams of enjoying the funfhine of life. Befides, there are many huf- bands fo devoid of fenfe and parental affection, that during the firft effervefcence of voluptuous fondnefs they refufe to let their wives fuckle their children. They are only to drefs and live to pleafe them : and love—even innocent love, foon finks into lafcivioufnefs, when the exercife of a duty is facrificed to its indulgence.

Perfonal attachment is a very happy founda- tion for friendfhip ; yet, when even two virtuous

young

young people marry, it would, perhaps, be happy if some circumstances checked their passion ; if the recollection of some prior attachment, or disappointed affection, made it on one side, at least, rather a match founded on esteem. In that case they would look beyond the present moment, and try to render the whole of life respectable, by forming a plan to regulate a friendship which only death ought to dissolve.

Friendship is a serious affection ; the most sublime of all affections, because it is founded on principle, and cemented by time. The very reverse may be said of love. In a great degree, love and friendship cannot subsist in the same bosom ; even when inspired by different objects they weaken or destroy each other, and for the same object can only be felt in succession. The vain fears and fond jealousies, the winds which fan the flame of love, when judiciously or artfully tempered, are both incompatible with the tender confidence and sincere respect of friendship.

Love, such as the glowing pen of genius has traced, exists not on earth, or only resides in those exalted, fervid imaginations that have sketched such dangerous pictures. Dangerous, because they not only afford a plausible excuse, to the voluptuary who disguises sheer sensuality under a sentimental veil ; but as they spread affectation, and take from the dignity of virtue. Virtue, as the very word imports, should have an appearance of seriousness, if not austerity ; and to endeavour to trick her out in the garb of pleasure, because the epithet has been used as another name for beauty, is to exalt her on a quicksand ; a most

insidious

infidious attempt to haften her fall by apparent refpect. Virtue and pleafure are not, in fact, fo nearly allied in this life as fome eloquent writers have laboured to prove. Pleafure prepares the fading wreath, and mixes the intoxicating cup; but the fruit which virtue gives, is the recompence of toil: and, gradually feen as it ripens, only affords calm fatisfaction; nay, appearing to be the refult of the natural tendency of things, it is fcarcely obferved. Bread, the common food of life, feldom thought of as a bleffing, fupports the conftitution and preferves health; ftill feafts delight the heart of man, though difeafe and even death lurk in the cup or dainty that elevates the fpirits or tickles the palate. The lively heated imagination, in the fame ftyle, draws the picture of love, as it draws every other picture, with thofe glowing colours, which the daring hand will fteal from the rainbow that is directed by a mind, condemned in a world like this, to prove its noble origin by panting after unattainable perfection; ever purfuing what it acknowledges to be a fleeting dream. An imagination of this vigorous caft can give exiftence to infubftantial forms, and ftability to the fhadowy reveries which the mind naturally falls into when realities are found vapid. It can then depict love with celeftial charms, and dote on the grand ideal object—it can imagine a degree of mutual affection that fhall refine the foul, and not expire when it has ferved as a 'fcale to heavenly;' and, like devotion, make it abforb every meaner affection and defire. In each others arms, as in a temple, with its fummit loft in the clouds, the world is to be fhut out, and every
thought

thought and wiſh, that do not nurture pure affection and permanent virtue.——Permanent virtue! alas! Rouſſeau, reſpectable viſionary! thy
paradiſe would ſoon be violated by the entrance of
ſome unexpected gueſt. Like Milton's it would
only contain angels, or men ſunk below the dignity of rational creatures. Happineſs is not material, it cannot be ſeen or felt! Yet the eager
purſuit of the good which every one ſhapes to
his own fancy, proclaims man the lord of this
lower world, and to be an intelligent creature,
who is not to receive, but to acquire happineſs.
They, therefore, who complain of the deluſions
of paſſion, do not recollect that they are exclaiming againſt a ſtrong proof of the immortality of
the ſoul.

But leaving ſuperiour minds to correct themſelves, and pay dearly for their experience, it is
neceſſary to obſerve, that it is not againſt ſtrong,
perſevering paſſions; but romantic wavering feelings that I wiſh to guard the female heart by
exerciſing the underſtanding: for theſe paradiſia-
cal reveries are oftener the effect of idleneſs than
of a lively fancy.

Women have ſeldom ſufficient ſerious employment to ſilence their feelings; a round of little
cares, or vain purſuits frittering away all ſtrength
of mind and organs, they become naturally only
objects of ſenſe.——In ſhort, the whole tenour of
female education (the education of ſociety) tends
to render the beſt diſpoſed romantic and incon-
ſtant; and the remainder vain and mean. In
the preſent ſtate of ſociety this evil can ſcarcely
be remedied, I am afraid, in the ſlighteſt degree;

I 3   ſhould

should a more laudable ambition ever gain ground they may be brought nearer to nature and reason; and become more virtuous and useful as they grow more respectable.

But, I will venture to assert that their reason will never acquire sufficient strength to enable it to regulate their conduct, whilst the making an appearance in the world is the first wish of the majority of mankind. To this weak wish the natural affections, and the most useful virtues are sacrificed. Girls marry merely to *better them-selves*, to borrow a significant vulgar phrase, and have such perfect power over their hearts as not to permit themselves to *fall in love* till a man with a superiour fortune offers. On this subject I mean to enlarge in a future chapter; it is only necessary to drop a hint at present, because women are so often degraded by suffering the selfish prudence of age to chill the ardour of youth.

From the same source flows an opinion that young girls ought to dedicate great part of their time to needle-work; yet, this employment contracts their faculties more than any other that could have been chosen for them, by confining their thoughts to their persons. Men order their clothes to be made, and have done with the subject; women make their own clothes, necessary or ornamental, and are continually talking about them; and their thoughts follow their hands. It is not indeed the making of necessaries that weakens the mind; but the frippery of dress. For when a woman in the lower rank of life makes her husband's and children's clothes, she does her duty, this is a part of her business;

but

but when women work only to drefs better than they could otherwife afford, it is worfe than fheer lofs of time. To render the poor virtuous they muft be employed, and women in the middle rank of life, did they not ape the fafhions of the nobility, without catching their eafe, might employ them, whilft they themfelves managed their families, inftructed their children, and exercifed their own minds. Gardening, experimental philofophy, and literature, would afford them fubjects to think of and matter for converfation, that in fome degree would exercife their underftandings. The converfation of French women, who are not fo rigidly nailed to their chairs to twift lappets, and knot ribbons, is frequently fuperficial; but, I contend, that it is not half fo infipid as that of thofe Englifh women whofe time is fpent in making caps, bonnets, and the whole mifchief of trimmings, not to mention fhopping, bargain-hunting, &c. &c. and it is the decent, prudent women, who are moft degraded by thefe practices; for their motive is fimply vanity. The wanton who exercifes her tafte to render her perfon alluring, has fomething more in view.

These obfervations all branch out of a general one, which I have before made, and which cannot be too often infifted upon, for, fpeaking of men, women, or profeffions, it will be found that the employment of the thoughts fhapes the character both generally and individually. The thoughts of women ever hover round their perfons, and is it furprifing that their perfons are reckoned moft valuable? Yet fome degree of

I 4 liberty

liberty of mind is neceffary even to form the perfon ; and this may be one reafon why fome gentle wives have fo few attractions befide that of fex.
Add to this, fedentary employments render the
majority of women fickly—and falfe notions of
female excellence make them proud of this delicacy, though it be another fetter, that by calling
the attention continually to the body, cramps
the activity of the mind.

Women of quality feldom do any of the manual part of their drefs, confequently only their
tafte is exercifed, and they acquire, by thinking
lefs of the finery, when the bufinefs of their toilet is over, that eafe, which feldom appears in
the deportment of women, who drefs merely for
the fake of dreffing. In fact, the obfervation
with refpect to the middle rank, the one in which
talents thrive beft, extends not to women ; for
thofe of the fuperiour clafs, by catching, at leaft,
a fmattering of literature, and converfing more
with men, on general topics, acquire more knowledge than the women who ape their fafhions
and faults without fharing their advantages.
With refpect to virtue, to ufe the word in a comprehenfive fenfe, I have feen moft in low life.
Many poor women maintain their children by
the fweat of their brow, and keep together families that the vices of the fathers would have fcat-
tered abroad ; but gentle-women are too indolent
to be actively virtuous, and are foftened rather
than refined by civilization. Indeed, the good
fenfe which I have met with, among the poor
women who have had few advantages of education, and yet have acted heroically, ftrongly con-
firmed

firmed me in the opinion that trifling employments have rendered woman a trifler. Men, taking her * body, the mind is left to ruft ; fo that while phyfical love enervates man, as being his favourite recreation, he will endeavour to enflave woman :—and, who can tell, how many generations may be neceflary to give vigour to the virtue and talents of the freed pofterity of abject flaves † ?

In tracing the caufes that, in my opinion, have degraded woman, I have confined my obfervations to fuch as univerfally act upon the morals and manners of the whole fex, and to me it appears clear that they all fpring from want of underftanding. Whether this arife from a phyfical or accidental weaknefs of faculties, time alone can determine ; for I fhall not lay any great ftrefs on the example of a few women ‡ who, from having received a mafculine education, have acquired courage and refolution ; I only contend that the men who have been placed in fimilar fituations, have acquired a fimilar character—I fpeak of bodies of men, and that men of genius and talents have ftarted out of a clafs, in which women have never yet been placed.

* ‘ I take her body,’ fays Ranger.

† ‘ Suppofing that women are voluntary flaves—flavery of any kind is
‘ unfavourable to human happinefs and improvement.’   _Knox's Effays._

‡ Sappho, Eloifa, Mrs. Macauley, the Emprefs of Ruffia, Madame d’Eon, &c. Thefe, and many more, may be reckoned exceptions ; and, are not all heroes, as well as heroines, exceptions to general rules ? I wifh to fee women neither heroines nor brutes ; but reafonable creatures.

CHAP.

C H A P. V.

ANIMADVERSIONS ON SOME OF THE WRITERS WHO HAVE RENDERED WOMEN OBJECTS OF PITY, BORDERING ON CONTEMPT.

THE opinions fpecioufly fupported, in fome modern publications on the female character and education, which have given the tone to moft of the obfervations made, in a more curfory manner, on the fex, remain now to be examined.

S E C T. I.

I SHALL begin with Roufſeau, and give a fketch of the character of women, in his own words, interfperfing comments and reflections. My comments, it is true, will all fpring from a few fimple principles, and might have been deduced from what I have already faid; but the artificial ftructure has been raifed with fo much ingenuity, that it feems neceffary to attack it in a more circumftantial manner, and make the application myfelf.

Sophia, fays Roufſeau, fhould be as perfect a woman as Emilius is a man, and to render her fo, it is neceffary to examine the character which nature has given to the fex.

He then proceeds to prove that woman ought to be weak and paffive, becaufe fhe has lefs bodily ftrength than man ; and, from hence infers,

infers, that she was formed to please and to be
subject to him ; and that it is her duty to render
herself *agreeable* to her master—this being the
grand end of her existence*. Still, however, to
give a little mock dignity to sensual desire, he in-
sists that man should not exert his strength, but
depend on the will of the woman, when he seeks
for pleasure with her.

' Hence we deduce a third consequence from
' the different constitutions of the sexes ; which
' is, that the strongest should be masters in ap-
' pearance, and be dependent in fact on the
' weakest ; and that not from any frivolous prac-
' tice of gallantry or vanity of protectorship, but
' from an invariable law of nature, which, fur-
' nishing woman with a greater facility to excite
' desires than she has given man to satisfy them,
' makes the latter dependent on the good pleasure
' of the former, and compels him to endeavour
' to please in his turn, *in order to obtain her con-*
' *sent that he should be strongest* †. On these oc-
' casions, the most delightful circumstance a man
' finds in his victory is, to doubt whether it was
' the woman's weakness that yielded to his supe-
' riour strength, or whether her inclinations
' spoke in his favour : the females are also gen-
' erally artful enough to leave this matter in
' doubt. The understanding of women answers in
' this respect perfectly to their constitution : so far
' from being ashamed of their weakness, they
' glory in it ; their tender muscles make no re-
' sistance ; they affect to be incapable of lifting
' the

* I have already inserted the passage, page 88.
† What nonsense !

‘ the fmalleft burthens, and would blufh to be
‘ thought robuft and ftrong. To what purpofe
‘ is all this ? Not merely for the fake of appear-
‘ ing delicate, but through an artful precaution :
‘ it is thus they provide an excufe beforehand,
‘ and a right to be feeble when they think it ex-
‘ pedient*.’

I have quoted this paffage, left my readers
fhould fufpect that I warped the author's reafoning to fupport my own arguments. I have already afferted that in educating women thefe fundamental principles lead to a fyftem of cunning
and lafcioufnefs.

Suppofing woman to have been formed only
to pleafe, and be fubject to man, the conclufion
is juft, fhe ought to facrifice every other confideration to render herfelf agreeable to him : and let
this brutal defire of felf-prefervation be the grand
fpring of all her actions, when it is proved to be
the iron bed of fate, to fit which her character
fhould be ftretched or contracted, regardlefs of
all moral or phyfical diftinctions. But, if, as I
think, may be demonftrated, the purpofes, of
even this life, viewing the whole, are fubverted
by practical rules built upon this ignoble bafe, I
may be allowed to doubt whether woman was
created for man : and, though the cry of irreli-
gion, or even atheifm, be raifed againft me, I will
fimply declare, that were an angel from heaven
to tell me that Mofes's beautiful, poetical cof-
mogony, and the account of the fall of man,
were literally true, I could not believe what my
reafon told me was derogatory to the character of
the

* Rouffeau's Emilius, Vol. III. p. 168,

the Supreme Being : and, having no fear of the devil before mine eyes, I venture to call this a suggestion of reason, instead of resting my weakness on the broad shoulders of the first seducer of my frail sex.

'It being once demonstrated,' continues Rousseau, 'that man and woman are not, nor ought 'to be, constituted alike in temperament and 'character, it follows of course that they should 'not be educated in the same manner. In pur- 'suing the directions of nature, they ought in- 'deed to act in concert, but they should not be 'engaged in the same employments : the end of 'their pursuits should be the same, but the means 'they should take to accomplish them, and of 'consequence their tastes and inclinations, should 'be different*.'

* * * * * * * * * * * *

'Whether I consider the peculiar destination 'of the sex, observe their inclinations, or remark 'their duties, all things equally concur to point 'out the peculiar method of education best adapt- 'ed to them. Woman and man were made for 'each other, but their mutual dependence is not 'the same. The men depend on the women 'only on account of their desires ; the women 'on the men both on account of their desires 'and their necessities : we could subsist better 'without them than they without us†.'

* * * * * * * * * * *

'For

* Rousseau's Emilius, Vol. III. p. 176.
† Rousseau's Emilius, Vol. III. p. 179.

'For this reason, the education of the women
'should be always relative to the men.   To
'please, to be useful to us, to make us love and
'esteem them, to educate us when young, and
'take care of us when grown up, to advise, to
'console us, to render our lives easy and agreea-
'ble : these are the duties of women at all times,
'and what they should be taught in their infan-
'cy.   So long as we fail to recur to this princi-
'ple, we run wide of the mark, and all the pre-
'cepts which are given them contribute neither
'to their happiness nor our own*.'

.   .   .   .

'Girls are from their earliest infancy fond of
'dress.   Not content with being pretty, they
'are desirous of being thought so ; we see, by all
'their little airs, that this thought engages their
'attention ; and they are hardly capable of un-
'derstanding what is said to them, before they
'are to be governed by talking to them of what
'people will think of their behaviour.   The
'same motive, however, indiscreetly made use of
'with boys, has not the same effect : provided
'they are let to pursue their amusements at plea-
'sure, they care very little what people think of
'them.   Time and pains are necessary to sub-
'ject boys to this motive.
'Whencesoever girls derive this first lesson, it
'is a very good one.   As the body is born, in a
'manner before the soul, our first concern should
'be to cultivate the former ; this order is common

---

* Rousseau's Emilius, Vol. III. p. 181.

' mon to both fexes, but the object of that cul-
' tivation is different. In the one fex it is the
' developement of corporeal powers ; in the oth-
' er, that of perfonal charms : not that either
' the quality of ftrength or beauty ought to be
' confined exclufively to one fex ; but only that
' the order of the cultivation of both is in that
' refpect reverfed. Women certainly require as
' much ftrength as to enable them to move and
' act gracefully, and men as much addrefs as to
' qualify them to act with eafe.'

. . . .

' Children of both fexes have a great many
' amufements in common ; and fo they ought ;
' have they not alfo many fuch when they are
' grown up ? Each fex has alfo its peculiar tafte
' to diftinguifh in this particular. Boys love
' fports of noife and activity ; to beat the drum,
' to whip the top, and to drag about their little
' carts : girls, on the other hand, are fonder of
' things of fhow and ornament ; fuch as mirrours,
' trinkets, and dolls : the doll is the peculiar
' amufement of the females ; from whence we fee
' their tafte plainly adapted to their deftination.
' The phyfical part of the art of pleafing lies in
' drefs ; and this is all which children are ca-
' pacitated to cultivate of that art.'

. . . .

' Here then we fee a primary propenfity firm-
' ly eftablifhed, which you need only purfue and
                                        ' regulate.

' regulate. The little creature will doubtleſs be
' very deſirous to know how to dreſs up her doll,
' to make its ſleeve-knots, its flounces, its
' head-dreſs, &c. ſhe is obliged to have ſo much
' recourſe to the people about her, for their aſ-
' ſiſtance in theſe articles, that it would be much
' more agreeable to her to owe them all to her
' own induſtry. Hence we have a good reaſon for
' the firſt leſſons that are uſually taught theſe young
' females : in which we do not appear to be ſet-
' ting them a taſk, but obliging them, by in-
' ſtructing them in what is immediately uſeful to
' themſelves. And, in fact, almoſt all of them
' learn with reluctance to read and write ; but
' very readily apply themſelves to the uſe of their
' needles. They imagine themſelves already grown
' up, and think with pleaſure that ſuch qualifica-
' tions will enable them to decorate themſelves.'

This is certainly only an education of the body ;
but Rouſſeau is not the only man who has indirectly ſaid that merely the perſon of a *young* woman, without any mind, unleſs animal ſpirits
come under that deſcription, is very pleaſing. To
render it weak, and what ſome may call beautiful, the underſtanding is neglected, and girls
forced to ſit ſtill, play with dolls and liſten to
fooliſh converſations ;—the effect of habit is inſiſted upon as an undoubted indication of nature.
I know it was Rouſſeau's opinion that the firſt
years of youth ſhould be employed to form the
body, though in educating Emilius he deviates
from this plan ; yet, the difference between
ſtrengthening the body, on which ſtrength of
mind in a great meaſure depends, and only giving it an eaſy motion, is very wide.

Rouſſeau's

Rousseau's observations, it is proper to remark, were made in a country where the art of pleasing was refined only to extract the grossness of vice. He did not go back to nature, or his ruling appetite disturbed the operations of reason, else he would not have drawn these crude inferences.

In France boys and girls, particularly the latter, are only educated to please, to manage their persons, and regulate their exterior behaviour; and their minds are corrupted, at a very early age, by the worldly and pious cautions they receive to guard them against immodesty. I speak of past times. The very confessions which mere children were obliged to make, and the questions asked by the holy men, I assert these facts on good authority, were sufficient to impress a sexual character; and the education of society was a school of coquetry and art. At the age of ten or eleven; nay, often much sooner, girls began to coquet, and talked, unreproved, of establishing themselves in the world by marriage.

In short, they were made women, almost from their very birth, and compliments were listened to instead of instruction. These, weakening the mind, Nature was supposed to have acted like a step-mother, when she formed this after-thought of creation.

Not allowing them understanding, however, it was but consistent to subject them to authority independent of reason; and to prepare them for this subjection, he gives the following advice:

'Girls ought to be active and diligent; nor is
'that all; they should also be early subjected to
'restraint. This misfortune, if it really be one,

K   'is

' is inseparable from their sex ; nor do they ever
' throw it off but to suffer more cruel evils. They
' must be subject, all their lives, to the most
' constant and severe restraint, which is that of
' decorum : it is, therefore necessary to accustom
' them early to such confinement, that it may not
' afterwards cost them too dear ; and to the sup-
' pression of their caprices, that they may the
' more readily submit to the will of others. If,
' indeed, they are fond of being always at work,
' they should be sometimes compelled to lay it
' aside. Dissipation, levity, and inconstancy, are
' faults that readily spring up from their first pro-
' pensities, when corrupted or perverted by too
' much indulgence. To prevent this abuse, we
' should learn them, above all things, to lay a due
' restraint on themselves. The life of a modest
' woman is reduced, by our absurd institutions,
' to a perpetual conflict with herself : not but it
' is just that this sex should partake of the suffer-
' ings which arise from those evils it hath caused
' us.'

And why is the life of a modest woman a perpetual conflict ? I should answer, that this very
system of education makes it so. Modesty, temperance, and self-denial, are the sober offspring of
reason ; but when sensibility is nurtured at the
expense of the understanding, such weak beings
must be restrained by arbitrary means, and be subjected to continual conflicts; but give their activity of mind a wider range, and nobler passions
and motives will govern their appetites and sentiments.

' The

' The common attachment and regard of a
' mother, nay, mere habit, will make her belov-
' ed by her children, if she does nothing to incur
' their hate. Even the constraint she lays them
' under, if well directed, will increase their af-
' fection, instead of lessening it ; because a state
' of dependence being natural to the sex, they
' perceive themselves formed for obedience.'

This is begging the question ; for servitude
not only debases the individual, but its effects
seem to be transmitted to posterity. Considering
the length of time that women have been dependent, is it surprising that some of them hug
their chains, and fawn like the spaniel ? ' These
dogs,' observes a naturalist, ' at first kept their
' ears erect ; but custom has superseded nature,
' and a token of fear is become a beauty.'

' For the same reason,' adds Rousseau, ' wo-
' men have, or ought to have, but little liberty ;
' they are apt to indulge themselves excessively in
' what is allowed them. Addicted in every thing
' to extremes, they are even more transported at
' their diversions than boys.'

The answer to this is very simple. Slaves and
mobs have always indulged themselves in the same
excesses, when once they broke loose from authority.—The bent bow recoils with violence,
when the hand is suddenly relaxed that forcibly
held it ; and sensibility, the play-thing of outward circumstances, must be subjected to authority, or moderated by reason.

' There results,' he continues, ' from this ha-
' bitual restraint a tractableness which the women
' have occasion for during their whole lives, as
' they

'they conftantly remain either under fubjection
'to the men, or to the opinions of mankind ;
'and are never permitted to fet themfelves above
'thofe opinions. The firft and moft important
'qualification in a woman is good-nature or fweet-
'nefs of temper : formed to obey a being fo im-
'perfect as man, often full of vices, and always
'full of faults, fhe ought to learn betimes even
'to fuffer injuftice, and to bear the infults of a
'hufband without complaint ; it is not for his
'fake, but her own, that fhe fhould be of a mild
'difpofition. The perverfenefs and ill-nature of
'the women only ferve to aggravate their own
'misfortunes, and the mifconduct of their huf-
'bands ; they might plainly perceive that fuch
'are not the arms by which they gain the fupe-
'riority.'

Formed to live with fuch an imperfect being
as man, they ought to learn from the exercife of
their faculties the neceffity of forbearance ; but
all the facred rights of humanity are violated by
infifting on blind obedience ; or, the moft facred rights belong _only_ to man.

The being who patiently endures injuftice, and
filently bears infults, will foon become unjuft, or
unable to difcern right from wrong. Befides, I
deny the fact, this is not the true way to form or
meliorate the temper ; for, as a fex, men have
better tempers than women, becaufe they are occupied by purfuits that intereft the head as well
as the heart ; and the fteadinefs of the head gives
a healthy temperature to the heart. People of
fenfibility have feldom good tempers. The formation of the temper is the cool work of reafon,

when,

when, as life advances, she mixes with happy art, jarring elements. I never knew a weak or ignorant person who had a good temper, though that constitutional good humour, and that docility, which fear stamps on the behaviour, often obtains the name. I say behaviour, for genuine meekness never reached the heart or mind, unless as the effect of reflection; and that simple restraint produces a number of peccant humours in domestic life, many sensible men will allow, who find some of these gentle irritable creatures, very troublesome companions.

' Each sex, he further argues, ' should preserve ' its peculiar tone and manner; a meek husband ' may have a wife impertinent; but mildness of ' disposition on the woman's side will always ' bring a man back to reason, at least if he be not ' absolutely a brute, and will sooner or later tri-' umph over him.' True, the mildness of reason; but abject fear always inspires contempt; and tears are only eloquent when they flow down fair cheeks.

Of what materials can that heart be composed, which can melt when insulted, and instead of revolting at injustice, kiss the rod? Is it unfair to infer that her virtue is built on narrow views and selfishness, who can caress a man, with true feminine softness, the very moment when he treats her tyrannically? Nature never dictated such insincerity;—and though prudence of this sort be termed a virtue, morality becomes vague when any part is supposed to rest on falsehood. These are mere expedients, and expedients are only useful for the moment.

Let

Let the husband beware of trusting too implicitly to this servile obedience ; for if his wife can with winning sweetness caress him when angry, and when she ought to be angry, unless contempt had stifled a natural effervescence, she may do the same after parting with a lover. These are all preparations for adultery ; or, should the fear of the world, or of hell, restrain her desire of pleasing other men, when she can no longer please her husband, what substitute can be found by a being who was only formed, by nature and art, to please man ? what can make her amends for this privation, or where is she to seek for a fresh employment ? where find sufficient strength of mind to determine to begin the search, when her habits are fixed, and vanity has long ruled her chaotic mind ?

But this partial moralist recommends cunning systematically and plausibly.

‘ Daughters should be always submissive ;
‘ their mothers, however, should not be inexora-
‘ ble.   To make a young person tractable, she
‘ ought not to be made unhappy ; to make her
‘ modest she ought not to be rendered stupid.
‘ On the contrary, I should not be displeased at
‘ her being permitted to use some art, not to elude
‘ punishment in case of disobedience, but to ex-
‘ empt herself from the necessity of obeying.   It
‘ is not necessary to make her dependence bur-
‘ densome, but only to let her feel it.   Subtilty
‘ is a talent natural to the sex ; and, as I am per-
‘ suaded, all our natural inclinations are right
‘ and good in themselves, I am of opinion this
‘ should be cultivated as well as the others : it is
‘ requisite for us only to prevent its abuse.’
                                    ‘ Whatever

' Whatever is, is right,' he then proceeds triumphantly to infer. Granted ;—yet, perhaps, no aphorifm ever contained a more paradoxical affertion. It is a folemn truth with refpect to God. He, reverentially I fpeak, fees the whole at once, and faw its juft proportions in the womb of time ; but man, who can only infpect difjointed parts, finds many things wrong ; and it is a part of the fyftem, and therefore right, that he fhould endeavour to alter what appears to him to be fo, even while he bows to the Wifdom of his Creator, and refpects the darknefs he labours to difperfe.

The inference that follows is juft fuppofing the principle to be found. ' The fuperiority of ' addrefs, peculiar to the female fex, is a very ' equitable indemnification for their inferiority ' in point of ftrength : without this, woman ' would not be the companion of man ; but his ' flave : it is by her fuperiour art and ingenuity ' that fhe preferves her equality, and governs him ' while fhe affects to obey. Woman has every ' thing againft her, as well our faults, as her own ' timidity and weaknefs ; fhe has nothing in her ' favour, but her fubtilty and her beauty. Is it ' not very reafonable, therefore, fhe fhould culti- ' vate both ?' Greatnefs of mind can never dwell with cunning, or addrefs, for I fhall not differ about words, when their direct fignification is infincerity and falfehood ; but content myfelf with obferving, that if any clafs of mankind are to be educated by rules not ftrictly deducible from truth, virtue is an affair of convention. How could Rouffeau dare to affert, after giving

K 4   this

this advice, that in the grand end of exiſtence the object of both ſexes ſhould be the ſame, when he well knew that the mind, formed by its purſuits, is expanded by great views ſwallowing up little ones, or that it becomes itſelf little ?

Men have ſuperiour ſtrength of body ; but were it not for miſtaken notions of beauty, women would acquire ſufficient to enable them to earn their own ſubſiſtence, the true definition of independence ; and to bear thoſe bodily inconveniences and exertions that are requiſite to ſtrengthen the mind.

Let us then, by being allowed to take the ſame exerciſe as boys, not only during infancy, but youth, arrive at perfection of body, that we may know how far the natural ſuperiority of man extends. For what reaſon or virtue can be expected from a creature when the ſeed-time of life is neglected ? None—did not the winds of heaven caſually ſcatter many uſeful ſeeds in the fallow ground.

‘ Beauty cannot be acquired by dreſs, and co-
‘ quetry is an art not ſo early and ſpeedily attain-
‘ ed. While girls are yet young, however, they
‘ are in a capacity to ſtudy agreeable geſture, a
‘ pleaſing modulation of voice, an eaſy carriage
‘ and behaviour ; as well as to take the advan-
‘ tage of gracefully adapting their looks and atti-
‘ tudes to time, place, and occaſion. Their ap-
‘ plication, therefore, ſhould not be ſolely con-
‘ fined to the arts of induſtry and the needle,
‘ when they come to diſplay other talents, whoſe
‘ utility is already apparent.’

‘ For

' For my part, I would have a young English-
' woman cultivate her agreeable talents, in order
' to pleafe her future hufband, with as much care
' and affiduity as a young Circaffian cultivates
' her's, to fit her for the haram of an eaftern
' bafhaw.'

To render women completely infignificant, he
adds—' The tongues of women are very voluble ;
' they fpeak earlier, more readily, and more agree-
' ably, than the men ; they are accufed alfo of
' fpeaking much more : but fo it ought to be,
' and I fhould be very ready to convert this re-
' proach into a compliment ; their lips and eyes
' have the fame activity, and for the fame reafon.
' A man fpeaks of what he knows, a woman of
' what pleafes her ; the one requires knowledge,
' the other tafte ; the principal object of a man's
' difcourfe fhould be what is ufeful, that of a wo-
' man's what is agreeable. There ought to be
' nothing in common between their different
' converfation but truth.'

' We ought not, therefore, to reftrain the prat-
' tle of girls, in the fame manner as we fhould
' that of boys, with that fevere queftion ; *To what
' purpofe are you talking ?* but by another, which
' is no lefs difficult to anfwer, *How will your dif-
' courfe be received ?* In infancy, while they are
' as yet incapable to difcern good from evil, they
' ought to obferve it, as a law, never to fay any
' thing difagreeable to thofe whom they are fpeak-
' ing to : what will render the practice of this
' rule alfo the more difficult, is, that it muft ever
' be fubordinate to the former, of never fpeaking
' falfely or telling an untruth.' To govern the

tongue

tongue in this manner muſt require great addreſs indeed ; and it is too much practiſed both by men and women.—Out of the abundance of the heart how few ſpeak ! So few, that I, who love ſimplicity, would gladly give up politeneſs for a quarter of the virtue that has been ſacrificed to an equivocal quality which at beſt ſhould only be the poliſh of virtue.

But, to complete the ſketch. ' It is eaſy to ' be conceived, that if male children are not in a ' capacity to form any true notions of religion, ' thoſe ideas muſt be greatly above the concep- ' tion of the females : it is for this very reaſon, ' I would begin to ſpeak to them the earlier on ' this ſubject ; for if we were to wait till they ' were in a capacity to diſcuſs methodically ſuch ' profound queſtions, we ſhould run a riſk of ' never ſpeaking to them on this ſubject as long ' as they lived. Reaſon in women is a practi- ' cal reaſon, capacitating them artfully to diſcov- ' er the means of attaining a known end, but ' which would never enable them to diſcover ' that end itſelf. The ſocial relations of the ' ſexes are indeed truly admirable : from their ' union there reſults a moral perſon, of which ' woman may be termed the eyes, and man the ' hand, with this dependence on each other, that ' it is from the man that the woman is to learn ' what ſhe is to ſee, and it is of the woman that ' man is to learn what he ought to do. If wo- ' man could recur to the firſt principles of things ' as well as man, and man was capacitated to en- ' ter into their *minutiæ* as well as woman, always ' independent of each other, they would live in ' perpetual

' perpetual difcord, and their union could not
' fubfift. But in the prefent harmony which
' naturally fubfifts between them, their different
' faculties tend to one common end ; it is diffi-
' cult to fay which of them conduces the moft
' to it : each follows the impulfe of the other ;
' each is obedient, and both are mafters.'

' As the conduct of a woman is fubfervient to
' the public opinion, her faith in matters of re-
' ligion fhould, for that very reafon, be fubject
' to authority. *Every daughter ought to be of the*
' *fame religion as her mother, and every wife to be*
' *of the fame religion as her hufband : for, though*
' *fuch religion fhould be falfe, that docility which*
' *induces the mother and daughter to fubmit to the*
' *order of nature, take away, in the fight of God,*
' *the criminality of their error*.'* As ' they are
' not in a capacity to judge for themfelves, they
' ought to abide by the decifion of their fathers
' and hufbands as confidently as by that of the
' church.'

' As authority ought to regulate the religion of
' the women, it is not fo needful to explain to
' them the reafons for their belief, as to lay down
' precifely the tenets they are to believe : for the
' creed, which prefents only obfcure ideas to the
' mind, is the fource of fanaticifm ; and that
' which prefents abfurdities, leads to infidelity.'

Abfolute, uncontroverted authority, it feems,
muft fubfift fomewhere : but is not this a direct
and

---

* What is to be the confequence, if the mother's and hufband's opinion
fhould *chance* not to agree ? An ignorant perfon cannot be reafoned out
of an error—and when *perfuaded* to give up one prejudice for another the
mind is unfettled. Indeed, the hufband may not have any religion to
teach her, though in fuch a fituation fhe will be in great want of a fupport to her virtue, independent of worldly confiderations.

and exclusive appropriation of reason ? The *rights*
of humanity have been thus confined to the male
line from Adam downwards. Rousseau would
carry his male aristocracy still further, for he insinuates, that he should not blame those, who
contend for leaving woman in a state of the most
profound ignorance, if it were not necessary in
order to preserve her chastity and justify the man's
choice, in the eyes of the world, to give her a little knowledge of men, and the customs produced
by human passions ; else she might propagate at
home without being rendered less voluptuous and
innocent by the exercise of her understanding :
excepting, indeed, during the first year of marriage, when she might employ it to dress like Sophia. ' Her dress is extremely modest in ap-
' pearance, and yet very coquettish in fact : she
' does not make a display of her charms, she con-
' ceals them ; but in concealing them, she knows
' how to affect your imagination. Every one
' who sees her, will say, There is a modest and
' discreet girl ; but while you are near her, your
' eyes and affections wander all over her person, so
' that you cannot withdraw them ; and you would
' conclude, that every part of her dress, simple as
' it seems, was only put in its proper order to be
' taken to pieces by the imagination.' Is this
modesty ? Is this a preparation for immortality ?
Again.——What opinion are we to form of a system of education, when the author says of his heroine, ' that with her, doing things well, is but
' a *secondary* concern ; her principal concern is to
' do them *neatly*.'

Secondary,

Secondary, in fact, are all her virtues and qualities, for, respecting religion, he makes her parents thus address her, accustomed to submission—
' Your husband will instruct you in good time.'

After thus cramping a woman's mind, if, in order to keep it fair, he has not made it quite a blank, he advises her to reflect, that a reflecting man may not yawn in her company, when he is tired of caressing her.—What has she to reflect about who must obey ? and would it not be a refinement on cruelty only to open her mind to make the darkness and misery of her fate *visible* ? Yet, these are his sensible remarks ; how consistent with what I have already been obliged to quote, to give a fair view of the subject, the reader may determine.

' They who pass their whole lives in working
' for their daily bread, have no ideas beyond their
' business or their interest, and all their under-
' standing seems to lie in their fingers' ends.
' This ignorance is neither prejudicial to their in-
' tegrity nor their morals ; it is often of service
' to them. Sometimes, by means of reflection,
' we are led to compound with our duty, and we
' conclude by substituting a jargon of words, in
' the room of things. Our own conscience is
' the most enlightened philosopher. There is no
' need to be acquainted with Tully's offices, to
' make a man of probity : and perhaps the most
' virtuous woman in the world, is the least ac-
' quainted with the definition of virtue. But it
' is no less true, that an improved understanding
' can only render society agreeable ; and it is a
' melancholy thing for a father of a family, who
' is

' is fond of home, to be obliged to be always
' wrapped up in himself, and to have nobody
' about him to whom he can impart his senti-
' ments.

' Besides, how should a woman void of re-
' flection be capable of educating her children ?
' How should she discern what is proper for
' them ? How should she incline them to those
' virtues she is unacquainted with, or to that
' merit of which she has no idea ? She can only
' sooth or chide them ; render them insolent or
' timid ; she will make them formal coxcombs,
' or ignorant blockheads ; but will never make
' them sensible or amiable.'   How indeed should
she, when her husband is not always at hand to
lend her his reason ?—when they both together make but one moral being.   A blind will,
' eyes without hands, ' would go a very little way ;
and perchance his abstract reason, that should
concentrate the scattered beams of her practical
reason, may be employed in judging of the fla-
vour of wine, descanting on the sauces most proper for turtle ; or, more profoundly intent at a
card-table, he may be generalizing his ideas as he
bets away his fortune, leaving all the *minutiæ* of
education to his help-mate or to chance.

But, granting that woman ought to be beautiful, innocent and silly, to render her a more alluring and indulgent companion ;—what is her
understanding sacrificed for ? And why is all this
preparation necessary only, according to Rousseau's own account, to make her the mistress of
her husband, a very short time ? For no man ever
insisted more on the transient nature of love.

                                        Thus

Thus speaks the philosopher. 'Sensual pleasures 'are transient. The habitual state of the affec- 'tions always lose by their gratification. The im- 'agination, which decks the object of our desires, 'is lost in fruition. Excepting the Supreme Be- 'ing, who is self-existent, there is nothing beau- 'tiful but what is ideal.'

But he returns to his unintelligible paradoxes again, when he thus addresses Sophia. 'Emili- 'us, in becoming your husband, is become your 'master; and claims your obedience. Such is ' the order of nature. When a man is married, 'however, to such a wife as Sophia, it is proper 'he should be directed by her; this is also agreea- 'ble to the order of nature: it is, therefore, to 'give you as much authority over his heart as his 'sex gives him over your person, that I have made 'you the arbiter of his pleasures. It may cost 'you, perhaps, some disagreeable self-denial; but 'you will be certain of maintaining your empire 'over him, if you can preserve it over yourself— 'what I have already observed, also, shows me, 'that this difficult attempt does not surpass your 'courage.

'Would you have your husband constantly at 'your feet? keep him at some distance from 'your person. You will long maintain the au- 'thority in love, if you know but how to render 'your favours rare and valuable. It is thus you 'may employ even the arts of coquetry in the 'service of virtue, and those of love in that of 'reason.'

I shall close my extracts with a just description of a comfortable couple. 'And yet you must
' not

' not imagine, that even such management will
' always suffice. Whatever precaution be taken,
' enjoyment will, by degrees, take off the edge of
' passion. But when love hath lasted as long as
' possible, a pleasing habitude supplies its place,
' and the attachment of a mutual confidence suc-
' ceeds to the transports of passion. Children
' often form a more agreeable and permanent con-
' nection between married people than even love
' itself. When you cease to be the mistress of
' Emilius, you will continue to be his wife and
' friend, you will be the mother of his chil-
' dren*.'

Children, he truly observes, form a much more
permanent connection between married people
than love. Beauty, he declares, will not be valued, or even seen, after a couple have lived six
months together ; artificial graces and coquetry
will likewise pall on the senses : why then does
he say that a girl should be educated for her husband with the same care as for an eastern haram ?

I now appeal from the reveries of fancy and refined licentiousness to the good sense of mankind,
whether, if the object of education be to prepare
women to become chaste wives and sensible mothers, the methods so plausibly recommended in the
foregoing sketch, be the one best calculated to produce those ends ? Will it be allowed that the
surest way to make a wife chaste, is to teach her to
practise the wanton arts of a mistress, termed
virtuous coquetry, by the sensualist, who can no
longer relish the artless charms of sincerity, or
taste the pleasure arising from a tender intimacy,
                                                    when

* Rousseau's Emilius.

when confidence is unchecked by suspicion, and rendered interesting by sense?

The man who can be contented to live with a pretty, useful companion, without a mind, has lost in voluptuous gratifications a taste for more refined enjoyments; he has never felt the calm satisfaction, that refreshes the parched heart, like the silent dew of heaven,—of being beloved by one who could understand him.—In the society of his wife he is still alone, unless when the man is sunk in the brute. ' The charm of life,' says a grave philosophical reasoner, is ' sympathy; ' nothing pleases us more than to observe in oth- ' er men a fellow-feeling with all the emotions ' of our own breast.'

But, according to the tenour of reasoning, by which women are kept from the tree of know- ledge, the important years of youth, the useful- ness of age, and the rational hopes of futurity, are all to be sacrificed to render women an object of desire for a *short* time. Besides, how could Rous- feau expect them to be virtuous and constant when reason is neither allowed to be the foundation of their virtue, nor truth the object of their inquir- ies?

But all Rousseau's errors in reasoning arose from sensibility, and sensibility to their charms women are very ready to forgive! When he should have reasoned he became impassioned, and reflection in- flamed his imagination instead of enlightening his understanding. Even his virtues also led him farther astray; for, born with a warm constitu- tion and lively fancy, nature carried him toward the other sex with such eager fondness, that he

L.   soon

foon became lafcivious. Had he given way to thefe defires, the fire would have extinguifhed itfelf in a natural manner ; but virtue, and a romantic kind of delicacy, made him practife felfdenial ; yet, when fear, delicacy, or virtue, reftrained him, he debauched his imagination, and reflecting on the fenfations to which fancy gave force, he traced them in the moft glowing colours, and funk them deep into his foul.

He then fought for folitude, not to fleep with the man of nature ; or calmly inveftigate the caufes of things under the fhade where Sir Ifaac Newton indulged contemplation, but merely to indulge his feelings. And fo warmly has he painted, what he forcibly felt, that, interefting the heart and inflaming the imagination of his readers ; in proportion to the ftrength of their fancy, they imagine that their underftanding is convinced when they only fympathize with a poetic writer, who fkilfully exhibits the objects of fenfe, moft voluptuoufly fhadowed or gracefully veiled—And thus making us feel, whilft dreaming that we reafon, erroneous conclufions are left in the mind.

Why was Rouffeau's life divided between ecftacy and mifery ? Can any other anfwer be given than this, that the effervefcence of his imagination produced both ; but, had his fancy been allowed to cool, it is poffible that he might have acquired more ftrength of mind. Still, if the purpofe of life be to educate the intellectual part of man, all with refpect to him was right ; yet, had not death led to a nobler fcene of action, it is probable that he would have enjoyed more

equal

equal happiness on earth, and have felt the calm sensations of the man of nature instead of being prepared for another stage of existence by nourishing the passions which agitate the civilized man.

But peace to his manes! I war not with his ashes, but his opinions. I war only with the sensibility that led him to degrade woman by making her the slave of love.

> ———' Curs'd vassalage,
> ' First idoliz'd till love's hot fire be o'er,
> ' Then slaves to those who courted us before.
>
> *Dryden.*

The pernicious tendency of those books, in which the writers insidiously degrade the sex whilst they are prostrate before their personal charms, cannot be too often or too severely exposed.

Let us, my dear contemporaries, arise above such narrow prejudices! If wisdom is desirable on its own account, if virtue, to deserve the name, must be founded on knowledge; let us endeavour to strengthen our minds by reflection, till our heads become a balance for our hearts; let us not confine all our thoughts to the petty occurrences of the day, nor our knowledge to an acquaintance with our lovers' or husbands' hearts; but let the practice of every duty be subordinate to the grand one of improving our minds, and preparing our affections for a more exalted state!

Beware then, my friends, of suffering the heart to be moved by every trivial incident: the reed is shaken by a breeze, and annually dies, but the oak stands firm, and for ages braves the storm!

Were

Were we, indeed, only created to flutter our hour out and die—why let us then indulge fenfibility, and laugh at the feverity of reafon—Yet, alas ! even then we fhould want ftrength of body and mind, and life would be loft in feverifh pleafures or wearifome languor.

But the fyftem of education, which I earneftly wifh to fee exploded, feems to prefuppofe what ought never to be taken for granted, that virtue fhields us from the cafualties of life ; and that fortune, flipping off her bandage, will fmile on a well-educated female, and bring in her hand an Emilius or a Telemachus. Whilft, on the contrary, the reward which virtue promifes to her votaries is confined, it is clear, to their own bofoms ; and often muft they contend with the moft vexatious worldly cares, and bear with the vices and humours of relations for whom they can never feel a friendfhip.

There have been many women in the world who, inftead of being fupported by the reafon and virtue of their fathers and brothers, have ftrengthened their own minds by ftruggling with their vices and follies ; yet have never met with a hero, in the fhape of a hufband ; who, paying the debt that mankind owed them, might chance to bring back their reafon to its natural dependent ftate, and reftore the ufurped prerogative, of rifing above opinion, to man.

SECT. II.

DR. FORDYCE's fermons have long made a part of a young woman's library ; nay, girls at
fchool

ſchool are allowed to read them; but I ſhould inſtantly diſmiſs them from my pupil's, if I wiſhed to ſtrengthen her underſtanding, by leading her to form ſound principles on a broad baſis; or, were I only anxious to cultivate her taſte; though they muſt be allowed to contain many ſenſible obſervations.

Dr. Fordyce may have had a very laudable end in view; but theſe diſcourſes are written in ſuch an affected ſtyle, that were it only on that account, and had I nothing to object againſt his *melliſluous* precepts, I ſhould not allow girls to peruſe them, unleſs I deſigned to hunt every ſpark of nature out of their compoſition, melting every human quality into female weakneſs and artificial grace. I ſay artificial, for true grace ariſes from ſome kind of independence of mind.

Children, careleſs of pleaſing, and only anxious to amuſe themſelves, are often very graceful; and the nobility who have moſtly lived with inferiours, and always had the command of money, acquire a graceful eaſe of deportment, which ſhould rather be termed habitual grace of body, than that ſuperiour gracefulneſs which is truly the expreſſion of the mind. This mental grace, not noticed by vulgar eyes, often flaſhes acroſs a rough countenance, and irradiating every feature, ſhows ſimplicity and independence of mind.—It is then we read characters of immortality in the eye, and ſee the ſoul in every geſture, though when at reſt, neither the face nor limbs may have much beauty to recommend them; or the behaviour, any thing peculiar to attract univerſal attention. The maſs of mankind, however, look for more

tangible beauty; yet fimplicity is, in general, admired, when people do not confider what they
admire; and can there be fimplicity without
fincerity? But, to have done with remarks that
are in fome meafure defultory, though naturally
excited by the fubject—

In declamatory periods Dr. Fordyce fpins out
Roufleau's eloquence; and in moft fentimental
rant, details his opinions refpecting the female
character, and the behaviour which woman ought
to affume to render her lovely.

He fhall fpeak for himfelf, for thus he makes
Nature addrefs man. ' Behold thefe fmiling in-
' nocents, whom I have graced with my faireft
' gifts, and committed to your protection; be-
' hold them with love and refpect; treat them
' with tendernefs and honour. They are timid
' and want to be defended. They are frail; O
' do not take advantage of their weaknefs! Let
' their fears and blufhes endear them. Let their
' confidence in you never be abufed.——But is it
' poffible, than any of you can be fuch barbarians,
' fo fupremely wicked, as to abufe it? Can you
' find in your hearts * to defpoil the gentle, truft-
' ing creatures of their treafure, or do any thing
' to ftrip them of their native robe of virtue?
' Curft be the impious hand that would dare to
' violate the unblemifhed form of Chaftity! Thou
' wretch! thou ruffian! forbear; nor venture to
' provoke heaven's fierceft vengeance.' I know
not any comment that can be made ferioufly on
this curious paffage, and I could produce many
                                                 fimilar

---

* Can you?—Can you? would be the moft emphatical comment, were
it drawled out in a whining voice.

fimilar ones; and fome, fo very fentimental, that I have heard rational men ufe the word indecent, when they mentioned them with difguft.

Throughout there is a difplay of cold artificial feelings, and that parade of fenfibility which boys and girls fhould be taught to defpife as the fure mark of a little vain mind. Florid appeals are made to heaven, and to the *beauteous innocents*, the faireft images of heaven here below, whilft fober fenfe is left far behind.—This is not the language of the heart, nor will it ever reach it, though the ear may be tickled.

I fhall be told, perhaps, that the public have been pleafed with thefe volumes.—True—and Hervey's Meditations are ftill read, though he equally finned againft fenfe and tafte.

I particularly object to the lover-like phrafes of pumped up paffion, which are every where interfperfed. If women be ever allowed to walk without leading-ftrings, why muft they be cajoled into virtue by artful flattery and fexual compliments ?—Speak to them the language of truth and fobernefs, and away with the lullaby ftrains of condefcending endearment ! Let them be taught to refpect themfelves as rational creatures, and not led to have a paffion for their own infipid perfons. It moves my gall to hear a preacher defcanting on drefs and needle-work ; and ftill more, to hear him addrefs the *Britifh fair, the faireft of the fair*, as if they had only feelings.

Even recommending piety he ufes the following argument. ' Never, perhaps, does a fine ' woman ftrike more deeply, than when, compo- ' fed into pious recollection, and poffeffed with

' the

‘ the nobleſt conſiderations, ſhe aſſumes, without
‘ knowing it, ſuperiour dignity and new graces ;
‘ ſo that the beauties of holineſs ſeem to radiate
‘ about her, and the by-ſtanders are almoſt indu-
‘ ced to fancy her already worſhipping amongſt
‘ her kindred angels !’ Why are women to be
thus bred up with a deſire of conqueſt ? the very epithet, uſed in this ſenſe, gives me a ſickly
qualm ! Does religion and virtue offer no ſtrong-
er motives, no brighter reward ? Muſt they always be debaſed by being made to conſider the
ſex of their companions ? Muſt they be taught
always to be pleaſing ? And when levelling their
ſmall artillery at the heart of man, is it neceſſary
to tell them that a little ſenſe is ſufficient to render their attention *incredibly ſoothing* ? ‘ As a
‘ ſmall degree of knowledge entertains in a wo-
‘ man, ſo from a woman, though for a different
‘ reaſon, a ſmall expreſſion of kindneſs delights,
‘ particularly if ſhe have beauty !’ I ſhould have
ſuppoſed for the ſame reaſon.

Why are girls to be told that they reſemble
angels ; but to ſink them below women ? Or,
that a gentle innocent female is an object that
comes nearer to the idea which we have formed
of angels than any other. Yet they are told, at
the ſame time, that they are only like angels when
they are young and beautiful ; conſequently, it is
their perſons, not their virtues, that procure them
this homage.

Idle empty words ! What can ſuch deluſive
flattery lead to, but vanity and folly ? The lover,
it is true, has a poetic licence to exalt his miſ-
treſs ; his reaſon is the bubble of his paſſion, and
he

he does not utter a falsehood when he borrows the language of adoration. His imagination may raise the idol of his heart, unblamed, above humanity; and happy would it be for women, if they were only flattered by the men who loved them; I mean who loved the individual, not the sex; but should a grave preacher interlard his discourses with such fooleries?

In sermons or novels, however, voluptuousness is always true to its text. Men are allowed by moralists to cultivate, as Nature directs, different qualities, and assume the different characters, that the same passions, modified almost to infinity, give to each individual. A virtuous man may have a choleric or a sanguine constitution, be gay or grave, unreproved; be firm till he is almost overbearing, or, weakly submissive, have no will or opinion of his own; but all women are to be levelled, by meekness and docility, into one character of yielding softness and gentle compliance.

I will use the preacher's own words. 'Let 'it be observed, that in your sex manly exercises 'are never graceful; that in them a tone and fig-'ure, as well as an air and deportment, of the 'masculine kind, are always forbidding; and that 'men of sensibility desire in every woman soft 'features, and a flowing voice, a form, not ro-'bust, and demeanour delicate and gentle.'

Is not the following portrait—the portrait of a house slave? 'I am astonished at the folly of 'many women, who are still reproaching their 'husbands for leaving them alone, for preferring 'this or that company to theirs, for treating
'them

' them with this and the other mark of difregard
' or indifference ; when, to fpeak the truth, they
' have themfelves in a great meafure to blame.
' Not that I would juftify the men in any thing
' wrong on their part.   But had you behaved to
' them with more *refpectful obfervance*, and a
' more *equal tendernefs* ; *ftudying their humours*,
' *overlooking their miftakes, fubmitting to their*
' *opinions* in matters indifferent, paffing by little
' inftances of unevennefs, caprice, or paffion,
' giving *foft* anfwers to hafty words, complain-
' ing as feldom as poffible, and making it your
' daily care to relieve their anxieties and prevent
' their wifhes, to enliven the hour of dulnefs,
' and call up the ideas of felicity : had you pur-
' fued this conduct, I doubt not but you would
' have maintained and even increafed their efteem,
' fo far as to have fecured every degree of influ-
' ence that could conduce to their virtue, or
' your mutual fatisfaction ; and your houfe might
' at this day have been the abode of domeftic
' blifs.'   Such a woman ought to be an angel—
or fhe is an afs—for I difcern not a trace of the
human character, neither reafon nor paffion in
this domeftic drudge, whofe being is abforbed
in that of a tyrant's.

Still Dr. Fordyce muft have very little acquaintance with the human heart, if he really
fuppofed that fuch conduct would bring back
wandering love, inftead of exciting contempt.
No, beauty, gentlenefs, &c. &c. may gain a
heart ; but efteem, the only lafting affection,
can alone be obtained by virtue fupported by reafon.   It is refpect for the understanding that
keeps alive tendernefs for the perfon.   As

As these volumes are so frequently put into the hands of young people, I have taken more notice of them than, strictly speaking, they deserve; but as they have contributed to vitiate the taste, and enervate the understanding of many of my fellow-creatures, I could not pass them silently over.

S E C T. III.

Such paternal solicitute pervades Dr. Gregory's Legacy to his Daughters, that I enter on the task of criticism with affectionate respect; but as this little volume has many attractions to recommend it to the notice of the most respectable part of my sex, I cannot silently pass over arguments that so speciously support opinions which, I think, have had the most baneful effect on the morals and manners of the female world.

His easy familiar style is particularly suited to the tenor of his advice, and the melancholy tenderness which his respect for the memory of a beloved wife, diffuses through the whole work, renders it very interesting; yet there is a degree of concise elegance conspicuous in many passages that disturbs this sympathy; and we pop on the author, when we only expected to meet the— father.

Besides, having two objects in view, he seldom adhered steadily to either; for wishing to make his daughters amiable, and fearing lest unhappiness should only be the consequence, of instilling sentiments that might draw them out of the track of common life without enabling them to act

with

with consonant independence and dignity, he checks the natural flow of his thoughts, and neither advises one thing nor the other.

In the preface he tells them a mournful truth, ' that they will hear, at least once in their lives, ' the genuine sentiments of a man who has no in- ' terest in deceiving them.'

Hapless woman ! what can be expected from thee when the beings on whom thou art said naturally to depend for reason and support, have all an interest in deceiving thee ! This is the root of the evil that has shed a corroding mildew on all thy virtues ; and blighting in the bud thy opening faculties, has rendered thee the weak thing thou art ! It is this separate interest—this insidious state of warfare, that undermines morality, and divides mankind !

If love have made some women wretched— how many more has the cold unmeaning intercourse of gallantry rendered vain and useless ! yet this heartless attention to the sex is reckoned so manly, so polite, that till society is very differently organized, I fear, this vestige of gothic manners will not be done away by a more reasonable and affectionate mode of conduct. Besides, to strip it of its imaginary dignity, I must observe, that in the most uncivilized European states this lip-service prevails in a very great degree, accompanied with extreme dissoluteness of morals. In Portugal, the country that I particularly allude to, it takes place of the most serious moral obligations ; for a man is seldom assassinated when in the company of a woman. The savage hand of rapine is unnerved by this chivalrous spirit ; and,

if

if the ftroke of vengeance cannot be ftayed—the lady is entreated to pardon the rudenefs and depart in peace, though fprinkled, perhaps, with her hufband's or brother's blood.

I fhall pafs over his ftrictures on religion, becaufe I mean to difcufs that fubject in a feparate chapter.

The remarks relative to behaviour, though many of them very fenfible, I entirely difapprove of, becaufe it appears to me to be beginning, as it were, at the wrong end. A cultivated underftanding, and an affectionate heart, will never want ftarched rules of decorum—fomething more fubftantial than feemlinefs will be the refult ; and, without underftanding the behaviour here recommended, would be rank affectation. Decorum, indeed, is the one thing needful !—decorum is to fupplant nature, and banifh all fimplicity and variety of character out of the female world. Yet what good end can all this fuperficial counfel produce ? It is, however, much eafier to point out this or that mode of behaviour, than to fet the reafon to work ; but, when the mind has been ftored with ufeful knowledge, and ftrengthened by being employed, the regulation of the behaviour may fafely be left to its guidance.

Why, for inftance, fhould the following caution be given when art of every kind muft contaminate the mind ; and why entangle the grand motives of action, which reafon and religion equally combine to enforce, with pitiful worldly fhifts and flight of hand tricks to gain the applaufe of gaping taftelefs fools ? ' Be even cautious in dif-

'playing

' playing your good fenfe*.   It will be thought
' you affume a fuperiority over the reft of the
' company—But if you happen to have any
' learning, keep it a profound fecret, efpecially
' from the men, who generally look with a jeal-
' ous and malignant eye on a woman of great
' parts, and a cultivated underftanding.'   If men
of real merit, as he afterwards obferves, are fuperiour to this meannefs, where is the neceffity
that the behaviour of the whole fex fhould be
modulated to pleafe fools, or men, who having
little claim to refpect as individuals, choofe to
keep clofe in their phalanx.   Men, indeed, who
infift on their common fuperiority, having only
this fexual fuperiority, are certainly very excufable.

There would be no end to rules for behaviour,
if it be proper always to adopt the tone of the
company; for thus, for ever varying the key, a
flat would often pafs for a *natural* note.

Surely it would have been wifer to have advifed
women to improve themfelves till they rofe above
the fumes of vanity; and then to let the public
opinion come round—for where are rules of ac-
commodation to ftop? The narrow path of truth
and virtue inclines neither to the right nor left—
it is a ftraight-forward bufinefs, and they who
are earneftly purfuing their road, may bound over
many decorous prejudices, without leaving modefty behind.   Make the heart clean, and give
the head employment, and I will venture to predict that there will be nothing offenfive in the
behaviour.   The

* Let women once acquire good fenfe—and if it deferve the name, it
will teach them; or, of what ufe will it be? how to employ it.

The air of fashion, which many young people are so eager to attain, always strikes me like the studied attitudes of some modern prints, copied with tasteless servility after the antiques ;—the soul is left out, and none of the parts are tied together by what may properly be termed character. This varnish of fashion, which seldom sticks very close to sense, may dazzle the weak ; but leave nature to itself, and it will seldom disgust the wise. Besides, when a woman has sufficient sense not to pretend to any thing which she does not understand in some degree, there is no need of determining to hide her talents under a bushel. Let things take their natural course, and all will be well.

It is this system of dissimulation, throughout the volume, that I despise. Women are always to *seem* to be this and that—yet virtue might apostrophize them, in the words of Hamlet—Seems! I know not seems !—Have that within that passeth show !—

Still the same tone occurs ; for in another place, after recommending, without sufficiently discriminating delicacy, he adds, ‘ The men will ‘ complain of your reserve. They will assure ‘ you that a franker behaviour would make you ‘ more amiable. But, trust me, they are not sin- ‘ cere when they tell you so.—I acknowledge, ‘ that on some occasions it might render you more ‘ agreeable as companions, but it would make you ‘ less amiable as women : an important distinc- ‘ tion, which many of your sex are not aware of.

This desire of being always women, is the very consciousness that degrades the sex. Excepting with

with a lover, I muſt repeat with emphaſis, a former obſervation,—it would be well if they were
only agreeable or rational companions.—But in
this reſpect his advice is even inconſiſtent with a
paſſage˙ which I mean to quote with the moſt
marked approbation.

'The ſentiment that a woman may allow all
'innocent freedoms, provided her virtue is ſe-
'cure, is both groſsly indelicate and dangerous,
'and has proved fatal to many of your ſex.' With
this opinion I perfectly coincide. A man, or a
woman, of any feeling, muſt always wiſh to convince a beloved object that it is the careſſes of the
individual, not the ſex, that is received and returned with pleaſure; and that the heart, rather
than the ſenſes, is moved. Without this natural
delicacy, love becomes a ſelfiſh perſonal gratification that ſoon degrades the character.

I carry this ſentiment ſtill further. Affection, when love is out of the queſtion, authoriſes
many perſonal endearments, that naturally flowing from an innocent heart, give life to the behaviour; but the perſonal intercourſe of appetite,
gallantry, or vanity, is deſpicable. When a man
ſqueezes the hand of a pretty woman, handing
her to a carriage, whom he has never ſeen before,
ſhe will conſider ſuch an impertinent freedom in
the light of an inſult, if ſhe have any true delicacy, inſtead of being flattered by this unmeaning
homage to beauty. Theſe are the privileges of
friendſhip, or the momentary homage which the
heart pays to virtue, when it flaſhes ſuddenly on
the notice—mere animal ſpirits have no claim to
the kindneſſes of affection.

Wiſhing

Wishing to feed the affections with what is now the food of vanity, I would fain persuade my sex to act from simpler principles. Let them merit love, and they will obtain it, though they may never be told that—' The power of a fine woman ' over the hearts of men, of men of the finest ' parts, is even beyond what she conceives.'

I have already noticed the narrow cautions with respect to duplicity, female softness, delicacy of constitution ; for these are the changes which he rings round without ceasing—in a more decorous manner, it is true, than Rousseau ; but it all comes home to the same point, and whoever is at the trouble to analyze these sentiments, will find the first principles not quite so delicate as the superstructure.

The subject of amusements is treated in too cursory a manner ; but with the same spirit.

When I treat of friendship, love, and marriage, it will be found that we materially differ in opinion ; I shall not then forestall what I have to observe on these important subjects ; but confine my remarks to the general tenor of them, to that cautious family prudence, to those confined views of partial unenlightened affection, which exclude pleasure and improvement, by vainly wishing to ward off sorrow and error—and by thus guarding the heart and mind, destroy also all their energy. It is far better to be often deceived than never to trust ; to be disappointed in love than never to love ; to lose a husband's fondness than forfeit his esteem.

Happy would it be for the world, and for individuals, of course, if all this unavailing solici-

M   tude

tude to attain worldly happinefs, on a confined plan, were turned into an anxious defire to improve the underftanding.—' Wifdom is the principal ' thing : *therefore* get wifdom ; and with all thy ' gettings get underftanding.'—' How long, ye ' fimple ones, will ye love fimplicity, and hate ' knowledge ?' faith Wifdom to the daughters of men !

S E C T. IV.

I DO not mean to allude to all the writers who have written on the fubject of female manners— it would, in fact, be only beating over the old ground, for they have in general, written in the fame ftrain ; but attacking the boafted prerogative of man—the prerogative that may emphatically be called the iron fceptre of tyranny, the original fin of tyrants, I declare againft all power built on prejudices, however hoary.

If the fubmiffion demanded be founded on juftice —there is no appealing to a higher power—for God is Juftice itfelf. Let us then, as children of the fame parent, if not baftardized by being the younger born, reafon together, and learn to fubmit to the authority of reafon—when her voice is diftinctly heard. But, if it be proved, that this throne of prerogative only refts on a chaotic mafs of prejudices, that have no inherent princi-ple of order to keep them together, or on an el-ephant, tortoife, or even the mighty fhoulders of a fon of the earth, they may efcape, who dare to brave the confequence, without any breach of du-ty, without finning againft the order of things.

Whilft

Whilſt reaſon raiſes man above the brutal herd, and death is big with promiſes, they alone are ſubject to blind authority who have no reliance on their own ſtrength. ' They are free—who will be free* !'—

The being who can govern itſelf has nothing to fear in life ; but if any thing is dearer than its own reſpect, the price muſt be paid to the laſt farthing. Virtue, like every thing valuable, muſt be loved for herſelf alone ; or ſhe will not take up her abode with us. She will not impart that peace, ' which paſſeth underſtanding,' when ſhe is merely made the ſtilts of reputation ; and reſpected, with phariſaical exactneſs, becauſe ' honeſty is the beſt policy.

That the plan of life which enables us to carry ſome knowledge and virtue into another world, is the one beſt calculated to enſure content in this, cannot be denied ; yet few people act according to this principle, though it be univerſally allowed that it admit not of diſpute. Preſent pleaſure, or preſent power, carry before it theſe ſober convictions ; and it is for the day, not for life, that man bargains with happineſs. How few !—how very few ! have ſufficient foreſight, or reſolution, to endure a ſmall evil at the moment, to avoid a greater hereafter.

Woman in particular, whoſe virtue † is built on mutual prejudices, ſeldom attains to this greatneſs of mind ; ſo that, becoming the ſlave of her own feelings, ſhe is eaſily ſubjugated by thoſe of
M 2   others.

---

* ' He is the free man, whom the *truth* makes free !'   *Cowper.*

† I mean to uſe a word that comprehends more than chaſtity the ſexual virtue.

others. Thus degraded, her reason, her misty reason ! is employed rather to burnish than to snap her chains.

Indignantly have I heard women argue in the same track as men, and adopt the sentiments that brutalize them, with all the pertinacity of ignorance.

I must illustrate my assertion by a few examples. Mrs. Piozzi, who often repeated by rote, what she did not understand, comes forward with Johnsonian periods.

'Seek not for happiness in singularity; and
' dread a refinement of wisdom as a deviation into
' folly.' Thus she dogmatically addresses a new
married man ; and to elucidate this pompous ex-
ordium, she adds, ' I said that the person of your
' lady would not grow more pleasing to you, but
' pray let her never suspect that it grows less so ;
' that a woman will pardon an affront to her un-
' derstanding much sooner than one to her per-
' son, is well known ; nor will any of us con-
' tradict the assertion. All our attainments, all
' our arts, are employed to gain and keep the
' heart of man ; and what mortification can ex-
' ceed the disappointment, if the end be not ob-
' tained ? There is no reproof however pointed,
' no punishment however severe, that a woman
' of spirit will not prefer to neglect ; and if she
' can endure it without complaint, it only proves
' that she means to make herself amends by the at-
' tention of others for the slights of her husband !'
These are truly masculine sentiments.—' All
' our *arts* are employed to gain and keep the
' heart of man :'—and what is the inference ?—
if

if her perfon, and was there ever a perfon, though formed with Medicifan fymmetry, that was not flighted ? be neglected, fhe will make herfelf amends by endeavouring to pleafe other men. Noble morality! But thus is the underftanding of the whole fex affronted, and their virtue deprived of the common bafis of virtue. A woman muft know, that her perfon cannot be as pleafing to her hufband as it was to her lover, and if fhe be offended with him for being a human creature, fhe may as well whine about the lofs of his heart as about any other foolifh thing.—And this very want of difcernment or unreafonable anger, proves that he could not change his fondnefs for her perfon into affection for her virtues or refpect for her underftanding.

Whilft women avow, and act up to fuch opinions, their underftandings, at leaft, deferve the contempt and obloquy that men, *who never* infult their perfons, have pointedly levelled at the female mind. And it is the fentiments of thefe polite men, who do not wifh to be encumbered with mind, that vain women thoughtlefsly adopt. Yet they fhould know, that infulted reafon alone can fpread that *facred* referve about the perfon, which renders human affections, for human affections have always fome bafe alloy, as permanent as is confiftent with the grand end of exiftence— the attainment of virtue.

The Baronefs de Stael fpeaks the fame language as the lady juft cited, with more enthufiafm. Her eulogium on Rouffeau was accidentally put into my hands, and her fentiments, the fentiments of too many of my fex, may ferve as the text for

a few comments. 'Though Roufſeau,' ſhe obſerves, 'has endeavoured to prevent women from
' interfering in public affairs, and acting a bril-
' liant part in the theatre of politics ; yet in ſpeak-
' ing of them, how much has he done it to their
' ſatisfaction ! If he wiſhed to deprive them of
' ſome rights foreign to their ſex, how has he
' for ever reſtored to them all thoſe to which it
' has a claim ? And in attempting to diminiſh
' their influence over the deliberations of men,
' how ſacredly has he eſtabliſhed the empire they
' have over their happineſs ! In aiding them to
' deſcend from an uſurped throne, he has firmly
' ſeated them upon that to which they were deſ-
' tined by nature ; and though he be full of in-
' dignation againſt them when they endeavour
' to reſemble men, yet when they come before
' him with all the *charms, weakneſſes, virtues* and
' *errors,* of their ſex, his reſpect for their *perſons*
' amounts almoſt to adoration. True !—For
never was there a ſenſualiſt who paid more fer-
vent adoration at the ſhrine of beauty. So devout, indeed, was his reſpect for the perſon, that
excepting the virtue of chaſtity, for obvious rea-
ſons, he only wiſhed to ſee it embelliſhed by
charms, weakneſſes, and errors. He was afraid
leſt the auſterity of reaſon ſhould diſturb the ſoft
playfulneſs of love. The maſter wiſhed to have
a meretricious ſlave to fondle, entirely dependent
on his reaſon and bounty ; he did not want a companion, whom he ſhould be compelled to eſteem,
or a friend to whom he could confide the care of
his children's education, ſhould death deprive
them of their father, before he had fulfilled the
ſacred

sacred task. He denies woman reason, shuts her out from knowledge, and turns her aside from truth; yet his pardon is granted, because ' he admits the passion of love.' It would require some ingenuity to shew why women were to be under such an obligation to him for thus admitting love; when it is clear that he admits it only for the relaxation of men, and to perpetuate the species; but he talked with passion, and that powerful spell worked on the sensibility of a young encomiast. ' What signifies it,' pursues this rhapsodist, ' to women, that his reason disputes with them the empire, when his heart is ' devotedly theirs.' It is not empire,—but equality, that they should contend for. Yet, if they only wished to lengthen out their sway, they should not entirely trust to their persons, for though beauty may gain a heart, it cannot keep it, even while the beauty is in full bloom, unless the mind lend, at least, some graces.

When women are once sufficiently enlightened to discover their real interest, on a grand scale, they will, I am persuaded, be very ready to resign all the prerogatives of love, that are not mutual, speaking of them as lasting prerogatives, for the calm satisfaction of friendship, and the tender confidence of habitual esteem. Before marriage they will not assume any insolent airs, nor afterwards abjectly submit; but endeavouring to act like reasonable creatures, in both situations, they will not be tumbled from a throne to a stool.

Madame Genlis has written several entertaining books for children; and her Letters on Education afford many useful hints, that sensible par-

ents

ents will certainly avail themselves of ; but her views are narrow, and her prejudices as unreasonable as strong.

I shall pass over her vehement argument in favour of the eternity of future punishments, because I blush to think that a human being should ever argue vehemently in such a cause, and only make a few remarks on her absurd manner of making the parental authority supplant reason. For every where does she inculcate not only *blind* submission to parents ; but to the opinion of the world*.

She tells a story of a young man engaged by his father's express desire to a girl of fortune. Before the marriage could take place, she is deprived of her fortune, and thrown friendless on the world. The father practises the most infamous arts to separate his son from her, and when the son detects his villany, and, following the dictates of honour, marries the girl, nothing but misery ensues, because forsooth he married *without* his father's consent. On what ground can religion or morality rest when justice is thus set at defiance ? In the same style she represents an accomplished young woman, as ready to marry any body that her *mamma* pleased to recommend ; and, as actually marrying the young man of her own choice, without feeling any emotions of passions, because

that

---

* A person is not to act in this or that way, though convinced they are right in so doing, because some equivocal circumstances may lead the world to *suspect* that they acted from different motives.—This is sacrificing the substance for a shadow. Let people but watch their own hearts, and act rightly, as far as they can judge, and they may patiently wait till the opinion of the world comes round. It is best to be directed by a simple motive—for justice has too often been sacrificed to propriety ;—another word for convenience.

that a well educated girl had not time to be in love. Is it possible to have much respect for a system of education that thus insults reason and nature?

Many similar opinions occur in her writings, mixed with sentiments that do honour to her head and heart. Yet so much superstition is mixed with her religion, and so much worldly wisdom with her morality, that I should not let a young person read her works, unless I could afterwards converse on the subjects, and point out the contradictions.

Mrs. Chapone's Letters are written with such good sense, and unaffected humility, and contain so many useful observations, that I only mention them to pay the worthy writer this tribute of respect. I cannot, it is true, always coincide in opinion with her; but I always respect her.

The very word respect brings Mrs. Macaulay to my remembrance. The woman of the greatest abilities, undoubtedly, that this country has ever produced.—And yet this woman has been suffered to die without sufficient respect being paid to her memory.

Posterity, however, will be more just; and remember that Catharine Macaulay was an example of intellectual acquirements supposed to be incompatible with the weakness of her sex. In her style of writing, indeed, no sex appears, for it is like the sense it conveys, strong and clear.

I will not call her's a masculine understanding, because I admit not of such an arrogant assumption of reason; but I contend that it was a sound one, and that her judgment, the matured fruit of

profound

profound thinking, was a proof that a woman can acquire judgment, in the full extent of the word. Poſſeſſing more penetration than ſagacity, more underſtanding than fancy, ſhe writes with ſober energy and argumentative cloſeneſs ; yet ſympathy and benevolence give an intereſt to her ſentiments, and that vital heat to arguments, which forces the reader to weigh them*.

When I firſt thought of writing theſe ſtrictures I anticipated Mrs. Macaulay's approbation, with a little of that ſanguine ardour, which it has been the buſineſs of my life to depreſs ; but ſoon heard with the ſickly qualm of diſappointed hope ; and the ſtill ſeriouſneſs of regret—that ſhe was no more !

SECT. V.

Taking a view of the different works which have been written on education, Lord Cheſter-field's Letters muſt not be ſilently paſſed over. Not that I mean to analyze his unmanly, im-moral ſyſtem, or even to cull any of the uſeful, ſhrewd remarks which occur in his frivolous correſpondence—No, I only mean to make a few reflections on the avowed tendency of them—the art of acquiring an early knowledge of the world. An art, I will venture to aſſert, that preys ſecret-ly, like the worm in the bud, on the expanding powers, and turns to poiſon the generous juices which ſhould mount with vigour in the youth-ful

* Coinciding in opinion with Mrs. Macaulay relative to many branches of education, I refer to her valuable work, inſtead of quoting her ſentiments to ſupport my own.

ful frame, infpiring warm affections and great re-
folves*.

For every thing, faith the wife man, there is a
feafon ;—and who would look for the fruits of
autumn during the genial months of fpring ? But
this is mere declamation, and I mean to reafon
with thofe worldly-wife inftructors, who, inftead of cultivating the judgment inftil prejudices, and render hard the heart that gradual experience would only have cooled. An early acquaintance with human infirmities ; or, what is termed
knowledge of the world, is the fureft way, in my
opinion, to contract the heart and damp the natural youthful ardour which produces not only great
talents, but great virtues. For the vain attempt
to bring forth the fruit of experience, before the
fapling has thrown out its leaves, only exhaufts
its ftrength, and prevents its affuming a natural
form, juft as the form and ftrength of fubfiding
metals are injured when the attraction of cohefion
is difturbed.

Tell me, ye who have ftudied the human mind,
is it not a ftrange way to fix principles by fhow-
ing young people that they are feldom ftable ?
And how can they be fortified by habits when
they are proved to be fallacious by example ?
Why is the ardour of youth thus to be damped,
and the luxuriancy of fancy cut to the quick ?
This dry caution may, it is true, guard a charac-

ter

* That children ought to be conftantly guarded againft the vices and
follies of the world, appears, to me, a very miftaken opinion ; for in the
courfe of my experience, and my eyes have looked abroad, I never knew
a youth educated in this manner, who had early imbibed thefe chilling
fufpicions, and repeated by rote the hefitating if of age, that did not prove
a felfifh character.

ter from worldly mifchances ; but will infallibly preclude excellence in either virtue or know-ledge*. The ftumbling-block thrown acrofs every path by fufpicion, will prevent any vigorous exertions of genius or benevolence, and life will be ftripped of its moft alluring charm long be-fore its calm evening, when man fhould retire to contemplation for comfort and fupport.

A young man who has been bred up with do-meftic friends, and led to ftore his mind with as much fpeculative knowledge as can be acquired by reading and the natural reflections which youthful ebullitions of animal fpirits and inftinct-ive feelings infpire, will enter the world with warm and erroneous expectations. But this ap-pears to be the courfe of nature ; and in morals, as well as in works of tafte, we fhould be ob-fervant of her facred indications, and not prefume to lead when we ought obfequioufly to follow.

In the world few people act from principle ; prefent feelings, and early habits, are the grand fprings : but how would the former be deaden-ed, and the latter rendered iron corroding fetters, if the world were fhewn to young people juft as it is ; when no knowledge of mankind or their own hearts, flowly obtained by experience, ren-dered them forbearing ? Their fellow creatures would not then be viewed as frail beings ; like themfelves condemned to ftruggle with human infirmities, and fometimes difplaying the light, and fometimes the dark fide of their character ;

extorting

---

* I have already obferved that an early knowledge of the world, obtain-ed in a natural way, by mixing in the world, has the fame effect : inftan-cing officers and women.

extorting alternate feelings of love and difguft ; but guarded againft as beafts of prey, till every enlarged focial feeling, in a word,—humanity, was eradicated.

In life, on the contrary, as we gradually difcover the imperfections of our nature, we difcover virtues, and various circumftances attach us to our fellow creatures, when we mix with them, and view the fame objects, that are never thought of in acquiring a hafty unnatural knowledge of the world. We fee a folly fwell into a vice, by almoft imperceptible degrees, and pity while we blame ; but, if the hideous monfter burft fuddenly on our fight, fear and difguft rendering us more fevere than man ought to be, might lead us with blind zeal to ufurp the character of omnipotence, and denounce damnation on our fellow mortals, forgetting that we cannot read the heart, and that we have feeds of the fame vices lurking in our own.

I have already remarked that we expect more from inftruction, than mere inftruction can produce : for, inftead of preparing young people to encounter the evils of life with dignity, and to acquire wifdom and virtue by the exercife of their own faculties, precepts are heaped upon precepts, and blind obedience required, when conviction fhould be brought home to reafon.

Suppofe, for inftance, that a young perfon in the firft ardour of friendfhip deifies the beloved object—what harm can arife from this miftaken enthufiaftic attachment ? Perhaps it is neceffary for virtue firft to appear in a human form to imprefs youthful hearts : the ideal model, which a

more

more matured and exalted mind looks up to, and shapes for itself, would elude their sight. He who loves not his brother whom he hath seen, how can he love God ? asked the wisest of men.

It is natural for youth to adorn the first object of its affection with every good quality, and the emulation produced by ignorance, or, to speak with more propriety, by inexperience, brings forward the mind capable of forming such an affection, and when, in the lapse of time, perfection is found not to be within the reach of mortals, virtue, abstractedly, is thought beautiful, and wisdom sublime. Admiration then gives place to friendship, properly so called, because it is cemented by esteem ; and the being walks alone only dependent on heaven for that emulous panting after perfection which ever glows in a noble mind. But this knowledge a man must gain by the exertion of his own faculties ; and this is surely the blessed fruit of disappointed hope ! for He who delighteth to diffuse happiness and shew mercy to the weak creatures, who are learning to know him, never implanted a good propensity to be a tormenting ignis fatuus.

Our trees are now allowed to spread with wild luxuriance, nor do we expect by force to combine the majestic marks of time with useful graces ; but wait patiently till they have struck deep their root, and braved many a storm.—Is the mind then, which, in proportion to its dignity, advances more slowly towards perfection, to be treated with less respect ? To argue from analogy, every thing around us is in a progressive state ; and when an unwelcome knowledge of life pro-

duces

duces almost a satiety of life, and we discover by the natural course of things that all that is done under the sun is vanity, we are drawing near the awful close of the drama. The days of activity and hope are over, and the opportunities which the first stage of existence has afforded of advancing in the scale of intelligence, must soon be summed up.—A knowledge at this period of the futility of life, or earlier, if obtained by experience, is very useful, because it is natural; but when a frail being is shewn the follies and vices of man, that he may be taught prudently to guard against the common casualties of life by sacrificing his heart—surely it is not speaking harshly to call it the wisdom of this world, contrasted with the nobler fruit of piety and experience.

I will venture a paradox, and deliver my opinion without reserve; if men were only born to form a circle of life and death, it would be wise to take every step that foresight could suggest to render life happy. Moderation in every pursuit would then be supreme wisdom; and the prudent voluptuary might enjoy a degree of content, though he neither cultivated his understanding nor kept his heart pure. Prudence, supposing we were mortal, would be true wisdom, or, to be more explicit, would procure the greatest portion of happiness, considering the whole of life, but knowledge beyond the conveniences of life would be a curse.

Why should we injure our health by close study? The exalted pleasure which intellectual pursuits afford would scarcely be equivalent to the hours of languor that follow; especially, if

it

It be neceſſary to take into the reckoning the doubts and diſappointments that cloud our reſearches. Vanity and vexation cloſe every inquiry : for the cauſe which we particularly wiſhed to diſcover flies like the horizen before us as we advance. The ignorant, on the contrary, reſemble children, and ſuppoſe, that if they could walk ſtraight forward they ſhould at laſt arrive where the earth and clouds meet. Yet, diſappointed as we are in our reſearches, the mind gains ſtrength by the exerciſe, ſufficient, perhaps, to comprehend the anſwers which, in another ſtep of exiſtence, it may receive to the anxious queſtions it aſked, when the underſtanding with feeble wing was fluttering round the viſible effects to dive into the hidden cauſe.

The paſſions alſo, the winds of life, would be uſeleſs, if not injurious, did the ſubſtance which compoſes our thinking being, after we have thought in vain, only become the ſupport of vegetable life, and invigorate a cabbage, or bluſh in a roſe. The appetites would anſwer every earthly purpoſe, and produce more moderate and permanent happineſs. But the powers of the ſoul that are of little uſe here, and, probably, diſturb our animal enjoyments, even while conſcious dignity makes us glory in poſſeſſing them, prove that life is merely an education, a ſtate of infancy, to which the only hopes worth cheriſhing ſhould not be ſacrificed. I mean, therefore, to infer, that we ought to have a preciſe idea of what we wiſh to attain by education, for the immortality of the ſoul is contradicted by the actions of many people who firmly profeſs the belief.

If

If you mean to fecure eafe and profperity on earth as the firft confideration, and leave futurity to provide for itfelf; you act prudently in giving your child an early infight into the weakneffes of his nature. You may not, it is true, make an Inkle of him; but do not imagine that he will ftick to more than the letter of the law, who has very early imbibed a mean opinion of human nature; nor will he think it neceffary to rife much above the common ftandard. He may avoid grofs vices, becaufe honefty is the beft policy; but he will never aim at attaining great virtues. The example of writers and artifts will illuftrate this remark.

I muft therefore venture to doubt whether what has been thought an axiom in morals may not have been a dogmatical affertion made by men who have coolly feen mankind through the medium of books, and fay, in direct contradiction to them, that the regulation of the paffions is not, always, wifdom. On the contrary, it fhould feem, that one reafon why men have fuperiour judgment, and more fortitude than women, is undoubtedly this, that they give a freer fcope to the grand paffions, and by more frequently going aftray enlarge their minds. If then by the exercife of their own* reafon they fix on fome ftable principle, they have probably to thank the force of their paffions, nourifhed by *falfe* views of life, and permitted to overleap the boundary that fecures content. But if, in the dawn of life, we could foberly furvey the fcenes before as in perfpective, and fee every

N   thing

* ' I find that all is but lip-wifdom which wants experience,' fays Sidney.

thing in its true colours, how could the passions gain sufficient strength to unfold the faculties?

Let me now as from an eminence survey the world stripped of all its false delusive charms. The clear atmosphere enables me to see each object in its true point of view, while my heart is still. I am calm as the prospect in a morning when the mists, slowly dispersing, silently unveil the beauties of nature, refreshed by rest.

In what light will the world now appear?—I rub my eyes and think, perchance, that I am just awaking from a lively dream.

I see the sons and daughters of men pursuing shadows, and anxiously wasting their powers to feed passions which have no adequate object—if the very excess of these blind impulses, pampered by that lying, yet constantly trusted guide, the imagination, did not, by preparing them for some other state, render short-sighted mortals wiser without their own concurrence; or, what comes to the same thing, when they were pursuing some imaginary present good.

After viewing objects in this light, it would not be very fanciful to imagine that this world was a stage on which a pantomime is daily performed for the amusement of superiour beings. How would they be diverted to see the ambitious man consuming himself by running after a phantom, and, ' pursuing the bubble fame in the can- ' non's mouth' that was to blow him to nothing: for when consciousness is lost, it matters not whether we mount in a whirlwind or descend in rain. And should they compassionately invigorate his sight and shew him the thorny path
which

which led to eminence, that like a quicksand
sinks as he afcends, difappointing his hopes when
almoft within his grafp, would he not leave to
others the honour of amufing them, and labour
to fecure the prefent moment, though from the
conftitution of his nature he would not find it
very eafy to catch the flying ftream? Such flaves
are we to hope and fear!

But, vain as the ambitious man's purfuits
would be, he is often ftriving for fomething more
fubftantial than fame—that indeed would be the
verieft meteor, the wildeft fire that could lure a
man to ruin.——What! renounce the moft trifling
gratification to be applauded when he fhould be
no more! Wherefore this ftruggle, whether man
is mortal or immortal, if that noble paffion did
not really raife the being above his fellows?——

And love! What diverting fcenes would it
produce—Pantaloon's tricks muft yield to more
egregious folly. To fee a mortal adorn an object with imaginary charms, and then fall down
and worfhip the idol which he had himfelf fet
up—how ridiculous! But what ferious confequences enfue to rob man of that portion of happinefs, which the Deity by calling him into exiftence has (or, on what can his attributes reft?)
indubitably promifed: would not all the purpofes of life have been much better fulfilled if he
had only felt what has been termed phyfical love?
And, would not the fight of the object, not feen
through the medium of the imagination, foon reduce the paffion to an appetite, if reflection, the
noble diftinction of man, did not give it force,
and make it an inftrument to raife him above this

earthy drofs, by teaching him to love the centre of all perfection ; whofe wifdom appears clearer and clearer in the works of nature, in proportion as reafon is illuminated and exalted by contemplation, and by acquiring that love of order which the ftruggles of paffion produce ?

The habit of reflection, and the knowledge attained by foftering any paffion, might be fhewn to be equally ufeful, though the object be proved equally fallacious ; for they would all appear in the fame light, if they were not magnified by the governing paffion implanted in us by the Author of all good, to call forth and ftrengthen the faculties of each individual, and enable it to attain all the experience that an infant can obtain, who does certain things, it cannot tell why.

I defcend from my height, and mixing with my fellow-creatures, feel myfelf hurried along the common ftream ; ambition, love, hope and fear, exert their wonted power, though we be convinced by reafon that their prefent and moft attractive promifes are only lying dreams ; but had the cold hand of circumfpection damped each generous feeling before it had left any permanent character, or fixed fome habit, what could be expected, but felfifh prudence and reafon juft rifing above inftinct ? Who that has read Dean Swift's difgufting defcription of the Yahoos, and infipid one of Houyhnhnm with a philofophical eye, can avoid feeing the futility of degrading the paffions, or making man reft in contentment ?

The youth fhould *act* ; for had he the experience of a grey head he would be fitter for death than life, though his virtues, rather refiding in
his

his head than his heart, could produce nothing great, and his underſtanding, prepared for this world, would not, by its noble flights, prove that it had a title to a better.

Beſides, it is not poſſible to give a young perſon a juſt view of life ; he muſt have ſtruggled with his own paſſions before he can eſtimate the force of the temptation which betrayed his brother into vice. Thoſe who are entering life, and thoſe who are departing, ſee the world from ſuch very different points of view, that they can ſeldom think alike, unleſs the unfledged reaſon of the former never attempted a ſolitary flight.

When we hear of ſome daring crime, it comes full on us in the deepeſt ſhade of turpitude, and raiſes indignation ; but the eye that gradually ſaw the darkneſs thicken, muſt obſerve it with more compaſſionate forbearance. The world cannot be ſeen by an unmoved ſpectator, we muſt mix in the throng, and feel as men feel before we can judge of their feelings. If we mean, in ſhort, to live in the world to grow wiſer and better, and not merely to enjoy the good things of life, we muſt attain a knowledge of others at the ſame time that we become acquainted with ourſelves— knowledge acquired any other way only hardens the heart and perplexes the underſtanding.

I may be told, that the knowledge thus acquired, is ſometimes purchaſed at too dear a rate. I can only anſwer that I very much doubt whether any knowledge can be attained without labour and ſorrow ; and thoſe who wiſh to ſpare their children both, ſhould not complain, if they are neither wiſe nor virtuous. They only aimed

at

at making them prudent ; and prudence, early in life, is but the cautious craft of ignorant self-love.

I have obferved that young people, to whofe education particular attention has been paid, have, in general, been very fuperficial and conceited, and far from pleafing in any refpect, becaufe they had neither the unfufpecting warmth of youth, nor the cool depth of age. I cannot help imputing this unnatural appearance principally to that hafty premature inftruction, which leads them prefumptuoufly to repeat all the crude notions they have taken upon truft, fo that the careful education which they received, makes them all their lives the flaves of prejudices.

Mental as well as bodily exertion is, at firft, irkfome ; fo much fo, that the many would fain let others both work and think for them. An obfervation which I have often made will illuftrate my meaning. When in a circle of ftrangers, or acquaintances, a perfon of moderate abilities afferts an opinion with heat, I will venture to affirm, for I have traced this fact home, very often, that it is a prejudice. Thefe echoes have a high refpect for the underftanding of fome relation or friend, and without fully comprehending the opinions, which they are fo eager to retail, they maintain them with a degree of obftinacy, that would furprife even the perfon who concocted them.

I know that a kind of fafhion now prevails of refpecting prejudices ; and when any one dares to face them, though actuated by humanity and armed by reafon, he is fupercilioufly afked whether his anceftors were fools. No, I fhould reply ;

opinions,

opinions, at firft, of every defcription, were all, probably, confidered, and therefore were founded on
fome reafon ; yet not unfrequently, of courfe, it
was rather a local expedient than a fundamental
principle, that would be reafonable at all times.
But, mofs-covered opinions affume the difpro-
portioned form of prejudices, when they are indolently adopted only becaufe age has given them
a venerable afpect, though the reafon on which
they were built ceafes to be a reafon, or cannot
be traced. Why are we to love prejudices, merely becaufe they are prejudices *? A prejudice is
a fond obftinate perfuafion for which we can give
no reafon ; for the moment a reafon can be given
for an opinion, it ceafes to be a prejudice, though
it may be an error in judgment : and are we then
advifed to cherifh opinions only to fet reafon at
defiance ? This mode of arguing, if arguing it
may be called, reminds me of what is vulgarly
termed a woman's reafon. For women fometimes declare that they love, or believe, certain
things, *becaufe* they love, or believe them.

It is impoffible to converfe with people to any
purpofe, who, in this ftyle, only ufe affirmatives
and negatives. Before you can bring them to a
point, to ftart fairly from, you muft go back to
the fimple principles that were antecedent to the
prejudices broached by power ; and it is ten to
one but you are ftopped by the philofophical affertion, that certain principles are as practically
falfe as they are abftractly true†. Nay, it may be

N 4 inferred,

* Vide Mr. Burke.

† ' Convince a man againft his will.
' He's of the fame opinion ftill.'

inferred, that reason has whispered some doubts, for it generally happens that people assert their opinions with the greatest heat when they begin to waver; striving to drive out their own doubts by convincing their opponent, they grow angry when those gnawing doubts are thrown back to prey on themselves.

The fact is, that men expect from education, what education cannot give. A sagacious parent or tutor may strengthen the body and sharpen the instruments by which the child is to gather knowledge; but the honey must be the reward of the individual's own industry. It is almost as absurd to attempt to make a youth wise by the experience of another, as to expect the body to grow strong by the exercise which is only talked of, or seen *. Many of those children whose conduct has been most narrowly watched, become the weakest men, because their instructors only instil certain notions into their minds, that have no other foundation than their authority; and if they are loved or respected, the mind is cramped in its exertions and wavering in its advances. The business of education in this case, is only to conduct the shooting tendrils to a proper pole; yet after laying precept upon precept, without allowing a child to acquire judgment itself, parents expect them to act in the same manner by this borrowed fallacious light, as if they had illuminated it themselves; and be, when they enter life, what their parents are at the close. They do not consider that the tree, and even the human

man

---

† ' One sees nothing when one is content to contemplate only; it is necessary to act oneself to be able to see how others act.'　*Rousseau.*

man body does not ftrengthen its fibres till it has reached its full growth.

There appears to be fomething analogous in the mind. The fenfes and the imagination give a form to the character, during childhood and youth ; and the underftanding, as life advances, gives firmnefs to the firft fair purpofes of fenfi- bility—till virtue, arifing rather from the clear conviction of reafon than the impulfe of the heart, morality is made to reft on a rock againft which the ftorms of paffion vainly beat.

I hope I fhall not be mifunderftood when I fay, that religion will not have this condenfing energy, unlefs it be founded on reafon. If it be merely the refuge of weaknefs or wild fanaticifm, and not a governing principle of conduct, drawn from felf-knowledge, and a rational opinion re- fpecting the attributes of God, what can it be expected to produce ? The religion which con- fifts in warming the affections, and exalting the imagination, is only the poetical part, and may afford the individual pleafure without rendering it a more moral being. It may be a fubftitute for worldly purfuits ; yet narrow, inftead of en- larging the heart : but virtue muft be loved as in itfelf fublime and excellent, and not for the advantages it procures or the evils it averts, if any great degree of excellence be expected. Men will not become moral when they only build airy caftles in a future world to compenfate for the difappointments which they meet with in this ; if they turn their thoughts from relative duties to religious reveries.

Moft

Most prospects in life are marred by the shuffling worldly wisdom of men, who, forgetting that they cannot serve God and mammon, endeavour to blend contradictory things.—If you wish to make your son rich, pursue one course—if you are only anxious to make him virtuous, you must take another; but do not imagine that you can bound from one road to the other without losing your way *.

* See an excellent essay on this subject by Mrs. Barbauld, in *Miscellaneous Pieces in Prose.*

C H A P.

C H A P. VI.

THE EFFECT WHICH AN EARLY ASSOCIA-
TION OF IDEAS HAS UPON THE CHARAC-
TER.

EDUCATED in the enervating ſtyle recommended by the writers on whom I have been
animadverting ; and not having a chance, from
their ſubordinate ſtate in ſociety, to recover their
loſt ground, is it ſurpriſing that women every
where appear a defect in nature ? Is it ſurpriſing,
when we conſider what a determinate effect an
early aſſociation of ideas has on the character,
that they neglect their underſtandings, and turn
all their attention to their perſons ?

The great advantages which naturally reſult
from ſtoring the mind with knowledge, are obvious from the following conſiderations. The
aſſociation of our ideas is either habitual or in-
ſtantaneous ; and the latter mode ſeems rather
to depend on the original temperature of the
mind than on the will. When the ideas, and
matters of fact, are once taken in, they lie by for
uſe, till ſome fortuitous circumſtance makes the
information dart into the mind with illuſtrative
force, that has been received at very different periods of our lives. Like the lightning's flaſh are
many recollections ; one idea aſſimilating and ex-
plaining another, with aſtoniſhing rapidity. I do
not now allude to that quick perception of truth,
which is ſo intuitive that it baffles reſearch, and
makes

makes us at a lofs to determine whether it is re-miniscence or ratiocination, loft fight of in its ce-lerity, that opens the dark cloud. Over thofe inftantaneous affociations we have little power; for when the mind is once enlarged by excurfive flights, or profound reflection, the raw materials will, in fome degree, arrange themfelves. The underftanding, it is true, may keep us from going out of drawing when we group our thoughts, or tranfcribe from the imagination the warm fketch-es of fancy; but the animal fpirits, the individu-al character, give the colouring. Over this fub-tile electric fluid*, how little power do we pof-fefs, and over it how little power can reafon ob-tain! Thefe fine intractable fpirits appear to be the effence of genius, and beaming in its eagle eye, produce in the moft eminent degree the hap-py energy of affociating thoughts that furprife, delight, and inftruct. Thefe are the glowing minds that concentrate pictures for their fellow-creatures; forcing them to view with intereft the objects reflected from the impaffioned imagina-tion, which they paffed over in nature.

I muft be allowed to explain myfelf. The generality of people cannot fee or feel poetically, they want fancy, and therefore fly from folitude in fearch of fenfible objects; but when an author lends them his eyes they can fee as he faw, and be amufed by images they could not felect, though lying before them.   Education

---

* I have fometimes, when inclined to laugh at materialifts, afked whe-ther, as the moft powerful effects in nature, are apparently produced by fluids, the magnetic, &c. the paffions might not be fine volatile fluids that embraced humanity, keeping the more refractory elementary parts togeth-er—or whether they were fimply a liquid fire that pervaded the more flug-gifh materials, giving them life and heat?

Education thus only supplies the man of genius with knowledge to give variety and contrast to his affociations ; but there is an habitual affociation of ideas, that grows ' with our growth,' which has a great effect on the moral character of mankind ; and by which a turn is given to the mind that commonly remains throughout life. So ductile is the understanding, and yet so stubborn, that the affociations which depend on adventitious circumstances, during the period that the body takes to arrive at maturity, can feldom be difentangled by reafon. One idea calls up another, its old affociate, and memory, faithful to the first impreffions, particularly when the intellectual powers are not employed to cool our senfations, retraces them with mechanical exactnefs.

This habitual flavery, to first impreffions, has a more baneful effect on the female than the male character, because bufinefs and other dry employments of the understanding, tend to deaden the feelings and break affociations that do violence to reafon. But females, who are made women of when they are mere children, and brought back to childhood when they ought to leave the go-cart for ever, have not fufficient strength of mind to efface the fuperinductions of art that have fmothered nature.

Every thing that they fee or hear ferves to fix impreffions, call forth emotions, and affociate ideas, that give a fexual character to the mind. Falfe notions of beauty and delicacy ftop the growth of their limbs and produce a fickly forenefs, rather than delicacy of organs ; and thus

weakened

weakened by being employed in unfolding inftead
of examining the firft affociations, forced on them
by every furrounding object, how can they attain
the vigour neceffary to enable them to throw off
their factitious character ?—where find ftrength
to recur to reafon and rife fuperiour to a fyftem
of oppreffion, that blafts the fair promifes of
fpring ? This cruel affociation of ideas, which
every thing confpires to twift into all their habits
of thinking, or, to fpeak with more precifion, of
feeling, receives new force when they begin to
act a little for themfelves ; for they then perceive
that it is only through their addrefs to excite
emotions in men, that pleafure and power are to
be obtained. Befides, all the books profeffedly
written for their inftruction, which make the
firft impreffion on their minds, all inculcate the
fame opinions. Educated then in worfe than
Egyptian bondage, it is unreafonable, as well as
cruel, to upbraid them with faults that can fcarcely be avoided, unlefs a degree of native vigour be
fuppofed, that falls to the lot of very few amongft
mankind.

For inftance, the fevereft farcafms have been
levelled againft the fex, and they have been ridiculed for repeating ' a fet of phrafes learnt by
' rote,' when nothing could be more natural, confidering the education they receive, and that their
' higheft praife is to obey, unargued'—the will of
man. If they are not allowed to have reafon
fufficient to govern their own conduct—why, all
they learn—muft be learned by rote ! And when
all their ingenuity is called forth to adjuft their
drefs, ' a paffion for a fcarlet coat,' is fo natural,
that

that it never furprifed me ; and, allowing Pope's fummary of their character to be juft, ' that every ' woman is at heart a rake,' why fhould they be bitterly cenfured for feeking a congenial mind, and preferring a rake to a man of fenfe ?

Rakes know how to work on their fenfibility, whilft the modeft merit of reafonable men has, of courfe, lefs effect on their feelings, and they cannot reach the heart by the way of the under-ftanding, becaufe they have few fentiments in common.

It feems a little abfurd to expect women to be more reafonable than men in their *likings*, and ftill to deny them the uncontrouled ufe of reafon. When do men *fall-in-love* with fenfe ? When do they, with their fuperiour powers and advanta-ges, turn from the perfon to the mind ? And how can they then expect women, who are only taught to obferve behaviour, and acquire manners rather than morals, to defpife what they have been all their lives labouring to attain ? Where are they fuddenly to find judgment enough to weigh pa-tiently the fenfe of an awkward virtuous man, when his manners, of which they are made criti-cal judges, are rebuffing, and his converfation cold and dull, becaufe it does not confift of pretty re-partees, or well turned compliments ? In order to admire or efteem any thing for a continuance, we muft, at leaft, have our curiofity excited by knowing, in fome degree, what we admire ; for we are unable to eftimate the value of qualities and virtues above our comprehenfion. Such a refpect, when it is felt, may be very fublime ; and the confufed confcioufnefs of humility may
render

render the dependent creature an interesting object, in some points of view ; but human love must have grosser ingredients ; and the person very naturally will come in for its share—and, an ample share it mostly has !

Love is, in a great degree, an arbitrary passion, and will reign, like some other stalking mischiefs, by its own authority, without deigning to reason ; and it may also be easily distinguished from esteem, the foundation of friendship, because it is often excited by evanescent beauties and graces, though to give an energy to the sentiment, something more solid must deepen their impression and set the imagination to work, to make the most fair—the first good.

Common passions are excited by common qualities.—Men look for beauty and the simper of good-humoured docility : women are captivated by easy manners ; a gentleman-like man seldom fails to please them, and their thirsty ears eagerly drink the insinuating nothings of politeness, whilst they turn from the unintelligible sounds of the charmer—reason, charm he never so wisely. With respect to superficial accomplishments, the rake certainly has the advantage ; and of these females can form an opinion, for it is their own ground. Rendered gay and giddy by the whole tenor of their lives, the very aspect of wisdom, or the severe graces of virtue, must have a lugubrious appearance to them ; and produce a kind of restraint from which they and love, sportive child, naturally revolt. Without taste, excepting of the lighter kind, for taste is the offspring of judgment, how can they discover

that

that true beauty and grace muſt ariſe from the play of the mind ? and how can they be expected to reliſh in a lover what they do not, or very imperfectly, poſſeſs themſelves ? The ſympathy that unites hearts, and invites to confidence, in them is ſo very faint, that it cannot take fire, and thus mount to paſſion. No, I repeat it, the love cheriſhed by ſuch minds, muſt have groſſer fuel.

The inference is obvious ; till women are led to exerciſe their underſtandings, they ſhould not be ſatirized for their attachment to rakes ; nor even for being rakes at heart, when it appears to be the inevitable conſequence of their education: They who live to pleaſe—muſt find their enjoyments, their happineſs, in pleaſure ! It is a trite, yet true remark, that we never do any thing well, unleſs we love it for its own ſake.

Suppoſing, however, for a moment, that women were, in ſome future revolution of time, to become, what I ſincerely wiſh them to be, even love would acquire more ſerious dignity, and be purified in its own fires ; and virtue giving true delicacy to their affections, they would turn with diſguſt from a rake. Reaſoning then, as well as feeling, the only province of woman, at preſent, they might eaſily guard againſt exteriour graces, and quickly learn to deſpiſe the ſenſibility that had been excited and hackneyed in the ways of women, whoſe trade was vice ; and allurements, wanton airs. They would recollect that the flame, one muſt uſe appropriated expreſſions, which they wiſhed to light up, had been exhauſted by luſt, and that the ſated appetite loſing all reliſh for pure and ſimple pleaſures, could only

O be

be roufed by licentious arts or variety. What
fatisfaction could a woman of delicacy promife
herfelf in a union with fuch a man, when the
very artleffnefs of her affection might appear in-
fiped ? Thus does Dryden defcribe the fituation,

> ———— ' Where love is duty, on the female fide,
> ' On theirs mere fenfual guft, and fought with furly pride.'

But one grand truth women have yet to learn,
though much it imports them to act accordingly. In the choice of a hufband, they fhould not
be led aftray by the qualities of a lover—for a lover the hufband, even fuppofing him to be wife and
virtuous, cannot long remain.

Were women more rationally educated, could
they take a more comprehenfive view of things,
they would be contented to love but once in their
lives ; and after marriage calmly let paffion fub-
fide into friendfhip—into that tender intimacy,
which is the beft refuge from care ; yet is built
on fuch pure, ftill affections, that idle jealoufies
would not be allowed to difturb the difcharge
of the fober duties of life, nor to engrofs the
thoughts that ought to be otherwife employed.
This is a ftate in which many men live ; but
few, very few women. And the difference may
eafily be accounted for, without recurring to a
fexual character. Men, for whom we are told
women were made, have too much occupied the
thoughts of women ; and this affociation has fo
entangled love with all their motives of action ;
and, to harp a little on an old ftring, having been
folely employed either to prepare themfelves to
excite love, or actually putting their leffons in
practice,

practice, they cannot live without love. But, when a sense of duty, or fear of shame, obliges them to restrain this pampered desire of pleasing beyond certain lengths, too far for delicacy, it is true, though far from criminality, they obstinately determine to love, I speak of the passion, their husbands to the end of the chapter—and then acting the part which they foolishly exacted from their lovers, they become abject wooers, and fond slaves.

Men of wit and fancy are often rakes; and fancy is the food of love. Such men will inspire passion. Half the sex, in its present infantile state, would pine for a Lovelace; a man so witty, so graceful, and so valiant: and can they *deserve* blame for acting according to principles so constantly inculcated? They want a lover, and protector; and, behold him kneeling before them —bravery prostrate to beauty! The virtues of a husband are thus thrown by love into the back ground, and gay hopes, or lively emotions, banish reflection till the day of reckoning comes; and come it surely will, to turn the sprightly lover into a surly suspicious tyrant, who contemptuously insults the very weakness he fostered. Or, supposing the rake reformed, he cannot quickly get rid of old habits. When a man of abilities is first carried away by his passions, it is necessary that sentiment and taste varnish the enormities of vice, and give a zest to brutal indulgences; but when the gloss of novelty is worn off, and pleasure palls upon the sense, lasciviousness becomes barefaced, and enjoyment only the desperate effort of weakness flying from re-

flection

flection as from a legion of devils. Oh! virtue
thou art not an empty name! All that life can
give—thou givest!

If much comfort cannot be expected from the
friendship of a reformed rake of superiour abilities, what is the consequence when he lacketh
sense, as well as principles? Verily misery, in
its most hideous shape. When the habits of
weak people are consolidated by time, a reformation is barely possible ; and actually makes the
beings miserable who have not sufficient mind
to be amused by innocent pleasure ; like the tradef-
man who retires from the hurry of business, nature presents to them only a universal blank ; and
the restless thoughts prey on the damped spirits*.
Their reformation, as well as his retirement, actually makes them wretched because it deprives
them of all employment, by quenching the hopes
and fears that set in motion their sluggish minds.

If such is the force of habit ; if such is the
bondage of folly, how carefully ought we to
guard the mind from storing up vicious associations ; and equally careful should we be to cultivate the understanding, to save the poor wight
from the weak dependent state of even harmless
ignorance. For it is the right use of reason alone
which makes us independent of every thing—excepting the unclouded Reason—' whose service
is perfect freedom.'
                                        CHAP.

* I have frequently seen this exemplified in women, whose beauty could
no longer be repaired. They have retired from the noisy scenes of dissipation ; but, unless they became methodists, the solitude of the select society of their family connexions or acquaintance, has presented only a fearful
void ; consequently, nervous complaints, and all the vapourish train of
idleness, rendered them quite as useless, and far more unhappy, than when
they joined the giddy throng.

C H A P. VII.

MODESTY.—COMPREHENSIVELY CONSIDER-
ED, AND NOT AS A SEXUAL VIRTUE.

MODESTY! Sacred offspring of fenfibility
and reafon!—true delicacy of mind!—may I
unblamed prefume to inveftigate thy nature, and
trace to its covert the mild charm, that mellow-
ing each harfh feature of a character, renders
what would otherwife only infpire cold admiration—lovely!—Thou that fmootheft the wrin-
kles of wifdom, and fofteneft the tone of the
fublimeft virtues till they all melt into humanity;—thou that fpreadeft the ethereal cloud that
furrounding love heightens every beauty, it half
fhades, breathing thofe coy fweets that fteal into
the heart, and charm the fenfes—modulate for
me the language of perfuafive reafon, till I roufe
my fex from the flowery bed, on which they fu-
pinely fleep life away!

In fpeaking of the affociation of our ideas, I
have noticed two diftinct modes; and in defining
modefty, it appears to me equally proper to dif-
criminate that purity of mind, which is the effect of chaftity, from a fimplicity of character
that leads us to form a juft opinion of ourfelves,
equally diftant from vanity or prefumption,
though by no means incompatible with a lofty
confcioufnefs of our own dignity. Modefty, in
the latter fignification of the term, is, that fobernefs of mind which teaches a man not to think
more highly of himfelf than he ought to think,

O 3   and

and fhould be diftinguifhed from humility, becaufe humility is a kind of felf-abafement.

A modeft man often conceives a great plan,
and tenacioufly adheres to it, confcious of his
own ftrength, till fuccefs gives it a fanction that
determines its character. Milton was not arrogant when he fuffered a fuggeftion of judgment
to efcape him that proved a prophefy ; nor was
General Wafhington when he accepted of the
command of the American forces. The latter
has always been characterized as a modeft man ;
but had he been merely humble, he would probably have fhrunk back irrefolute, afraid of truft-
ing to himfelf the direction of an enterprife, on
which fo much depended.

A modeft man is fteady, an humble man timid,
and a vain one prefumptuous :—this is the judgment, which the obfervation of many characters,
has led me to form. Jefus Chrift was modeft,
Mofes was humble, and Peter vain.

Thus, difcriminating modefty from humility
in one cafe, I do not mean to confound it with
bafhfulnefs in the other. Bafhfulnefs, in fact, is
fo diftinct from modefty, that the moft bafhful
lafs, or raw country lout, often becomes the moft
impudent ; for their bafhfulnefs being merely the
inftinctive timidity of ignorance, cuftom foon
changes it into affurance *.   The

* ' Such is the country-maiden's fright,
  ' When firft a red-coat is in fight ;
  ' Behind the door fhe hides her face ;
  ' Next time at diftance eyes the lace :
  ' She now can all his terrors ftand,
  ' Nor from his fqueeze withdraws her hand.
  ' She plays familiar in his arms,
  ' And ev'ry foldier hath his charms ;
  ' From tent to tent fhe fpreads her flame ;
  ' For cuftom conquers fear and fhame.'   GAY.

The shameless behaviour of the prostitutes, who infest the streets of London, raising alternate emotions of pity and disgust, may serve to illustrate this remark. They trample on virgin bashfulness with a sort of bravado, and glorying in their shame, become more audaciously lewd than men, however depraved, to whom this sexual quality has not been gratuitously granted, ever appear to be. But these poor ignorant wretches never had any modesty to lose, when they consigned themselves to infamy ; for modesty is a virtue not a quality. No, they were only bashful, shame-faced innocents ; and losing their innocence, their shame-facedness was rudely brushed off ; a virtue would have left some vestiges in the mind, had it been sacrificed to passion, to make us respect the grand ruin.

Purity of mind, or that genuine delicacy, which is the only virtuous support of chastity, is near akin to that refinement of humanity, which never resides in any but cultivated minds. It is something nobler than innocence ; it is the delicacy of reflection, and not the coyness of ignorance.

The reserve of reason, which, like habitual cleanliness, is seldom seen in any great degree, unless the soul is active, may easily be distinguished from rustic shyness or wanton skittishness ; and, so far from being incompatible with knowledge, it is its fairest fruit. What a gross idea of modesty had the writer of the following remark ! ‘ The lady who asked the question whether wo‘ men may be instructed in the modern system of ‘ botany, consistently with female delicacy ?—‘ was accused of ridiculous prudery : neverthe-

‘ less

' lefs, if fhe had propofed the queftion to me, I
' fhould certainly have anfwered—They cannot.'
Thus is the fair book of knowledge to be fhut
with an everlafting feal ! On reading fimilar paffages I have reverentially lifted up my eyes and
heart to Him who liveth for ever and ever, and
faid, O my Father, haft Thou by the very conftitution of her nature forbid Thy child to feek
Thee in the fair forms of truth ? And, can her
foul be fullied by the knowledge that awfully
calls her to Thee ?

I have then philofophically purfued thefe reflections till I inferred that thofe women who
have moft improved their reafon muft have the
moft modefty—though a dignified fedatenefs of
deportment may have fucceeded the playful, bewitching bafhfulnefs of youth *.

And thus have I argued.   To render chaftity
the virtue from which unfophifticated modefty
will naturally flow, the attention fhould be called
away from employments which only exercife the
fenfibility ; and the heart made to beat time to
humanity, rather than to throb with love.   The
woman who has dedicated a confiderable portion
of her time to purfuits purely intellectual, and
whofe affections have been exercifed by humane
plans of ufefulnefs, muft have more purity of
mind, as a natural confequence, than the ignorant beings whofe time and thoughts have been
occupied by gay pleafures or fchemes to conquer
hearts.

* Modefty, is the graceful calm virtue of maturity ; bafhfulnefs, the
charm of vivacious youth.

hearts*. The regulation of the behaviour is not modeſty, though thoſe who ſtudy rules of decorum are, in general, termed modeſt women. Make the heart clean, let it expand and feel for all that is human, inſtead of being narrowed by ſelfiſh paſſions ; and let the mind frequently contemplate ſubjects that exerciſe the underſtanding, without heating the imagination, and artleſs modeſty will give the finiſhing touches to the picture.

She who can diſcern the dawn of immortality, in the ſtreaks that ſhoot athwart the miſty night of ignorance, promiſing a clearer day, will reſpect, as a ſacred temple, the body that enſhrines ſuch an improvable ſoul. True love, likewiſe, ſpreads this kind of myſterious ſanctity round the beloved object, making the lover moſt modeſt when in her preſence†. So reſerved is affection that, receiving or returning perſonal endearments, it wiſhes, not only to ſhun the human eye, as a kind of profanation ; but to diffuſe an encircling cloudy obſcurity to ſhut out even the ſaucy ſparkling ſunbeams. Yet, that affection does not deſerve the epithet of chaſte, which does not receive

* I have converſed, as man with man, with medical men, on anatomical ſubjects ; and compared the proportions of the human body with artiſts— yet ſuch modeſty did I meet with, that I was never reminded by word or look of my ſex, of the abſurd rules which make modeſty a phariſaical cloak of weakneſs. And I am perſuaded that in the purſuit of knowledge women would never be inſulted by ſenſible men, and rarely by men of any deſcription, if they did not by mock modeſty remind them that they were women : actuated by the ſame ſpirit as the Portugueſe ladies, who would think their charms inſulted, if, when left alone with a man, he did not, at leaſt, attempt to be very familiar with their perſons. Men are not always men in the company of women, nor would women always remember that they are women, if they were allowed to aquire more underſtanding.

† Male or female ; for the world contains many modeſt men.

ceive a sublime gloom of tender melancholy, that allows the mind for a moment to stand still and enjoy the present satisfaction, when a consciousness of the Divine presence is felt—for this must ever be the food of joy !

As I have always been fond of tracing to its source in nature any prevailing custom, I have frequently thought that it was a sentiment of affection for whatever had touched the person of an absent or lost friend, which gave birth to that respect for relicks, so much abused by selfish priests. Devotion, or love, may be allowed to hallow the garments as well as the person ; for the lover must want fancy who has not a sort of sacred respect for the glove or slipper of his mistress. He could not confound them with vulgar things of the same kind. This fine sentiment, perhaps, would not bear to be analyzed by the experimental philosopher—but of such stuff is human rapture made up !—A shadowy phantom glides before us, obscuring every other object; yet when the soft cloud is grasped, the form melts into common air, leaving a solitary void, or sweet perfume, stolen from the violet, that memory long holds dear. But I have tripped unawares on fairy ground, feeling the balmy gale of spring stealing on me, though November frowns.

As a sex, women are more chaste than men, and as modesty is the effect of chastity, they may deserve to have this virtue ascribed to them in rather an appropriated sense ; yet, I must be allowed to add an hesitating if :—for I doubt whether chastity will produce modesty, though it may propriety of conduct, when it is merely a

respect

respect for the opinion of the world*, and when coquetry and the lovelorn tales of novelists employ the thoughts. Nay, from experience, and reason, I should be led to expect to meet with more modesty amongst men than women, simply because men exercise their understandings more than women.

But, with respect to propriety of behaviour, excepting one class of females, women have evidently the advantage. What can be more disgusting than that impudent dross of gallantry, thought so manly, which makes many men stare insultingly at every female they meet ? Is this respect for the sex ? This loose behaviour shews such habitual depravity, such weakness of mind, that it is vain to expect much public or private virtue, till both men and women grow more modest— till men, curbing a sensual fondness for the sex, or an affectation of manly assurance, more properly speaking, impudence, treat each other with respect—unless appetite or passion gives the tone, peculiar to it, to their behaviour. I mean even personal respect—the modest respect of humanity, and fellow-feeling—not the the libidinous mockery of gallantry, nor the insolent condescension of protectorship.

To carry the observation still further, modesty must heartily disclaim, and refuse to dwell with that debauchery of mind, which leads a man coolly to bring forward, without a blush, indecent allusions, or obscene witticisms, in the presence of a fellow creature ; women are now out
of

* The immodest behaviour of many married women, who are neverthe-less faithful to their husbands' beds, will illustrate this remark.

of the question, for then it is brutality. Respect for man, as man, is the foundation of every noble sentiment. How much more modest is the libertine who obeys the call of appetite or fancy, than the lewd joker who sets the table in a roar !

This is one of the many instances in which the sexual distinction respecting modesty has proved fatal to virtue and happiness. It is, however, carried still further, and woman, weak woman ! made by her education the slave of sensibility, is required, on the most trying occasions, to resist that sensibility. ‘ Can any thing,’ says Knox, ‘ be more absurd than keeping women in ‘ a state of ignorance, and yet so vehemently ‘ to insist on their resisting temptation ?’——Thus when virtue or honour make it proper to check a passion, the burden is thrown on the weaker shoulders, contrary to reason and true modesty, which, at least, should render the self-denial mutual, to say nothing of the generosity of bravery, supposed to be a manly virtue.

In the same strain runs Rousseau's and Dr. Gregory's advice respecting modesty, strangely miscalled ! for they both desire a wife to leave it in doubt whether sensibility or weakness led her to her husband's arms.——The woman is immodest who can let the shadow of such a doubt remain on her husband's mind a moment.

But to state the subject in a different light.—— The want of modesty, which I principally deplore as subversive of morality, arises from the state of warfare so strenuously supported by voluptuous men as the very essence of modesty, though, in fact, its bane ; because it is a refinement

ment

ment on senfual defire, that men fall into who
have not fufficient virtue to relifh the innocent
pleafures of love. A man of delicacy carries his
notions of modefty ftill further, for neither weaknefs nor fenfibility will gratify him—he looks
for affection.

Again ; men boaft of their triumphs over women, what do they boaft of ? Truly the creature
of fenfibility was furprifed by her fenfibility into
folly—into vice*; and the dreadful reckoning
falls heavily on her own weak head, when reafon
wakes. For where art thou to find comfort,
forlorn and difconfolate one ? He who ought to
have directed thy reafon, and fupported thy weaknefs, has betrayed thee ! In a dream of paffion
thou confentedft to wander through flowery
lawns, and heedlefly ftepping over the precipice
to which thy guide, inftead of guarding, lured
thee, thou ftarteft from thy dream only to face a
fneering, frowning world, and to find thyfelf
alone in a wafte, for he that triumphed in thy
weaknefs is now purfuing new conquefts ; but
for thee—there is no redemption on this fide the
grave ! And what refource haft thou in an enervated mind to raife a finking heart ?

But, if the fexes are really to live in a ftate of
warfare, if nature has pointed it out, let men act
nobly, or let pride whifper to them, that the
victory is mean when they merely vanquifh fenfibility. The real conqueft is that over affection
not taken by furprife—when, like Heloifa, a woman gives up all the world, deliberately, for love.
I do not now confider the wifdom or virtue of
such

* The poor moth fluttering round a candle, burns its wings.

such a sacrifice, I only contend that it was a sacrifice to affection, and not merely to sensibility, though she had her share.——And I must be allowed to call her a modest woman, before I dismiss this part of the subject, by saying, that till men are more chaste women will be immodest. Where, indeed, could modest women find husbands from whom they would not continually turn with disgust? Modesty must be equally cultivated by both sexes, or it will ever remain a sickly hot-house plant, whilst the affectation of it, the fig leaf borrowed by wantonness, may give a zest to voluptuous enjoyments.

Men will probably still insist that woman ought to have more modesty than man; but it is not dispassionate reasoners who will most earnestly oppose my opinion. No, they are the men of fancy, the favourites of the sex, who outwardly respect and inwardly despise the weak creatures whom they thus sport with. They cannot submit to resign the highest sensual gratification, nor even to relish the epicurism of virtue—self-denial.

To take another view of the subject, confining my remarks to women.

The ridiculous falsities * which are told to children, from mistaken notions of modesty, tend

very

---

* Children very early see cats with their kittens, birds with their young ones, &c. Why then are they not to be told that their mothers carry and nourish them in the same way? As there would then be no appearance of mystery they would never think of the subject more. Truth may always be told to children, if it be told gravely; but it is the immodesty of affected modesty, that does all the mischief; and this smoke heats the imagination by vainly endeavouring to obscure certain objects. If, indeed, children could be kept entirely from improper company, we should never allude to any such subjects; but as this is impossible, it is best to tell them the truth, especially as such information, not interesting them, will make no impression on their imagination.

very early to inflame their imaginations and set their little minds to work, respecting subjects, which nature never intended they should think of till the body arrived at some degree of maturity; then the passions naturally begin to take place of the senses, as instruments to unfold the understanding, and form the moral character.

In nurseries, and boarding-schools, I fear, girls are first spoiled; particularly in the latter. A number of girls sleep in the same room, and wash together. And, though I should be sorry to contaminate an innocent creature's mind by instilling false delicacy, or those indecent prudish notions, which early cautions respecting the other sex naturally engender, I should be very anxious to prevent their acquiring indelicate, or immodest habits; and as many girls have learned very indelicate tricks, from ignorant servants, the mixing them thus indiscriminately together, is very improper.

To say the truth women are, in general, too familiar with each other, which leads to that gross degree of familiarity that so frequently renders the marriage state unhappy. Why in the name of decency are sisters, female intimates, or ladies and their waiting-women, to be so grossly familiar as to forget the respect which one human creature owes to another? That squeamish delicacy which shrinks from the most disgusting offices when affection * or humanity lead us to watch at a sick pillow, is despicable. But, why

women

---

* Affection would rather make one choose to perform these offices, to spare the delicacy of a friend, by still keeping a veil over them, for the personal helplessness, produced by sickness, is of an humbling nature.

women in health should be more familiar with
each other than men are, when they boast of their
superiour delicacy, is a solecism in manners which
I could never solve.

In order to preserve health and beauty, I should
earnestly recommend frequent ablutions, to dignify my advice that it may not offend the fastidious ear; and, by example, girls ought to be taught
to wash and dress alone, without any distinction
of rank; and if custom should make them require some little assistance, let them not require
it till that part of the business is over which
ought never to be done before a fellow-creature; because it is an insult to the majesty of
human nature. Not on the score of modesty,
but decency; for the care which some modest
women take, making at the same time a display
of that care, not to let their legs be seen, is as
childish as immodest *.

I could proceed still further, till I animadverted on some still more indelicate customs, which
men never fall into. Secrets are told—where
silence ought to reign; and that regard to cleanliness, which some religious sects have, perhaps,
carried too far, especially the Essenes, amongst
the Jews, by making that an insult to God which
is only an insult to humanity, is violated in a
brutal manner. How can *delicate* women ob-
trude on notice that part of the animal economy,
which is so very disgusting? And is it not very
rational to conclude, that the women who have

not

---

* I remember to have met with a sentence, in a book of education, that
made me smile. ‘ It would be needless to caution you against putting your
‘ hand, by chance, under your neck-handkerchief; for a modest woman
‘ never did so!’

not been taught to refpect the human nature of their own fex, in thefe particulars, will not long refpect the mere difference of fex in their hufbands? After their maidenifh bafhfulnefs is once loft, I, in fact, have generally obferved, that women fall into old habits; and treat their hufbands as they did their fifters or female acquaintance.

Befides, women from neceffity, becaufe their minds are not cultivated, have recourfe very often to what I familiarly term bodily wit; and their intimacies are of the fame kind. In fhort, with refpect to both mind and body, they are too intimate. That decent perfonal referve which is the foundation of dignity of character, muft be kept up between women, or their minds will never gain ftrength or modefty.

On this account alfo, I object to many females being fhut up together in nurferies, fchools, or convents. I cannot recollect without indignation, the jokes and hoiden tricks, which knots of young women indulge themfelves in, when in my youth accident threw me, an awkward ruftic, in their way. They were almoft on a par with the double meanings, which fhake the convivial table when the glafs has circulated freely. But, it is vain to attempt to keep the heart pure, unlefs the head is furnifhed with ideas, and fet to work to compare them, in order to acquire judgment, by generalizing fimple ones; and modefty, by making the underftanding damp the fenfibility.

It may be thought that I lay too great a ftrefs on perfonal referve; but it is ever the handmaid of modefty. So that were I to name the graces that ought to adorn beauty, I fhould inftantly

P   exclaim,

exclaim, cleanliness, neatness, and personal reserve. It is obvious, I suppose, that the reserve I mean, has nothing sexual in it, and that I think it *equally* necessary in both sexes. So necessary, indeed, is that reserve and cleanliness which indolent women too often neglect, that I will venture to affirm that when two or three women live in the same house, the one will be most respected by the male part of the family, who reside with them, leaving love entirely out of the question, who pays this kind of habitual respect to her person.

When domestic friends meet in a morning, there will naturally prevail an affectionate seriousness, especially, if each look forward to the discharge of daily duties ; and, it may be reckoned fanciful, but this sentiment has frequently risen spontaneously in my mind, I have been pleased after breathing the sweet bracing morning air, to see the same kind of freshness in the countenances I particularly loved ; I was glad to see them braced, as it were, for the day, and ready to run their course with the sun. The greetings of affection in the morning are by these means more respectful than the familiar tenderness which frequently prolongs the evening talk. Nay, I have often felt hurt, not to say disgusted, when a friend has appeared, whom I parted with full dressed the evening before, with her clothes huddled on, because she chose to indulge herself in bed till the last moment.

Domestic affection can only be kept alive by these neglected attentions ; yet if men and women took half as much pains to dress habitually neat, as they do to ornament, or rather to disfigure,

figure, their perfons, much would be done to-wards the attainment of purity of mind. But women only drefs to gratify men of gallantry; for the lover is always beft pleafed with the fim-ple garb that fits clofe to the fhape. There is an impertinence in ornaments that rebuffs affection; becaufe love always clings round the idea of home.

As a fex, women are habitually indolent; and every thing tends to make them fo. I do not forget the fpurts of activity which fenfibility pro-duces; but as thefe flights of feelings only increafe the evil, they are not to be confounded with the flow, orderly walk of reafon. So great in reality is their mental and bodily indolence, that till their body be ftrengthened and their underftand-ing enlarged by active exertions, there is little reafon to expect that modefty will take place of bafhfulnefs. They may find it prudent to affume its femblance; but the fair veil will only be worn on gala days.

Perhaps there is not a virtue that mixes fo kindly with every other as modefty.—It is the pale moon-beam that renders more interefting every virtue it foftens, giving mild grandeur to the contracted horizon. Nothing can be more beautiful than the poetical fiction, which makes Diana with her filver crefcent, the goddefs of chaftity. I have fometimes thought, that wan-dering with fedate ftep in fome lonely recefs, a modeft dame of antiquity muft have felt a glow of confcious dignity when, after contemplating the foft fhadowy landfcape, fhe has invited with placid fervour the mild reflection of her fifters beams to turn to her chafte bofom.

A

A Chriftian has ftill nobler motives to incite her to preferve her chaftity and acquire modefty, for her body has been called the Temple of the living God ; of that God who requires more than modefty of mien. His eye fearcheth the heart ; and let her remember, that if fhe hopeth to find favour in the fight of purity itfelf, her chaftity muft be founded on modefty and not on worldly prudence ; or verily a good reputation will be her only reward ; for that awful intercourfe, that facred communication, which virtue eftablifhes between man and his Maker, muft give rife to the wifh of being pure as he is pure !

After the foregoing remarks, it is almoft fuperfluous to add, that I confider all thofe feminine airs of maturity, which fucceed bafhfulnefs, to which truth is facrificed, to fecure the heart of a hufband, or rather to force him to be ftill a lover when nature would, had fhe not been interrupted in her operations, have made love give place to friendfhip, as immodeft. The tendernefs which a man will feel for the mother of his children is an excellent fubftitute for the ardour of unfatisfied paffion ; but to prolong that ardour it is indelicate, not to fay immodeft, for women to feign an unnatural coldnefs of conftitution. Women as well as men ought to have the common appetites and paffions of their nature, they are only brutal when unchecked by reafon : but the obligation to check them is the duty of mankind, not a fexual duty. Nature, in thefe refpects, may fafely be left to herfelf ; let women only acquire knowledge and humanity, and love will

will teach them modesty*. There is no need of falsehoods, disgusting as futile, for studied rules of behaviour only impose on shallow observers; a man of sense soon sees through, and despises the affectation.

The behaviour of young people, to each other, as men and women, is the last thing that should be thought of in education. In fact, behaviour in most circumstances is now so much thought of, that simplicity of character is rarely to be seen : yet, if men were only anxious to cultivate each virtue, and let it take root firmly in the mind, the grace resulting from it, its natural exteriour mark, would soon strip affectation of its flaunting plumes ; because, fallacious as unstable, is the conduct that is not founded upon truth !

Would ye, O my sisters, really possess modesty, ye must remember that the possession of virtue, of any denomination, is incompatible with ignorance and vanity ! ye must acquire that soberness of mind, which the exercise of duties, and the pursuit of knowledge, alone inspire, or ye will still remain in a doubtful dependent situation, and only be loved whilst ye are fair ! The downcast eye, the rosy blush, the retiring grace, are all proper in their season ; but modesty, being the child of reason, cannot long exist with the sensibility that is not tempered by reflection. Besides, when love, even innocent love, is the whole employ of your lives, your hearts will be too soft to afford modesty that tranquil retreat, where she delights to dwell, in close union with humanity.

P 3   CHAP.

* The behaviour of many newly married women has often disgusted me. They seem anxious never to let their husbands forget the privilege of marriage ; and to find no pleasure in his society unless he is acting the lover. Short, indeed, must be the reign of love, when the flame is thus constantly blown up, without its receiving any solid fuel !

C H A P. VIII.

MORALITY UNDERMINED BY SEXUAL NO-
TIONS OF THE IMPORTANCE OF A GOOD
REPUTATION.

IT has long since occurred to me that advice respecting behaviour, and all the various modes of preserving a good reputation, which have been so strenuously inculcated on the female world, were specious poisons, that incrusting morality eat away the substance. And, that this measuring of shadows produced a false calculation, because their length depends so much on the height of the sun, and other adventitious circumstances.

From whence arises the easy fallacious behaviour of a courtier ? From his situation, undoubtedly : for standing in need of dependents, he is obliged to learn the art of denying without giving offence, and, of evasively feeding hope with the chameleon's food : thus does politeness sport with truth, and eating away the sincerity and humanity natural to man, produce the fine gentleman.

Women in the same way acquire, from a supposed necessity, an equally artificial mode of behaviour. Yet truth is not with impunity to be sported with, for the practised dissembler, at last, become the dupe of his own arts, loses that sagacity, which has been justly termed common sense ; namely, a quick perception of common truths : which are constantly received as such by the

the unfophifticated mind, though it might not have had fufficient energy to difcover them itfelf, when obfcured by local prejudices. The greater number of people take their opinions on truft to avoid the trouble of exercifing their own minds, and thefe indolent beings naturally adhere to the letter, rather than the fpirit of a law, divine or human. ' Women,' fays fome author, I cannot recolle&t who, ' mind not what only heaven fees.' Why, indeed fhould they ? it is the eye of man that they have been taught to dread—and if they can lull their Argus to fleep, they feldom think of heaven or themfelves, becaufe their reputation is fafe ; and it is reputation, not chaftity and all its fair train, that they are employed to keep free from fpot, not as a virtue, but to preferve their ftation in the world.

To prove the truth of this remark, I need only advert to the intrigues of married women particularly in high life, and in countries where women are fuitably married, according to their refpective ranks, by their parents. If an innocent girl become a prey to love, fhe is degraded forever, though her mind was not polluted by the arts which married women, under the convenient cloke of marriage, practife ; nor has fhe violated any duty—but the duty of refpecting herfelf. The married woman, on the contrary, breaks a moft facred engagement, and becomes a cruel mother when fhe is a falfe and faithlefs wife. If her hufband has ftill an affection for her, the arts which fhe muft practife to deceive him, will render her the moft contemptible of human beings ; and, at any rate, the contrivances neceffary to pre-

ferve

serve appearances, will keep her mind in that childifh, or vicious, tumult, which deftroys all its energy. Befides, in time, like thofe people who habitually take cordials to raife their fpirits, fhe will want an intrigue to give life to her thoughts, having loft all relifh for pleafures that are not highly feafoned by hope or fear.

Sometimes married women act ftill more audacioufly; I will mention an inftance.

A woman of quality, notorious for her gallantries, though as fhe ftill lived with her hufband, nobody chofe to place her in the clafs where fhe ought to have been placed, made a point of treating with the moft infulting contempt a poor timid creature, abafhed by a fenfe of her former weaknefs, whom a neighbouring gentleman had feduced and afterwards married. This woman had actually confounded virtue with reputation; and, I do believe, valued herfelf on the propriety of her behaviour before marriage, though when once fettled, to the fatisfaction of her family, fhe and her lord were equally faithlefs,—fo that the half alive heir to an immenfe eftate, came from heaven knows where!

To view this fubject in another light.

I have known a number of women who, if they did not love their hufbands, loved nobody elfe, give themfelves entirely up to vanity and diffipation, neglecting every domeftic duty; nay, even fquandering away all the money which fhould have been faved for their helplefs younger children, yet have plumed themfelves on their unfullied reputation, as if the whole compafs of their duty as wives and mothers was only to preserve

ferve it. Whilft other indolent women neglecting every perfonal duty, have thought that they
deferved their hufband's affection, becaufe they
afked in this refpect with propriety.

Weak minds are always fond of refting in the
ceremonials of duty, but morality offers much
fimpler motives ; and it were to be wifhed that
fuperficial moralifts had faid lefs refpecting behaviour, and outward obfervances, for unlefs virtue, of any kind, is built on knowledge, it will
only produce a kind of infipid decency. Refpect
for the opinion of the world, has, however, been
termed the principal duty of woman in the moft
exprefs words, for Rouffeau declares, 'that repu-
' tation is no lefs indifpenfable than chaftity.' ' A
' man,' adds he, ' fecure in his own good con-
' duct, depends only on himfelf, and may brave
' the public opinion ; but a woman, in behaving
' well, performs but half her duty ; as what is
' thought of her, is as important to her as what
' fhe really is. It follows hence, that the fyftem
' of a woman's education fhould, in this refpect,
' be directly contrary to that of ours. Opinion
' is the grave of virtue among the men ; but its
' throne among women.' It is ftrictly logical to
infer that the virtue that refts on opinion is merely worldly, and that it is the virtue of a being to
whom reafon has been denied. But, even with
refpect to the opinion of the world, I am convinced that this clafs of reafoners are miftaken.

This regard for reputation, independent of its
being one of the natural rewards of virtue, however, took its rife from a caufe that I have already
deplored as the grand fource of female depravity,

the

the impoffibility of regaining refpectability by a
return to virtue, though men preferve theirs during the indulgence of vice.   It was natural for
women then to endeavour to preferve what once
loft—was loft for ever, till this care fwallowing
up every other care, reputation for chaftity, became the one thing needful to the fex.   But vain
is the fcrupulofity of ignorance, for neither religion nor virtue, when they refide in the heart,
require fuch a puerile attention to mere ceremonies, becaufe the behaviour muft, upon the whole,
be proper, when the motive is pure.

To fupport my opinion I can produce very refpectable authority ; and the authority of a cool
reafoner ought to have weight to enforce confideration, though not to eftablifh a fentiment.
Speaking of the general laws of morality, Dr.
Smith obferves,—' That by fome very extraordi-
' nary and unlucky circumftance, a good man
' may come to be fufpected of a crime of which
' he was altogether incapable, and upon that ac-
' count be moft unjuftly expofed for the remain-
' ing part of his life to the horror and averfion of
' mankind.   By an accident of this kind he may
' be faid to lofe his all, notwithftanding his in-
' tegrity and juftice, in the fame manner as a
' cautious man, notwithftanding his utmoft cir-
' cumfpection, may be ruined by an earthquake
' or an inundation.   Accidents of the firft kind,
' however, are perhaps ftill more rare, and ftill
' more contrary to the common courfe of things
' than thofe of the fecond ; and it ftill remains
' true, that the practice of truth, juftice, and hu-
' manity, is a certain and almoft infallible method

' of

' of acquiring what those virtues chiefly aim at,
' the confidence and love of those we live with.
' A person may be easily misrepresented with re-
' gard to a particular action ; but it is scarcely
' possible that he should be so with regard to the
' general tenor of his conduct. An innocent man
' may be believed to have done wrong : this,
' however, will rarely happen. On the contra-
' ry, the established opinion of the innocence of
' his manners will often lead us to absolve him
' where he has really been in the fault, notwith-
' standing very strong presumptions.'

I perfectly coincide in opinion with this writer, for I verily believe that few of either sex
were ever despised for certain vices without de-
serving to be despised. I speak not of the ca-
lumny of the moment, which hangs over a character, like one of the dense fogs of November,
over this metropolis, till it gradually subsides
before the common light of day, I only contend that the daily conduct of the majority prevails to stamp their character with the impression
of truth. Quietly does the clear light, shining
day after day, refute the ignorant surmise, or ma-
licious tale, which has thrown dirt on a pure
character. A false light distorted, for a short
time, its shadow—reputation ; but it seldom fails
to become just when the cloud is dispersed that
produced the mistake in vision.

Many people, undoubtedly, in several respects
obtain a better reputation than, strictly speaking,
they deserve ; for unremitting industry will mostly reach its goal in all races. They who only
strive for this paltry prize, like the Pharisees,

who

who prayed at the corners of ftreets, to be feen of men, verily obtain the reward they feek ; for the heart of man cannot be read by man ! Still the fair fame that is naturally reflected by good actions, when the man is only employed to direct his fteps aright, regardlefs of the lookers-on, is, in general, not only more true, but more fure.

There are, it is true, trials when the good man muft appeal to God from the injuftice of man ; and amidft the whining candour or hiffings of envy, erect a pavilion in his own mind to retire to till the rumour be overpaft ; nay, the darts of undeferved cenfure may pierce an innocent tender bofom through with many forrows ; but thefe are all exceptions to general rules. And it is according to thefe common laws that human behaviour ought to be regulated. The eccentric orbit of the comet never influences aftronomical calculations refpecting the invariable order eftablifhed in the motion of the principal bodies of the folar fyftem.

I will then venture to affirm, that after a man is arrived at maturity, the general outline of his character in the world is juft, allowing for the before-mentioned exceptions to the rule. I do not fay that a prudent, worldly-wife man, with only negative virtues and qualities, may not fometimes obtain a more fmooth reputation than a wifer or a better man. So far from it, that I am apt to conclude from experience, that where the virtue of two people is nearly equal, the moft negative character will be liked beft by the world at large, whilft the other may have more friends in private life. But the hills and dales, clouds and

funfhine,

sunshine, conspicuous in the virtues of great men, set off each other ; and though they afford envious weakness a fairer mark to shoot at, the real character will still work its way to light, though bespattered by weak affection, or ingenious malice*.

With respect to that anxiety to preserve a reputation hardly earned, which leads sagacious people to analyze it, I shall not make the obvious comment ; but I am afraid that morality is very insidiously undermined, in the female world, by the attention being turned to the shew instead of the substance. A simple thing is thus made strangely complicated ; nay, sometimes virtue and its shadow are set at variance. We should never, perhaps, have heard of Lucretia, had she died to preserve her chastity instead of her reputation. If we really deserve our own good opinion we shall commonly be respected in the world ; but if we pant after higher improvement and higher attainments, it is not sufficient to view ourselves as we suppose that we are viewed by others, though this has been ingeniously argued, as the foundation of our moral sentiments†. Because each by-stander may have his own prejudices, beside the prejudices of his age or country. We should rather endeavour to view ourselves as we suppose that Being views us who seeth each thought ripen into action, and whose judgment never swerves from the eternal rule of right. Righteous are all his judgments—just as merciful !

The

---

* I allude to various biographical writings, but particularly to Boswell's Life of Johnson.

† Smith.

The humble mind that seeketh to find favour in His sight, and calmly examines its conduct when only His presence is felt, will seldom form a very erroneous opinion of its own virtues. During the still hour of self-collection the angry brow of offended justice will be fearfully deprecated, or the tie which draws man to the Deity will be recognized in the pure sentiment of reverential adoration, that swells the heart without exciting any tumultuous emotions. In these solemn moments man discovers the germ of those vices, which like the Java tree shed a pestiferous vapour around—death is in the shade! and he perceives them without abhorrence, because he feels himself drawn by some cord of love to all his fellow-creatures, for whose follies he is anxious to find every extenuation in their nature— in himself. If I, he may thus argue, who exercise my own mind, and have been refined by tribulation, find the serpent's egg in some fold of my heart, and crush it with difficulty, shall not I pity those who have stamped with less vigour, or who have heedlessly nurtured the insidious reptile till it poisoned the vital stream it sucked? Can I, conscious of my secret sins, throw off my fellow-creatures, and calmly see them drop into the chasm of perdition, that yawns to receive them.—No! no! The agonized heart will cry with suffocating impatience—I too am a man! and have vices, hid, perhaps, from human eye, that bend me to the dust before God, and loudly tell me, when all is mute, that we are formed of the same earth, and breathe the same element. Humanity thus rises naturally out of humility, and twists the cords of love

love that in various convolutions entangle the heart.

This sympathy extends still further, till a man well pleased observes force in arguments that do not carry conviction to his own bosom, and he gladly places in the fairest light, to himself, the shews of reason that have led others astray, rejoiced to find some reason in all the errors of man ; though before convinced that he who rules the day makes his sun to shine on all. Yet, shaking hands thus as it were with corruption, one foot on earth, the other with bold stride mounts to heaven, and claims kindred with superiour natures. Virtues, unobserved by man, drop their balmy fragrance at this cool hour, and the thirsty land, refreshed by the pure streams of comfort that suddenly gush out, is crowned with smiling verdure; this is the living green, on which that eye may look with complacency that is too pure to behold iniquity !

But my spirits flag ; and I must silently indulge the reverie these reflections lead to, unable to describe the sentiments, that have calmed my soul, when watching the rising sun, a soft shower drizzling through the leaves of neighbouring trees, seemed to fall on my languid, yet tranquil spirits, to cool the heart that had been heated by the passions which reason laboured to tame.

The leading principles which run through all my disquisitions, would render it unnecessary to enlarge on this subject, if a constant attention to keep the varnish of the character fresh, and in good condition, were not often inculcated as the sum total of female duty ; if rules to regulate

the

the behaviour, and to preserve the reputation, did not too frequently supersede moral obligations. But, with respect to reputation, the attention is confined to a single virtue—chastity. If the honour of a woman, as it is absurdly called, is safe, she may neglect every social duty ; nay, ruin her family by gaming and extravagance ; yet still present a shameless front—for truly she is an honourable woman !

Mrs. Macaulay has justly observed, that ' there ' is but one fault which a woman of honour may ' not commit with impunity.' She then justly, and humanely adds—' This has given rise to the ' trite and foolish observation, that the first fault ' against chastity in woman has a radical power ' to deprave the character. But no such frail be- ' ings come out of the hands of nature. The ' human mind is built of nobler materials than ' to be so easily corrupted ; and with all their ' disadvantages of situation and education, women ' seldom become entirely abandoned till they are ' thrown into a state of desperation, by the ven- ' omous rancour of their own sex.'

But, in proportion as this regard for the reputation of chastity is prized by women, it is despised by men : and the two extremes are equally destructive to morality.

Men are certainly more under the influence of their appetites than women ; and their appetites are more depraved by unbridled indulgence and the fastidious contrivances of satiety. Luxury has introduced a refinement in eating, that destroys the constitution ; and a degree of gluttony which is so beastly, that a perception of seemliness

nefs of behaviour muft be worn out before one
being could eat immoderately in the prefence of
another, and afterwards complain of the oppreffion that his intemperance naturally produced.
Some women, particularly French women, have
alfo loft a fenfe of decency in this refpect; for
they will talk very calmly of an indigeftion. It
were to be wifhed that idlenefs was not allowed
to generate, on the rank foil of wealth, thofe
fwarms of fummer infects that feed on putrefac-
tion, we fhould not then be difgufted by the fight
of fuch brutal exceffes.

There is one rule relative to behaviour that, I
think, ought to regulate every other; and it is
fimply to cherifh fuch an habitual refpect for
mankind as may prevent us from difgufting a
fellow-creature for the fake of a prefent indulgence. The fhameful indolence of many married
women, and others a little advanced in life, frequently leads them to fin againft delicacy. For,
though convinced that the perfon is the band of
union between the fexes, yet, how often do they
from fheer indolence, or, to enjoy fome trifling
indulgence, difguft?

The depravity of the appetite which brings
the fexes together, has had a ftill more fatal effect. Nature muft ever be the ftandard of tafte,
the guage of appetite—yet how grofsly is nature
infulted by the voluptuary. Leaving the refinements of love out of the queftion; nature, by
making the gratification of an appetite, in this
refpect, as well as every other, a natural and
imperious law to preferve the fpecies, exalts the
appetite, and mixes a little mind and affection

Q   with

with a fenfual guft. The feelings of a parent mingling with an inftinct merely animal, give it dignity ; and the man and woman often meeting on account of the child, a mutual intereft and affection is excited by the exercife of a common fympathy. Women then having neceffarily fome duty to fulfil, more noble than to adorn their perfons, would not contentedly be the flaves of cafual appetite ; which is now the fituation of a very confiderable number who are, literally fpeaking, ftanding difhes to which every glutton may have accefs.

I may be told that great as this enormity is, it only affects a devoted part of the fex—devoted for the falvation of the reft. But, falfe as every affertion might eafily be proved, that recommends the fanctioning a fmall evil to produce a greater good ; the mifchief does not ftop here, for the moral character, and peace of mind, of the chafter part of the fex, is undermined by the conduct of the very women to whom they allow no refuge from guilt : whom they inexorably confign to the exercife of arts that lure their hufbands from them, debauch their fons, and force them, let not modeft women ftart, to affume, in fome degree, the fame character themfelves. For I will venture to affert, that all the caufes of female weaknefs, as well as depravity, which I have already enlarged on, branch out of one grand caufe—want of chaftity in men.

This intemperance, fo prevalent, depraves the appetite to fuch a degree, that a wanton ftimulus is neceffary to roufe it ; but the parental defign of nature is forgotten, and the mere perfon,

and

and that for a moment, alone engroſſes the thoughts. So voluptuous, indeed, often grows the luſtful prowler, that he refines on female ſoftneſs. Something more ſoft than woman is then ſought for; till, in Italy and Portugal, men attend the levees of equivocal beings, to ſigh for more than female langour.

To ſatisfy this genus of men, women are made ſyſtematically voluptuous, and though they may not all carry their libertiniſm to the ſame height, yet this heartleſs intercourſe with the ſex, which they allow themſelves, depraves both ſexes, becauſe the taſte of men is vitiated; and women, of all claſſes, naturally ſquare their behaviour to gratify the taſte by which they obtain pleaſure and power. Women becoming, conſequently, weaker, in mind and body, than they ought to be, were one of the grand ends of their being taken into the account, that of bearing and nurſing children, have not ſufficient ſtrength to diſcharge the firſt duty of a mother; and ſacrificing to laſciviouſneſs the parental affection, that ennobles inſtinct, either deſtroy the embryo in the womb, or caſt it off when born. Nature in every thing demands reſpect, and thoſe who violate her laws ſeldom violate them with impunity. The weak enervated women who particularly catch the attention of libertines, are unfit to be mothers, though they may conceive; ſo that the rich ſenſualiſt, who has rioted among women, ſpreading depravity and miſery, when he wiſhes to perpetuate his name, receives from his wife only an half-formed being that inherits both its father's and mother's weakneſs.

Contraſting

Contrasting the humanity of the present age with the barbarism of antiquity, great stress has been laid on the savage custom of exposing the children whom their parents could not maintain ; whilst the man of sensibility, who thus, perhaps, complains, by his promiscuous amours produces a most destructive barrenness and contagious flagitiousness of manners. Surely nature never intended that women, by satisfying an appetite, should frustrate the very purpose for which it was implanted !

I have before observed, that men ought to maintain the women whom they have seduced ; this would be one means of reforming female manners, and stopping an abuse that has an equally fatal effect on population and morals. Another, no less obvious, would be to turn the attention of woman to the real virtue of chastity ; for to little respect has that woman a claim, on the score of modesty, though her reputation may be white as the driven snow, who smiles on the libertine whilst she spurns the victims of his lawless appetites and their own folly.

Besides, she has a taint of the same folly, pure as she esteems herself, when she studiously adorns her person only to be seen by men, to excite respectful sighs, and all the idle homage of what is called innocent gallantry. Did women really respect virtue for its own sake, they would not seek for a compensation in vanity, for the self-denial which they are obliged to practise to preserve their reputation, nor would they associate with men who set reputation at defiance.

The

The two fexes mutually corrupt and improve each other. This I believe to be an indifputable truth, extending it to every virtue. Chaftity, modefty, public fpirit, and all the noble train of virtues, on which focial virtue and happinefs is built, fhould be underftood and cultivated by all mankind, or they will be cultivated to little effect. And, inftead of furnifhing the vicious or idle with a pretext for violating fome facred duty, by terming it a fexual one, it would be wifer to fhew that nature has not made any difference, for that the unchafte man doubly defeats the purpofe of nature, by rendering women barren, and deftroying his own conftitution, though he avoids the fhame that purfues the crime in the other fex. Thefe are the phyfical confequences, the moral are ftill more alarming ; for virtue is only a nominal diftinction when the duties of citizens, hufbands, wives, fathers, mothers, and directors of families, become merely the felfifh ties of convenience.

Why then do philofophers look for public fpirit ? Public fpirit muft be nutured by private virtue, or it will refemble the factitious fentiment which makes women careful to preferve their reputation, and men their honour. A fentiment that often exifts unfupported by virtue, unfupported by that fublime morality which makes the habitual breach of one duty a breach of the whole moral law.

C H A P.

C H A P. IX.

OF THE PERNICIOUS EFFECTS WHICH ARISE
  FROM THE UNNATURAL DISTINCTIONS
  ESTABLISHED IN SOCIETY.

FROM the refpect paid to property flow, as
from a poifoned fountain, moft of the evils and
vices which render this world fuch a dreary fcene
to the contemplative mind. For it is in the moft
polifhed fociety that noifome reptiles and venom-
ous ferpents lurk under the rank herbage ; and
there is voluptuoufnefs pampered by the ftill ful-
try air, which relaxes every good difpofition before it ripens into virtue.

One clafs preffes on another ; for all are aiming
to procure refpect on account of their property :
and property, once gained, will procure the refpect due only to talents and virtue.   Men neglect the duties incumbent on man, yet are treated like demi-gods ; religion is alfo feparated from
morality by a ceremonial veil, yet men wonder
that the world is almoft, literally fpeaking, a den
of fharpers or oppreffors.

There is a homely proverb, which fpeaks a
fhrewd truth, that whoever the devil finds idle he
will employ. And what but habitual idlenefs
can hereditary wealth and titles produce ? For
man is fo conftituted that he can only attain a
proper ufe of his faculties by exercifing them,
and will not exercife them unlefs neceffity, of
fome kind, firft fet the wheels in motion.   Virtue

tue likewise can only be acquired by the difcharge of relative duties; but the importance of thefe facred duties will fcarcely be felt by the being who is cajoled out of his humanity by the flattery of fycophants. There muft be more equality eftablifhed in fociety, or morality will never gain ground, and this virtuous equality will not reft firmly even when founded on a rock, if one half of mankind are chained to its bottom by fate, for they will be continually undermining it through ignorance or pride.

It is vain to expect virtue from women till they are, in fome degree, independent of men; nay, it is vain to expect that ftrength of natural affection, which would make them good wives and mothers. Whilft they are abfolutely dependent on their hufbands they will be cunning, mean, and felfifh, and the men who can be gratified by the fawning fondnefs of fpaniel-like affection, have not much delicacy, for love is not to be bought, in any fenfe of the words, its filken wings are inftantly fhrivelled up when any thing befide a return in kind is fought. Yet whilft wealth enervates men; and women live, as it were, by their perfonal charms, how can we expect them to difcharge thofe ennobling duties which equally require exertion and felf-denial. Hereditary property fophifticates the mind, and the unfortunate victims to it, if I may fo exprefs myfelf, fwathed from their birth, feldom exert the locomotive faculty of body or mind; and, thus viewing every thing through one medium, and that a falfe one, they are unable to difcern in what true merit and happinefs confift.

Falfe,

Falfe, indeed, muft be the light when the drapery of fituation hides the man, and makes him
ftalk in mafquerade, dragging from one fcene of
diffipation to another the nervelefs limbs that
hang with ftupid liftneffnefs, and rolling round
the vacant eye which plainly tells us that there is
no mind at home.

I mean, therefore, to infer that the fociety is
not properly organized which does not compel
men and women to difcharge their refpective duties, by making it the only way to acquire that
countenance from their fellow-creatures, which
every human being wifhes fome way to attain.
The refpect, confequently, which is paid to
wealth and mere perfonal charms, is a true north-
eaft blaft, that blights the tender bloffoms of affection and virtue.   Nature has wifely attached
affections to duties, to fweeten toil, and to give
that vigour to the exertions of reafon which only
the heart can give.   But, the affection which is
put on merely becaufe it is the appropriated infig-
nia of a certain character, when its duties are not
fulfilled, is one of the empty compliments which
vice and folly are obliged to pay to virtue and
the real nature of things.

To illuftrate my opinion, I need only obferve,
that when a woman is admired for her beauty,
and fuffers herfelf to be fo far intoxicated by the
admiration fhe receives, as to neglect to difcharge
the indifpenfable duty of a mother, fhe fins againft
herfelf by neglecting to cultivate an affection that
would equally tend to make her ufeful and happy.   True happinefs, I mean all the contentment,
and virtuous fatisfaction, that can be fnatched in
                                                    this

this imperfect state, must arise from well regulated affections; and an affection includes a duty. Men are not aware of the misery they cause, and the vicious weakness they cherish, by only inciting women to render themselves pleasing; they do not consider that they thus make natural and artificial duties clash, by sacrificing the comfort and respectability of a woman's life to voluptuous notions of beauty, when in nature they all harmonize.

Cold would be the heart of a husband, were he not rendered unnatural by early debauchery, who did not feel more delight at seeing his child suckled by its mother, than the most artful wanton tricks could ever raise; yet this natural way of cementing the matrimonial tie, and twisting esteem with fonder recollections, wealth leads women to spurn. To preserve their beauty, and wear the flowery crown of the day, that gives them a kind of right to reign for a short time over the sex, they neglect to stamp impressions on their husbands' hearts, that would be remembered with more tenderness when the snow on the head began to chill the bosom, than even their virgin charms. The maternal solicitude of a reasonable affectionate woman is very interesting, and the chastened dignity with which a mother returns the caresses that she and her child receive from a father who has been fulfilling the serious duties of his station, is not only a respectable, but a beautiful sight. So singular, indeed, are my feelings, and I have endeavoured not to catch factitious ones, that after having been fatigued with the sight of insipid grandeur and the slavish ceremonies that with cumberous pomp supplied the place of domestic affections, I have turned to some other scene to relieve my eye by resting it on the refreshing green every where scattered by nature. I have then viewed with pleasure a woman nursing her children, and discharging the duties of her station with, perhaps, merely a servant maid to take off her hands the servile part of the household business. I have seen her prepare herself and children, with only the luxury of cleanliness, to receive her husband, who returning weary home in the evening found smiling babes and a clean hearth. My heart has loitered in the midst of the group, and has even throbbed with sympathetic emotion, when the scraping of the well known foot has raised a pleasing tumult.

Whilst my benevolence has been gratified by contemplating this artless picture, I have thought that a couple of this description, equally necessary and independent of each other, because each fulfilled the respective duties of their station, possessed all that life could give.—Raised sufficiently above abject poverty not to be obliged to weigh the consequence of every farthing they spend, and having sufficient to prevent their attending to a frigid system of economy, which narrows both heart and mind. I declare, so vulgar are my conceptions, that I know not what is wanted to render this the happiest as well as the most respectable situation in the world, but a taste for literature, to throw a little variety and interest into social converse, and some superfluous money to give to the needy and to buy books. For it is

not

not pleasant when the heart is opened by compassion and the head active in arranging plans of usefulness, to have a prim urchin continually twitching back the elbow to prevent the hand from drawing out an almost empty purse, whispering at the same time some prudential maxim about the priority of justice.

Destructive, however, as riches and inherited honours are to the human character, women are more debased and cramped, if possible, by them, than men, because men may still, in some degree, unfold their faculties by becoming soldiers and statesmen.

As soldiers, I grant, they can now only gather, for the most part, vain glorious laurels, whilst they adjust to a hair the European balance, taking especial care that no bleak northern nook or sound incline the beam. But the days of true heroism are over, when a citizen fought for his country like a Fabricius or a Washington, and then returned to his farm to let his virtuous fervour run in a more placid, but not a less salutary, stream. No, our British heroes are oftener sent from the gaming table than from the plow; and their passions have been rather inflamed by hanging with dumb suspense on the turn of a die, than sublimated by panting after the adventurous march of virtue in the historic page.

The statesman, it is true, might with more propriety quit the Faro Bank, or card-table, to guide the helm, for he has still but to shuffle and trick. The whole system of British politics, if system it may courteously be called, consisting in multiplying dependents and contriving taxes which

which grind the poor to pamper the rich ; thus a war, or any wild goose chace is, as the vulgar use the phrase, a lucky turn-up of patronage for the minister, whose chief merit is the art of keeping himself in place.

It is not necessary then that he should have bowels for the poor, so he can secure for his family the odd trick. Or should some shew of respect, for what is termed with ignorant ostentation an Englishman's birth-right, be expedient to bubble the gruff mastiff that he has to lead by the nose, he can make an empty shew, very safely, by giving his single voice, and suffering his light squadron to file off to the other side. And when a question of humanity is agitated he may dip a sop in the milk of human kindness, to silence Cerberus, and talk of the interest which his heart takes in an attempt to make the earth no longer cry for vengeance as it sucks in its children's blood, though his cold hand may at the very moment rivet their chains, by sanctioning the abominable traffick. A minister is no longer a minister than while he can carry a point, which he is determined to carry.—Yet it is not necessary that a minister should feel like a man, when a bold push might shake his seat.

But, to have done with these episodical observations, let me return to the more specious slavery which chains the very soul of woman, keeping her for ever under the bondage of ignorance.

The preposterous distinctions of rank, which render civilization a curse, by dividing the world between voluptuous tyrants, and cunning envious dependents, corrupt, almost equally, every
class

clafs of people, becaufe refpectability is not attached to the difcharge of the relative duties of life, but to the ftation, and when the duties are not fulfilled the affections cannot gain fufficient ftrength to fortify the virtue of which they are the natural reward. Still there are fome loopholes out of which a man may creep, and dare to think and act for himfelf; but for a woman it is an herculean tafk, becaufe fhe has difficulties peculiar to her fex to overcome, which require almoft fuper-human powers.

A truly benevolent legiflator always endeavours to make it the intereft of each individual to be virtuous; and thus private virtue becoming the cement of public happinefs, an orderly whole is confolidated by the tendency of all the parts towards a common centre. But, the private or public virtue of woman is very problematical; for Rouffeau, and a numerous lift of male writers, infift that fhe fhould all her life be fubjected to a fevere reftraint, that of propriety. Why fubject her to propriety—blind propriety, if fhe be capable of acting from a nobler fpring, if fhe be an heir of immortality? Is fugar always to be produced by vital blood? Is one half of the human fpecies, like the poor African flaves, to be fubject to prejudices that brutalize them, when principles would be a furer guard, only to fweeten the cup of man? Is not this indirectly to deny woman reafon? for a gift is a mockery, if it be unfit for ufe.

Women are, in common with men, rendered weak and luxurious by the relaxing pleafures which wealth procures; but added to this they

are

are made flaves to their perfons, and muft render them alluring that man may lend them his rea- fon to guide their tottering fteps aright. Or fhould they be ambitious, they muft govern their tyrants by finifter tricks, for without rights there cannot be any incumbent duties. The laws re- fpecting woman, which I mean to difcufs in a future part, make an abfurd unit of a man and his wife ; and then, by the eafy tranfition of only confidering him as refponfible, fhe is reduced to a mere cypher.

The being who difcharges the duties of its fta- tion is independent ; and, fpeaking of women at large, their firft duty is to themfelves as rational creatures, and the next, in point of importance, as citizens, is that, which includes fo many, of a mother. The rank in life which difpenfes with their fulfilling this duty, neceffarily degrades them by making them mere dolls. Or, fhould they turn to fomething more important than merely fitting drapery upon a fmooth block, their minds are only occupied by fome foft pla- tonic attachment ; or, the actual management of an intrigue may keep their thoughts in motion ; for when they neglect domeftic duties, they have it not in their power to take the field and march and counter-march like foldiers, or wrangle in the fenate to keep their faculties from rufting.

I know that as a proof of the inferiority of the fex, Rouffeau has exultingly exclaimed, How can they leave the nurfery for the camp !—And the camp has by fome moralifts been termed the fchool of the moft heroic virtues ; though, I think, it would puzzle a keen cafuift to prove the

the reasonableness of the greater number of wars that have dubbed heroes. I do not mean to consider this question critically; because, having frequently viewed these freaks of ambition as the first natural mode of civilization, when the ground must be torn up, and the woods cleared by fire and sword, I do not choose to call them pests; but surely the present system of war has little connection with virtue of any denomination, being rather the school of *finesse* and effeminacy, than of fortitude.

Yet, if defensive war, the only justifiable war, in the present advanced state of society, where virtue can shew its face and ripen amidst the rigours which purify the air on the mountain's top, were alone to be adopted as just and glorious, the true heroism of antiquity might again animate female bosoms.—But fair and softly, gentle reader, male or female, do not alarm thyself, for though I have contrasted the character of a modern soldier with that of a civilized woman, I am not going to advise them to turn their distaff into a musket, though I sincerely wish to see the bayonet converted into a pruning-hook. I only recreated an imagination, fatigued by contemplating the vices and follies which all proceed from a feculent stream of wealth that has muddied the pure rills of natural affection, by supposing that society will some time or other be so constituted, that man must necessarily fulfil the duties of a citizen, or be despised, and that while he was employed in any of the departments of civil life, his wife, also an active citizen, should be equally intent to manage her family, educate her children, and assist her neighbours. But,

But, to render her really virtuous and useful, she must not, if she discharge her civil duties, want, individually, the protection of civil laws; she must not be dependent on her husband's bounty for her subsistence during his life, or support after his death—for how can a being be generous who has nothing of its own ? or, virtuous, who is not free ? The wife, in the present state of things, who is faithful to her husband, and neither suckles nor educates her children, scarcely deserves the name of a wife, and has no right to that of a citizen. But take away natural rights, and there is of course an end of duties.

Women thus infallibly become only the wanton solace of men, when they are so weak in mind and body, that they cannot exert themselves, unless to pursue some frothy pleasure, or to invent some frivolous fashion. What can be a more melancholy sight to a thinking mind, than to look into the numerous carriages that drive helter-skelter about this metropolis in a morning full of pale-faced creatures who are flying from themselves. I have often wished, with Dr. Johnson, to place some of them in a little shop with half a dozen children looking up to their languid countenances for support. I am much mistaken, if some latent vigour would not soon give health and spirit to their eyes, and some lines drawn by the exercise of reason on the blank cheeks, which before were only undulated by dimples, might restore lost dignity to the character, or rather enable it to attain the true dignity of its nature. Virtue is not to be acquired even by speculation, much less by the negative supineness that wealth naturally generates. Besides,

Befides, when poverty is more difgraceful than even vice, is not morality cut to the quick ? Still to avoid mifconftruction, though I confider that women in the common walks of life are called to fulfil the duties of wives and mothers, by religion and reafon, I cannot help lamenting that women of a fuperiour caft have not a road open by which they can purfue more extenfive plans of ufefulnefs and independence. I may excite laughter, by dropping an hint, which I mean to purfue, fome future time, for I really think that women ought to have reprefentatives, inftead of being arbitrarily governed without having any direct fhare allowed them in the deliberations of goverment.

But, as the whole fyftem of reprefentation is now, in this country, only a convenient handle for defpotifm, they need not complain, for they are as well reprefented as a numerous clafs of hard working mechanics, who pay for the fupport of royalty when they can fcarcely ftop their children's mouths with bread. How are they reprefented whofe very fweat fupports the fplendid ftud of an heir apparent, or varnifhes the chariot of fome female favourite who looks down on fhame ? Taxes on the very neceffaries of life, enable an endlefs tribe of idle princes and princeffes to pafs with ftupid pomp before a gaping crowd, who almoft worfhip the very parade which cofts them fo dear. This is mere gothic grandeur, fomething like the barbarous ufelefs parade of having fentinels on horfeback at Whitehall, which I could never view without a mixture of contempt and indignation.

R

How

How strangely must the mind be sophisticated when this sort of state impresses it ! But, till these monuments of folly are levelled by virtue, similar follies will leaven the whole mass. For the same character, in some degree, will prevail in the aggregate of society : and the refinements of luxury, or the vicious repinings of envious poverty, will equally banish virtue from society, considered as the characteristic of that society, or only allow it to appear as one of the stripes of the harlequin coat, worn by the civilized man.

In the superiour ranks of life, every duty is done by deputies, as if duties could ever be waved, and the vain pleasures which consequent idleness forces the rich to pursue, appear so enticing to the next rank, that the numerous scramblers for wealth sacrifice every thing to tread on their heels. The most sacred trusts are then considered as sinecures, because they were procured by interest, and only sought to enable a man to keep *good company.* Women, in particular, all want to be ladies. Which is simply to have nothing to do, but listlessly to go they scarcely care where, for they cannot tell what.

But what have women to do in society ? I may be asked, but to loiter with easy grace ; surely you would not condemn them all to suckle fools and chronicle small beer ! No. Women might certainly study the art of healing, and be physicians as well as nurses. And midwifery, decency seems to allot to them, though I am afraid the word midwife, in our dictionaries, will soon give place to *accoucheur,* and one proof of the former delicacy of the sex be effaced from the language.   They

They might, alſo, ſtudy politics, and ſettle their benevolence on the broadeſt baſis ; for the reading of hiſtory will ſcarcely be more uſeful than the peruſal of romances, if read as mere bi-ography ; if the character of the times, the po-litical improvements, arts, &c. be not obſerved. In ſhort, if it be not conſidered as the hiſtory of man ; and not of particular men, who filled a niche in the temple of fame, and dropped into the black rolling ſtream of time, that ſilently ſweeps all before it, into the ſhapeleſs void called—eter-nity.—For ſhape, can it be called, ' that ſhape ' hath none ?'

Buſineſs of various kinds, they might likewiſe purſue, if they were educated in a more orderly manner, which might ſave many from common and legal proſtitution. Women would not then marry for a ſupport, as men accept of places un-der government, and neglect the implied duties ; nor would an attempt to earn their own ſubſiſt-ence, a moſt laudable one ! ſink them almoſt to the level of thoſe poor abandoned creatures who live by proſtitution. For are not milliners and mantua-makers reckoned the next claſs ? The few employments open to women, ſo far from being liberal, are menial ; and when a ſuperiour education enables them to take charge of the edu-cation of children as governeſſes, they are not treated like the tutors of ſons, though even cle-rical tutors are not always treated in a manner calculated to render them reſpectable in the eyes of their pupils, to ſay nothing of the private com-fort of the individual. But as women educated like gentlewomen, are never deſigned for the hu-

R 2

miliating

miliating situation which necessity sometimes forces them to fill ; these situations are considered in the light of a degradation ; and they know little of the human heart, who need to be told, that nothing so painfully sharpens the sensibility as such a fall in life.

Some of these women might be restrained from marrying by a proper spirit or delicacy, and others may not have had it in their power to escape in this pitiful way from servitude ; is not that government then very defective, and very unmindful of the happiness of one half of its members, that does not provide for honest, independent women, by encouraging them to fill respectable stations ? But in order to render their private virtue a public benefit, they must have a civil existence in the state, married or single ; else we shall continually see some worthy woman, whose sensibility has been rendered painfully acute by undeserved contempt, droop like ' the lily broken down by a plow-share.'

It is a melancholy truth ; yet such is the blessed effect of civilization ! the most respectable women are the most oppressed ; and, unless they have understandings far superiour to the common run of understandings, taking in both sexes, they must, from being treated like contemptible beings, become contemptible. How many women thus waste life away the prey of discontent, who might have practised as physicians, regulated a farm, managed a shop, and stood erect, supported by their own industry, instead of hanging their heads surcharged with the dew of sensibility, that consumes the beauty to which it at first

gave

gave luſtre ; nay, I doubt whether pity and love are ſo near akin as poets feign, for I have ſeldom ſeen much compaſſion excited by the helpleſſ-neſs of females, unleſs they were fair ; then, per-haps, pity was the ſoft handmaid of love, or the harbinger of luſt.

How much more reſpectable is the woman who earns her own bread by fulfilling any duty, than the moſt accompliſhed beauty !—beauty did I ſay ?—ſo ſenſible am I of the beauty of moral lovelineſs, or the harmonious propriety that at-tunes the paſſions of a well-regulated mind, that I bluſh at making the compariſon ; yet I ſigh to think how few women aim at attaining this re-ſpectability by withdrawing from the giddy whirl of pleaſure, or the indolent calm that ſtu-pifies the good ſort of women it ſucks in.

Proud of their weakneſs, however, they muſt always be protected, guarded from care, and all the rough toils that dignify the mind.—If this be the fiat of fate, if they will make themſelves inſigni-ficant and contemptible, ſweetly to waſte ' life ' away ' let them not expect to be valued when their beauty fades, for it is the fate of the faireſt flowers to be admired and pulled to pieces by the careleſs hand that plucked them. In how ma-ny ways do I wiſh, from the pureſt benevolence, to impreſs this truth on my ſex ; yet I fear that they will not liſten to a truth that dear bought experience has brought home to many an agitated boſom, nor willingly reſign the privileges of rank and ſex for the privileges of humanity, to which thoſe have no claim who do not diſcharge its duties.

R 3

Thoſe

Thofe writers are particularly ufeful, in my opinion, who make man feel for man, independent of the ftation he fills, or the drapery of factitious fentiments.   I then would fain convince reafonable men of the importance of fome of my remarks, and prevail on them to weigh difpaffionately the whole tenor of my obfervations.——I appeal to their underftandings ; and, as a fellow-creature claim, in the name of my fex, fome intereft in their hearts.   I entreat them to affift to emancipate their companion, to make her a help meet for them !

Would men but generoufly fnap our chains, and be content with rational fellowfhip inftead of flavifh obedience, they would find us more obfervant daughters, more affectionate fifters, more faithful wives, more reafonable mothers—in a word, better citizens.   We fhould then love them with true affection, becaufe we fhould learn to refpect ourfelves ; and the peace of mind of a worthy man would not be interrupted by the idle vanity of his wife, nor his babes fent to neftle in a ftrange bofom, having never found a home in their mother's.

C H A P.

C H A P. X.

PARENTAL AFFECTION.

PARENTAL affection is, perhaps, the blindest modification of perverfe felf-love; for we have not, like the French*, two terms to diftinguifh the purfuit of a natural and reafonable defire, from the ignorant calculations of weaknefs. Parents often love their children in the moft brutal manner, and facrifice every relative duty to promote their advancement in the world.——To promote, fuch is the perverfity of unprincipled prejudices, the future welfare of the very beings whofe prefent exiftence they embitter by the moft defpotic ftretch of power. Power, in fact, is ever true to its vital principle, for in every fhape it would reign without controul or inquiry. Its throne is built acrofs a dark abyfs, which no eye muft dare to explore, left the bafelefs fabric fhould totter under inveftigation. Obedience, unconditional obedience, is the catch-word of tyrants of every defcription, and to render ' affur-' ance doubly fure,' one kind of defpotifm fupports another. Tyrants would have caufe to tremble if reafon were to become the rule of duty in any of the relations of life, for the light might fpread till perfect day appeared. And when it did appear, how would men fmile at the fight of the bugbears at which they ftarted during the night of ignorance, or the twilight of timid inquiry.   Parental

R 4

* *L'amour propre. L'amour de foi même.*

Parental affection, indeed, in many minds, is but a pretext to tyrannize where it can be done with impunity, for only good and wise men are content with the respect that will bear discussion. Convinced that they have a right to what they insist on, they do not fear reason, or dread the sifting of subjects that recur to natural justice : because they firmly believe that the more enlightened the human mind becomes the deeper root will just and simple principles take. They do not rest in expedients, or grant that what is metaphysically true can be practically false ; but disdaining the shifts of the moment they calmly wait till time, sanctioning innovation, silences the hiss of selfishness or envy.

If the power of reflecting on the past, and darting the keen eye of contemplation into futurity, be the grand privilege of man, it must be granted that some people enjoy this prerogative in a very limited degree. Every thing now appears to them wrong ; and not able to distinguish the possible from the monstrous, they fear where no fear should find a place, running from the light of reason, as if it were a firebrand ; yet the limits of the possible have never been defined to stop the sturdy innovator's hand.

Woman, however, a slave in every situation to prejudice, seldom exerts enlightened maternal affection ; for she either neglects her children, or spoils them by improper indulgence. Besides, the affection of some women for their children is, as I have before termed it, frequently very brutish : for it eradicates every spark of humanity. Justice, truth, every thing is sacrificed by
these

thefe Rebekah's, and for the fake of their *own* children they violate the moft facred duties, forgetting the common relationfhip that binds the whole family on earth together. Yet, reafon feems to fay, that they who fuffer one duty, or affection, to fwallow up the reft, have not fufficient heart or mind to fulfil that one confcientioufly. It then lofes the venerable afpect of a duty, and affumes the fantaftic form of a whim.

As the care of children in their infancy is one of the grand duties annexed to the female character by nature, this duty would afford many forcible arguments for ftrengthening the female underftanding, if it were properly confidered.

The formation of the mind muft be begun very early, and the temper, in particular, requires the moft judicious attention—an attention which women cannot pay who only love their children becaufe they are their children, and feek no further for the foundation of their duty, than in the feelings of the moment. It is this want of reafon in their affections which makes women fo often run into extremes, and either be the moft fond or moft carelefs and unnatural mothers.

To be a good mother—a woman muft have fenfe, and that independence of mind which few women poffefs who are taught to depend entirely on their hufbands. Meek wives are, in general, foolifh mothers ; wanting their children to love them beft, and take their part, in fecret, againft the father, who is held up as a fcarecrow. If they are to be punifhed, though they have offended the mother, the father muft inflict the punifhment ; he muft be the judge in all difputes : but

I

I fhall more fully difcufs this fubject when I treat of private education, I now only mean to in-fift, that unlefs the underftanding of woman be enlarged, and her character rendered more firm, by being allowed to govern her own conduct, fhe will never have fufficient fenfe or command of temper to manage her children properly. Her parental affection, indeed, fcarcely deferves the name, when it does not lead her to fuckle her children, becaufe the difcharge of this duty is equally calculated to infpire maternal and filial affection : and it is the indifpenfable duty of men and women to fulfil the duties which give birth to affections that are the fureft prefervatives againft vice. Natural affection, as it is termed, I believe to be a very faint tie, affections muft grow out of the habitual exercife of a mutual fympathy ; and what fympathy does a mother exercife who fends her babe to a nurfe, and only takes it from a nurfe to fend it to a fchool ?

In the exercife of their maternal feelings pro-vidence has furnifhed women with a natural fub-ftitute for love, when the lover becomes only a friend and mutual confidence takes place of over-ftrained admiration—a child then gently twifts the relaxing cord, and a mutual care produces a new mutual fympathy.—But a child, though a pledge of affection, will not enliven it, if both father and mother are content to transfer the charge to hire-lings ; for they who do their duty by proxy fhould not murmur if they mifs the reward of duty—parental affection produces filial duty.

C H A P.

CHAP. XI.

DUTY TO PARENTS.

THERE seems to be an indolent propensity in man to make prescription always take place of reason, and to place every duty on an arbitrary foundation. The rights of kings are deduced in a direct line from the King of kings; and that of parents from our first parent.

Why do we thus go back for principles that should always rest on the same base, and have the same weight to-day that they had a thousand years ago—and not a jot more ? If parents discharge their duty they have a strong hold and sacred claim on the gratitude of their children; but few parents are willing to receive the respectful affection of their offspring on such terms. They demand blind obedience, because they do not merit a reasonable service : and to render these demands of weakness and ignorance more binding, a mysterious sanctity is spread round the most arbitrary principle ; for what other name can be given to the blind duty of obeying vicious or weak beings merely because they obeyed a powerful instinct ?

The simple definition of the reciprocal duty, which naturally subsists between parent and child, may be given in a few words : The parent who pays proper attention to helpless infancy has a right to require the same attention when the feebleness of age comes upon him. But to subju-

gate

gate a rational being to the mere will of another, after he is of age to anſwer to ſociety for his own conduct, is a moſt cruel and undue ſtretch of power ; and, perhaps, as injurious to morality as thoſe religious ſyſtems which do not allow right and wrong to have any exiſtence, but in the Divine will.

I never knew a parent who had paid more than common attention to his children, diſregarded *; on the contrary, the early habit of relying almoſt implicitly on the opinion of a reſpected parent is not eaſily ſhook, even when matured reaſon convinces the child that his father is not the wiſeſt man in the world. This weakneſs, for a weakneſs it is, though the epithet amiable may be tacked to it, a reaſonable man muſt ſteel himſelf againſt ; for the abſurd duty, too often inculcated, of obeying a parent only on account of his being a parent, ſhackles the mind, and prepares it for a ſlaviſh ſubmiſſion to any power but reaſon.

I diſtinguiſh between the natural and accidental duty due to parents.

The parent who ſeduouſly endeavours to form the heart and enlarge the underſtanding of his child, has given that dignity to the diſcharge of a duty, common to the whole animal world, that only reaſon can give. This is the parental affection of humanity, and leaves inſtinctive natural affection far behind. Such a parent acquires all the rights of the moſt ſacred friendſhip, and his advice, even when his child is advanced in life, demands ſerious conſideration.

With

* Dr. Johnſon makes the ſame obſervation.

With respect to marriage, though after one and twenty a parent seems to have no right to withhold his consent on any account; yet twenty years of solicitude call for a turn, and the son ought, at least, to promise not to marry for two or three years, should the object of his choice not entirely meet with the approbation of his first friend.

But, respect for parents is, generally speaking, a much more debasing principle; it is only a selfish respect for property. The father who is blindly obeyed, is obeyed from sheer weakness, or from motives that degrade the human character.

A great proportion of the misery that wanders, in hideous forms around the world, is allowed to rise from the negligence of parents; and still these are the people who are most tenacious of what they term a natural right, though it be subversive of the birth-right of man, the right of acting according to the direction of his own reason.

I have already very frequently had occasion to observe, that vicious or indolent people are always eager to profit by enforcing arbitrary privileges; and, generally, in the same proportion as they neglect the discharge of the duties which alone render the privileges reasonable. This is at the bottom a dictate of common sense, or the instinct of self-defence, peculiar to ignorant weakness; resembling that instinct, which makes a fish muddy the water it swims in to allude its enemy, instead of boldly facing it in the clear stream.

From

From the clear ſtream of argument, indeed, the ſupporters of preſcription, of every denomination, fly ; and, taking refuge in the darkneſs, which, in the language of ſublime poetry, has been ſuppoſed to ſurround the throne of Omnipotence, they dare to demand that implicit reſpect which is only due to His unſearchable ways. But, let me not be thought preſumptuous, the darkneſs which hides our God from us, only reſpects ſpeculative truths——it never obſcures moral ones, they ſhine clearly, for God is light, and never, by the conſtitution of our nature, requires the diſcharge of a duty, the reaſonableneſs of which does not beam on us when we open our eyes.

The indolent parent of high rank may, it is true, extort a ſhew of reſpect from his child, and females on the continent are particularly ſubject to the views of their families, who never think of conſulting their inclination, or providing for the comfort of the poor victims of their pride. The conſequence is notorious ; theſe dutiful daughters become adultereſſes, and neglect the education of their children, from whom they, in their turn, exact the ſame kind of obedience.

Females, it is true, in all countries, are too much under the dominion of their parents ; and few parents think of addreſſing their children in the following manner, though it is in this reaſonable way that Heaven ſeems to command the whole human race. It is your intereſt to obey me till you can judge for yourſelf ; and the Almighty Father of all has implanted an affection in me to ſerve as a guard to you whilſt your reaſon

ſon

fon is unfolding ; but when your mind arrives at maturity, you muſt only obey me, or rather reſpect my opinions, ſo far as they coincide with the light that is breaking in'on your own mind.

A ſlaviſh bondage to parents cramps every faculty of the mind ; and Mr. Locke very judiciouſly obſerves, that ' if the mind be curbed and ' humbled too much in children ; if their ſpirits ' be abaſed and broken much by too ſtrict an hand ' over them ; they loſe all their vigour and in- ' duſtry.' This ſtrict hand may in ſome degree account for the weakneſs of women ; for girls, from various cauſes, are more kept down by their parents, in every ſenſe of the word, than boys. The duty expected from them is, like all the duties arbitrarily impoſed on women, more from a ſenſe of propriety, more out of reſpect for decorum than reaſon ; and thus taught ſlaviſhly to ſubmit to their parents, they are prepared for the ſlavery of marriage. I may be told that a number of women are not ſlaves in the marriage ſtate. True, but they then become tyrants ; for it is not rational freedom, but a lawleſs kind of power reſembling the authority exerciſed by the favourites of abſolute monarchs, which they obtain by debaſing means. I do not, likewiſe, dream of inſinuating that either boys or girls are always ſlaves, I only inſiſt that when they are obliged to ſubmit to authority blindly, their faculties are weakened, and their tempers rendered imperious or abject. I alſo lament that parents, indolently availing themſelves of a ſuppoſed privilege, damp the firſt faint glimmering of reaſon, rendering at the ſame time the duty, which they are ſo anxious

ious to enforce, an empty name; becaufe they will not let it reft on the only bafis on which a duty can reft fecurely : for unlefs it be founded on knowledge, it cannot gain fufficient ftrength to refift the fqualls of paffion, or the filent fapping of felf-love. But it is not the parents who have given the fureft proof of their affection for their children, or, to fpeak more properly, who by fulfilling their duty, have allowed a natural parental affection to take root in their hearts, the child of excifed fympathy and reafon, and not the over-weening offspring of felfifh pride, who moft vehemently infift on their children fubmitting to their will merely becaufe it is their will. On the contrary, the parent, who fets a good example, patiently lets that example work ; and it feldom fails to produce its natural effect—filial refpect.

Children cannot be taught too early to fubmit to reafon, the true definition of that neceffity, which Rouffeau infifted on, without defining it ; for to fubmit to reafon is to fubmit to the nature of things, and to that God, who formed them fo, to promote our real intereft.

Why fhould the minds of children be warped as they juft begin to expand, only to favour the indolence of parents, who infift on a privilege without being willing to pay the price fixed by nature? I have before had occafion to obferve, that a right always includes a duty, and I think it may, likewife, fairly be inferred, that they forfeit the right, who do not fulfil the duty.

It is eafier, I grant, to command than reafon ; but it does not follow from hence that children cannot comprehend the reafon why they are made

to

to do certain things habitually ; for, from a steady adherence to a few simple principles of conduct flows that salutary power which a judicious parent gradually gains over a child's mind. And this power becomes strong indeed, if tempered by an even display of affection brought home to the child's heart. For I believe, as a general rule, it must be allowed that the affection which we inspire always resembles that we cultivate ; so that natural affections, which have been supposed almost distinct from reason, may be found more nearly connected with judgment than is commonly allowed. Nay, as another proof of the necessity of cultivating the female understanding, it is but just to observe, that the affections seem to have a kind of animal capriciousness when they merely reside in the heart.

It is the irregular exercise of parental authority that first injures the mind, and to these irregularities girls are more subject than boys. The will of those who never allow their will to be disputed, unless they happen to be in a good humour, when they relax proportionally, is almost always unreasonable. To elude this arbitrary authority girls very early learn the lessons which they afterwards practise on their husbands ; for I have frequently seen a little sharp-faced miss rule a whole family, excepting that now and then mamma's anger will burst out of some accidental cloud ; either her hair was ill dressed*, or she had lost more money at cards, the night before, than

S   she

---

* I myself heard a little girl once say to a servant, ' My mamma has ' been scolding me finely this morning, because her hair was not dressed ' to please her.' Though this remark was pert, it was just. And what respect could a girl acquire for such a parent without doing violence to reason ?

she was willing to own to her husband ; or some such moral cause of anger.

After observing sallies of this kind, I have been led into a melancholy train of reflection respecting females, concluding that when their first affection must lead them astray, or make their duties clash till they rest on mere whims and customs, little can be expected from them as they advance in life. How indeed can an instructor remedy this evil ? for to teach them virtue on any solid principle is to teach them to despise their parents. Children cannot, ought not, to be taught to make allowance for the faults of their parents, because every such allowance weakens the force of reason in their minds, and makes them still more indulgent to their own. It is one of the most sublime virtues of maturity that leads us to be severe with respect to ourselves, and forbearing to others ; but children should only be taught the simple virtues, for if they begin too early to make allowance for human passions and manners, they wear off the fine edge of the criterion by which they should regulate their own, and become unjust in the same proportion as they grow indulgent.

The affections of children, and weak people, are always selfish ; they love others, because others love them, and not on account of their virtues. Yet, till esteem and love are blended together in the first affection, and reason made the foundation of the first duty, morality will stumble at the threshold. But, till society is very differently constituted, parents, I fear, will still insist on being obeyed, because they will be obeyed, and constantly endeavour to settle that power on a Divine right which will not bear the investigation of reason. CHAP.

C H A P. XII.

ON NATIONAL EDUCATION.

THE good effects refulting from attention to private education will ever be very confined, and the parent who really puts his own hand to the plow, will always, in fome degree, be difappointed, till education become a grand national concern. A man cannot retire into a defart with his child, and if he did he could not bring himfelf back to childhood, and become the proper friend and play-fellow of an infant or youth. And when children are confined to the fociety of men and women, they very foon acquire that kind of premature manhood which ftops the growth of every vigorous power of mind or body. In order to open their faculties they fhould be excited to think for themfelves; and this can only be done by mixing a number of children together, and making them jointly purfue the fame objects.

A child very foon contracts a benumbing indolence of mind, which he has feldom fufficient vigour afterwards to fhake off, when he only afks a queftion inftead of feeking for information, and then relies implicitly on the anfwer he receives. With his equals in age this could never be the cafe, and the fubjects of inquiry, though they might be influenced, would not be entirely under the direction of men, who frequently damp, if not deftroy, abilities, by bringing them forward too haftily : and too haftily they will infallibly

be

be brought forward, if the child be confined to the society of a man, however fagacious that man may be.

Befides, in youth the feeds of every affection fhould be fown, and the refpectful regard, which is felt for a parent, is very different from the focial affections that are to conftitute the happinefs of life as it advances. Of thefe equality is the bafis, and an intercourfe of fentiments unclogged by that obfervant ferioufnefs which prevents difputation, though it may not enforce fubmiffion. Let a child have ever fuch an affection for his parent, he will always languifh to play and chat with children ; and the very refpect which he entertains, for filial efteem always has a dafh of fear mixed with it, will, if it do not teach him cunning, at leaft prevent him from pouring out the little fecrets which firft open the heart to friendfhip and confidence, gradually leading to more expanfive benevolence. Added to this, he will never acquire that frank ingenuoufnefs of behaviour, which young people can only attain by being frequently in fociety where they dare to fpeak what they think ; neither afraid of being reproved for their prefumption, nor laughed at for their folly.

Forcibly impreffed by the reflections which the fight of fchools, as they are at prefent conducted, naturally fuggefted, I have formerly delivered my opinion rather warmly in favour of a private education ; but further experience has led me to view the fubject in a different light. I ftill, however, think fchools, as they are now regulated, the hotbeds of vice and folly, and the

knowledge

knowledge of human nature, fuppofed to be attained there, merely cunning felfifhnefs.

At fchool boys become gluttons and flovens, and, inftead of cultivating domeftic affections, very early rufh into the libertinifm which deftroys the conftitution before it is formed ; hardening the heart as it weakens the underftanding.

I fhould, in fact, be averfe to boarding-fchools, if it were for no other reafon than the unfettled ftate of mind which the expectation of the vacations produce. On thefe the children's thoughts are fixed with eager anticipating hopes, for, at leaft, to fpeak with moderation, half of the time, and when they arrive they are fpent in total diffipation and beaftly indulgence.

But, on the contrary, when they are brought up at home, though they may purfue a plan of ftudy in a more orderly manner than can be adopted when near a fourth part of the year is actually fpent in idlenefs, and as much more in regret and anticipation ; yet they there acquire too high an opinion of their own importance, from being allowed to tyrannize over fervants, and from the anxiety expreffed by moft mothers, on the fcore of manners, who, eager to teach the accomplifhments of a gentleman, ftifle, in their birth, the virtues of a man. Thus brought into company when they ought to be ferioufly employed, and treated like men when they are ftill boys, they become vain and effeminate.

The only way to avoid two extremes equally injurious to morality, would be to contrive fome way of combining a public and private education. Thus to make men citizens two natural fteps

S 3

might

might be taken, which feem directly to lead to the defired point ; for the domeftic affections, that firft open the heart to the various modifications of humanity, would be cultivated, whilft the children were neverthelefs allowed to fpend great part of their time, on terms of equality, with other children.

I ftill recollect, with pleafure, the country day fchool ; where a boy trudged in the morning, wet or dry, carrying his books, and his dinner, if it were at a confiderable diftance ; a fervant did not then lead mafter by the hand, for, when he had once put on coat and breeches, he was allowed to fhift for himfelf, and return alone in the evening to recount the feats of the day clofe at the parental knee. His father's houfe was his home, and was ever after fondly remembered ; nay, I appeal to fome fuperiour men, who were educated in this manner, whether the recollection of fome fhady lane where they conned their leffon ; or, of fome ftile, where they fat making a kite, or mending a bat, has not endeared their country to them ?

But, what boy ever recollected with pleafure the years he fpent in clofe confinement, at an academy near London ? unlefs, indeed, he fhould, by chance, remember the poor fcarecrow of an ufher, whom he tormented ; or, the tartman, from whom he caught a cake, to devour it with the cattifh appetite of felfifhnefs. At boarding-fchools of every defcription, the relaxation of the junior boys is mifchief ; and of the fenior, vice. Befides, in great fchools, what can be more pre-judicial to the moral character than the fyftem of tyranny and abject flavery which is eftablifhed

amongft

amongſt the boys, to ſay nothing of the ſlavery to forms, which makes religion worſe than a farce ? For what good can be expected from the youth who receives the ſacrament of the Lord's ſupper, to avoid forfeiting half a guinea, which he probably afterwards ſpends in ſome ſenſual manner ? Half the employment of the youths is to elude the neceſſity of attending public worſhip ; and well they may, for ſuch a conſtant repetition of the ſame thing muſt be a very irkſome reſtraint on their natural vivacity. As theſe ceremonies have the moſt fatal effect on their morals, and as a ritual performed by the lips, when the heart and mind are far away, is not now ſtored up by our church as a bank to draw on for the fees of the poor ſouls in purgatory, why ſhould they not be aboliſhed ?

But the fear of innovation, in this country, extends to every thing.—This is only a covert fear, the apprehenſive timidity of indolent ſlugs, who guard, by ſliming it over, the ſnug place, which they conſider in the light of an hereditary eſtate ; and eat, drink, and enjoy themſelves, inſtead of fulfilling the duties, excepting a few empty forms, for which it was endowed. Theſe are the people who moſt ſtrenuouſly inſiſt on the will of the founder being obſerved, crying out againſt all reformation, as if it were a violation of juſtice. I am now alluding particularly to the relicks of popery retained in our colleges, when the proteſtant members ſeem to be ſuch ſticklers for the eſtabliſhed church ; but their zeal never makes them loſe ſight of the ſpoil of ignorance, which rapacious prieſts of ſuperſtitious memory

have

have scraped together. No, wise in their generation, they venerate the prescriptive right of
possession, as a strong hold, and still let the sluggish bell tinkle to prayers, as during the days
when the elevation of the host was supposed to
atone for the sins of the people, left one reformation should lead to another, and the spirit kill the
letter. These Romish customs have the most
baneful effect on the morals of our clergy; for
the idle vermin who two or three times a day
perform in the most slovenly manner a service
which they think useless, but call their duty,
soon lose a sense of duty. At college, forced to
attend or evade public worship, they acquire an
habitual contempt for the very service, the performance of which is to enable them to live in
idleness. It is mumbled over as an affair of business, as a stupid boy repeats his task, and frequently the college cant escapes from the preacher the moment after he has left the pulpit; and
even whilst he is eating the dinner which he
earned in such a dishonest manner.

Nothing, indeed, can be more irreverent than
the cathedral service as it is now performed in
this country, nor does it contain a set of weaker
men than those who are the slaves of this childish
routine. A disgusting skeleton of the former
state is still exhibited; but all the solemnity that
interested the imagination, if it did not purify the
heart, is stripped off. The performance of high
mass on the continent must impress every mind,
where a spark of fancy glows, with that awful
melancholy, that sublime tenderness, so near akin
to devotion. I do not say that these devotional
feelings

feelings are of more ufe, in a moral fenfe, than any other emotion of tafte ; but I contend that the theatrical pomp which gratifies our fenfes, is to be preferred to the cold parade that infults the underftanding without reaching the heart.

Amongft remarks on national education, fuch obfervations cannot be mifplaced, efpecially as the fupporters of thefe eftablifhments, degenerated into puerilities, affect to be the champions of religion.—Religion, pure fource of comfort in this vale of tears ! how has thy clear ftream been muddied by the dabblers, who have prefumptu-oufly endeavoured to confine in one narrow channel, the living waters that ever flow towards God —the fublime ocean of exiftence ! What would life be without that peace which the love of God, when built on humanity, alone can impart ? Every earthly affection turns back, at intervals, to prey upon the heart that feeds it ; and the pureft ef-fufions of benevolence, often rudely damped by man, muft mount as a free-will offering to Him who gave them birth, whofe bright image they faintly reflect.

In public fchools, however, religion, confound-ed with irkfome ceremonies and unreafonable re-ftraints, affumes the moft ungracious afpect : not the fober auftere one that commands refpect whilft it infpires fear ; but a ludicrous caft, that ferves to point a pun. For, in fact, moft of the good ftories and fmart things which enliven the fpirits that have been concentrated at whift, are manufactured out of the incidents to which the very men labour to give a droll turn who coun-tenance the abufe to live on the fpoil.

There

There is not, perhaps, in the kingdom, a more dogmatical, or luxurious fet of men, than the pedantic tyrants who refide in colleges and prefide at public fchools. The vacations are equally injurious to the morals of the mafters and pupils, and the intercourfe, which the former keep up with the nobility, introduces the fame vanity and extravagance into their families, which banifh domeftic duties and comforts from the lordly manfion, whofe ftate is awkwardly aped on a fmaller fcale. The boys, who live at a great expenfe with the mafters and affiftants, are never domefticated, though placed there for that purpofe ; for, after a filent dinner, they fwallow a hafty glafs of wine, and retire to plan fome mifchievous trick, or to ridicule the perfon or manners of the very people they have juft been cringing to, and whom they ought to confider as the reprefentatives of their parents.

Can it then be a matter of furprife that boys become felfifh and vicious who are thus fhut out from focial converfe ? or that a mitre often graces the brow of one of thefe diligent paftors ?

The defire of living in the fame ftyle, as the rank juft above them, infects each individual and every clafs of people, and meannefs is the concomitant of this ignoble ambition ; but thofe profeffions are moft debafing whofe ladder is patronage : yet, out of one of thefe profeffions the tutors of youth are, in general, chofen. But, can they be expected to infpire independent fentiments, whofe conduct muft be regulated by the cautious prudence that is ever on the watch for preferment ?

So

So far, however, from thinking of the morals of boys, I have heard feveral mafters of fchools argue, that they only undertook to teach Latin and Greek; and that they had fulfilled their duty, by fending fome good fcholars to college.

A few good fcholars, I grant, may have been formed by emulation and difcipline; but to bring forward thefe clever boys, the health and morals of a number have been facrificed. The fons of our gentry and wealthy commoners are moftly educated at thefe feminaries, and will any one pretend to affert that the majority, making every allowance, come under the defcription of tolerable fcholars?

It is not for the benefit of fociety that a few brilliant men fhould be brought forward at the expenfe of the multitude. It is true, that great men feem to ftart up, as great revolutions occur, at proper intervals, to reftore order, and to blow afide the clouds that thicken over the face of truth; but let more reafon and virtue prevail in fociety, and thefe ftrong winds would not be neceffary. Public education, of every denomination, fhould be directed to form citizens; but if you wifh to make good citizens, you muft firft exercife the affections of a fon and a brother. This is the only way to expand the heart; for public affections, as well as public virtues, muft ever grow out of the private character, or they are merely meteors that fhoot athwart a dark fky and difappear as they are gazed at and admired.

Few, I believe, have had much affection for mankind, who did not firft love their parents, their brothers, fifters, and even the domeftic brutes,

brutes, whom they firſt played with. The exerciſe of youthful ſympathies forms the moral
temperature ; and it is the recollection of theſe
firſt affections and purſuits that gives life to thoſe
that are afterwards more under the direction of
reaſon. In youth, the fondeſt friendſhips are
formed, the genial juices mounting at the ſame
time, kindly mix ; or, rather the heart, tempered
for the reception of friendſhip, is accuſtomed to
ſeek for pleaſure in ſomething more noble than
the churliſh gratification of appetite.

In order then to inſpire a love of home and domeſtic pleaſures, children ought to be educated at
home, for riotous holidays only make them fond
of home for their own ſakes. Yet, the vacations, which do not foſter domeſtic affections,
continually diſturb the courſe of ſtudy, and render any plan of improvement abortive which includes temperance ; ſtill, were they aboliſhed,
children would be entirely ſeparated from their
parents, and I queſtion whether they would become better citizens by ſacrificing the preparato-
ry affections, by deſtroying the force of relation-
ſhips that render the marriage ſtate as neceſſary as
reſpectable. But, if a private education produces
ſelf-importance, or inſulates a man in his family,
the evil is only ſhifted, not remedied.

This train of reaſoning brings me back to a
ſubject, on which I mean to dwell, the neceſſity
of eſtabliſhing proper day-ſchools.

But, theſe ſhould be national eſtabliſhments,
for whilſt ſchool-maſters are dependent on the
caprice of parents, little exertion can be expected
from them, more than is neceſſary to pleaſe ignorant

norant people. Indeed, the neceſſity of a maſter's giving the parents ſome ſample of the boys
abilities, which during the vacation is ſhewn to
every viſitor*, is productive of more miſchief
than would at firſt be ſuppoſed. For they are
ſeldom done entirely, to ſpeak with moderation,
by the child itſelf ; thus the maſter countenances
falſehood, or winds the poor machine up to ſome
extraordinary exertion, that injures the wheels,
and ſtops the progreſs of gradual improvement.
The memory is loaded with unintelligible words,
to make a ſhew of, without the underſtanding's
acquiring any diſtinct ideas : but only that education deſerves emphatically to be termed cultivation of mind, which teaches young people how
to begin to think. The imagination ſhould not
be allowed to debauch the underſtanding before
it gained ſtrength, or vanity will become the
forerunner of vice : for every way of exhibiting
the acquirements of a child is injurious to its
moral character.

How much time is loſt in teaching them to
recite what they do not underſtand ? whilſt ſeated on benches, all in their beſt array, the mam-
mas liſten with aſtoniſhment to the parrot-like
prattle, uttered in ſolemn cadences, with all the
pomp of ignorance and folly. Such exhibitions
only ſerve to ſtrike the ſpreading fibres of vanity
through the whole mind ; for they neither teach
children to ſpeak fluently, nor behave gracefully.
So far from it, that theſe frivolous purſuits might
comprehenſively be termed the ſtudy of affectation ;

---

* I now particularly allude to the numerous academies in, and about
London, and to the behaviour of the trading part of this great city.

tion ; for we now rarely see a simple, bashful boy, though few people of taste were ever disgusted by that awkward sheepishness so natural to the age, which schools and an early introduction into society, have changed into impudence and apish grimace.

Yet, how can these things be remedied whilst school-masters depend entirely on parents for a subsistence ; and when so many rival schools hang out their lures, to catch the attention of vain fathers and mothers, whose parental affection only leads them to wish that their children should outshine those of their neighbours ?

Without great good luck, a sensible, conscientious man, would starve before he could raise a school, if he disdained to bubble weak parents by practising the secret tricks of the craft.

In the best regulated schools, however, where swarms are not crammed together, many bad habits must be acquired ; but, at common schools, the body, heart, and understanding, are equally stunted, for parents are often only in quest of the cheapest school, and the master could not live, if he did not take a much greater number than he could manage himself ; nor will the scanty pittance, allowed for each child, permit him to hire ushers sufficient to assist in the discharge of the mechanical part of the business. Besides, whatever appearance the house and garden may make, the children do not enjoy the comfort of either, for they are continually reminded by irksome restrictions that they are not at home, and the state-rooms, garden, &c. must be kept in order for the recreation of the parents ; who, of a

Sunday,

Sunday, vifit the fchool, and are impreffed by the very parade that renders the fituation of their children uncomfortable.

With what difguft have I heard fenfible women, for girls are more reftrained and cowed than boys, fpeak of the wearifome confinement, which they endured at fchool. Not allowed, perhaps, to ftep out of one broad walk in a fuberb garden, and obliged to pace with fteady deportment ftupidly backwards and forwards, holding up their heads and turning out their toes, with fhoulders braced back, inftead of bounding, as nature directs to complete her own defign, in the various attitudes fo conducive to health *. The pure animal fpirits, which make both mind and body fhoot out, and unfold the tender bloffoms of hope, are turned four, and vented in vain wifhes, or pert repinings, that contract the faculties and fpoil the temper; elfe they mount to the brain, and fharpening the underftanding before it gains proportionable ftrength, produce that pitiful cunning which difgracefully characterizes the female mind—and I fear will ever characterize it whilft women remain the flaves of power !

The

---

* I remember a circumftance that once came under my own obfervation, and raifed my indignation. I went to vifit a little boy at a fchool where young children were prepared for a larger one. The mafter took me into the fchool-room, &c. but whilft I walked down a broad gravel walk, I could not help obferving that the grafs grew very luxuriantly on each fide of me. I immediately afked the child fome queftions, and found that the poor boys were not allowed to ftir off the walk, and that the mafter fometimes permitted fheep to be turned in to crop the untrodden grafs. The tyrant of this domain ufed to fit by a window that overlooked the prifon yard, and one nook turning from it, where the unfortunate babes could fport freely, he enclofed, and planted it with potatoes. The wife likewife was equally anxious to keep the children in order, left they fhould dirty or tear their clothes.

The little respect which the male world pay to chastity is, I am persuaded, the grand source of many of the physical and moral evils that torment mankind, as well as of the vices and follies that degrade and destroy women; yet at school, boys infallibly lose that decent bashfulness, which might have ripened into modesty, at home.

And what nasty indecent tricks do they also learn from each other, when a number of them pig together in the same bedchamber, not to speak of the vices, which render the body weak whilst they effectually prevent the acquisition of any delicacy of mind. The little attention paid to the cultivation of modesty, amongst men, produces great depravity in all the relationships of society; for, not only love—love that ought to purify the heart, and first call forth all the youthful powers, to prepare the man to discharge the benevolent duties of life, is sacrificed to premature lust; but, all the social affections are deadened by the selfish gratifications, which very early pollute the mind, and dry up the generous juices of the heart. In what an unnatural manner is innocence often violated; and what serious consequences ensue to render private vices a public pest. Besides, an habit of personal order, which has more effect on the moral character, than is, in general, supposed, can only be acquired at home, where that respectable reserve is kept up which checks the familiarity, that sinking into beastliness, undermines the affection it insults.

I have already animadverted on the bad habits which females acquire when they are shut up together;

gether; and, I think, that the obfervation may fairly be extended to the other fex, till the natural inference is drawn which I have had in view throughout—that to improve both fexes they ought, not only in private families, but in public fchools, to be educated together. If marriage be the cement of fociety, mankind fhould all be educated after the fame model, or the intercourfe of the fexes will never deferve the name of fellowfhip, nor will women ever fulfil the peculiar duties of their fex, till they become enlightened citizens, till they become free by being enabled to earn their own fubfiftence, independent of men; in the fame manner, I mean, to prevent mifconftruction, as one man is independent of another. Nay, marriage will never be held facred till women, by being brought up with men, are prepared to be their companions rather than their miftreffes; for the mean doublings of cunning will ever render them contemptible, whilft oppreffion renders them timid. So convinced am I of this truth, that I will venture to predict that virtue will never prevail in fociety till the virtues of both fexes are founded on reafon; and, till the affections common to both are allowed to gain their due ftrength by the difcharge of mutual duties.

Were boys and girls permitted to purfue the fame ftudies together, thofe graceful decencies might early be inculcated which produce modefty without thofe fexual diftinctions that taint the mind. Leffons of politenefs, and that formulary of decorum, which treads on the heels of falfehood, would be rendered ufelefs by habitual pro-

T   priety

priety of behaviour. Not indeed, put on for vi-
fitors like the courtly robe of politenefs, but the
fober effect of cleanlinefs of mind. Would not
this fimple elegance of fincerity be a chafte homage paid to domeftic affections, far furpaffing the
meretricious compliments that fhine with falfe
luftre in the heartlefs intercourfe of fafhionable
life ? But, till more underftanding preponderate
in fociety, there will ever be a want of heart and
tafte, and the harlot's *rouge* will fupply the place
of that celeftial fuffufion which only virtuous affections can give to the face. Gallantry, and
what is called love, may fubfift without fimplicity of character ; but the main pillars of friendfhip, are refpect and confidence—efteem is never
founded on it cannot tell what !

A tafte for the fine arts requires great cultivation ; but not more than a tafte for the virtuous
affections ; and both fuppofe that enlargement of
mind which opens fo many fources of mental
pleafure. Why do people hurry to noify fcenes,
and crowded circles ? I fhould anfwer, becaufe
they want activity of mind, becaufe they have not
cherifhed the virtues of the heart. They only,
therefore, fee and feel in the grofs, and continually pine after variety, finding every thing that is
fimple infipid.

This argument may be carried further than philofophers are aware of, for if nature deftined woman, in particular, for the difcharge of domeftic
duties, fhe made her fufceptible of the attached
affections in a great degree. Now women are
notorioufly fond of pleafure ; and, naturally muft
be fo according to my definition, becaufe they
cannot

cannot enter into the minutiæ of domeſtic taſte ; lacking judgment, the foundation of all taſte. For the underſtanding, in ſpite of ſenſual cavillers, reſerves to itſelf the privilege of conveying pure joy to the heart.

With what a languid yawn have I ſeen an admirable poem thrown down, that a man of true taſte returns to, again and again with rapture ; and, whilſt melody has almoſt ſuſpended reſpiration, a lady has aſked me where I bought my gown. I have ſeen alſo an eye glanced coldly over a moſt exquiſite picture, reſt, ſparkling with pleaſure, on a caricature rudely ſketched ; and whilſt ſome terrific feature in nature has ſpread a ſublime ſtillneſs through my ſoul, I have been deſired to obſerve the pretty tricks of a lap-dog, that my perverſe fate forced me to travel with. Is it ſurpriſing that ſuch a taſteleſs being ſhould rather careſs this dog than her children ? Or, that ſhe ſhould prefer the rant of flattery to the ſimple accents of ſincerity ?

To illuſtrate this remark I muſt be allowed to obſerve, that men of the firſt genius and moſt cultivated minds, have appeared to have the higheſt reliſh for the ſimple beauties of nature ; and they muſt have forcibly felt, what they have ſo well deſcribed, the charm, which natural affections, and unſophiſticated feelings ſpread round the human character. It is this power of looking into the heart, and reſponſively vibrating with each emotion, that enables the poet to perſonify each paſſion, and the painter to ſketch with a pencil of fire.

True

True taſte is ever the work of the underſtanding employed in obſerving natural effects ; and till women have more underſtanding, it is vain to expect them to poſſeſs domeſtic taſte. Their lively ſenſes will ever be at work to harden their hearts, and the emotions ſtruck out of them will continue to be vivid and tranſitory, unleſs a proper education ſtores their mind with knowledge.

It is the want of domeſtic taſte, and not the acquirement of knowledge, that takes women out of their families, and tears the ſmiling babe from the breaſt that ought to afford it nouriſhment. Women have been allowed to remain in ignorance, and ſlaviſh dependence, many, very many years, and ſtill we hear of nothing but their fondneſs of pleaſure and ſway, their preference of rakes and ſoldiers, their childiſh attachments to toys, and the vanity that makes them value accompliſhments more than virtues.

Hiſtory brings forward a fearful catalogue of the crimes which their cunning has produced, when the weak ſlaves have had ſufficient addreſs to overreach their maſters. In France, and in how many other countries, have men been the luxurious deſpots, and women the crafty miniſters ?—Does this prove that ignorance and dependence domeſticate them ? Is not their folly the by-word of the libertines, who relax in their ſociety ; and do not men of ſenſe continually lament that an immoderate fondneſs for dreſs and diſſipation carries the mother of a family for ever from home. Their hearts have not been debauched by knowledge, nor their minds led aſtray by ſcientific purſuits ; yet, they do not fulfil the pecu-

liar

liar duties which as women they are called upon by nature to fulfil. On the contrary, the state of warfare which subsists between the sexes, makes them employ those wiles, that frustrate the more open designs of force.

When, therefore, I call women slaves, I mean in a political and civil sense ; for, indirectly they obtain too much power, and are debased by their exertions to obtain illicit sway.

Let an enlightened nation * then try what effect reason would have to bring them back to nature, and their duty ; and allowing them to share the advantages of education and government with man, see whether they will become better, as they grow wiser and become free. They cannot be injured by the experiment ; for it is not in the power of man to render them more insignificant than they are at present.

To render this practicable, day schools, for particular ages, should be established by government, in which boys and girls might be educated together. The school for the younger children, from five to nine years of age, ought to be absolutely free and open to all classes†. A sufficient number of masters should also be chosen by a select committee, in each parish, to whom any complaint of negligence, &c. might be made, if signed by six of the children's parents.

Ushers would then be unnecessary ; for I believe experience will ever prove that this kind of subordinate authority is particularly injurious to

T 3 the

* France.

† Treating this part of the subject, I have borrowed some hints from a very sensible pamphlet, written by the late bishop of Autun on Public Education.

the morals of youth. What, indeed, can tend to deprave the character more than outward fub-miſſion and inward contempt? Yet how can boys be expected to treat an uſher with reſpect, when the maſter ſeems to conſider him in the light of a ſervant, and almoſt to countenance the ridicule which becomes the chief amuſement of the boys during the play hours.

But nothing of this kind could occur in an elementary day ſchool, where boys and girls, the rich and poor, ſhould meet together. And to prevent any of the diſtinctions of vanity, they ſhould be dreſſed alike, and all obliged to ſubmit to the ſame diſcipline, or leave the ſchool. The ſchool-room ought to be ſurrounded by a large piece of ground, in which the children might be uſefully exerciſed, for at this age they ſhould not be confined to any ſedentary employment for more than an hour at a time. But theſe relaxations might all be rendered a part of elementary educa-tion, for many things improve and amuſe the ſenſes, when introduced as a kind of ſhow, to the principles of which, dryly laid down, children would turn a deaf ear. For inſtance, botany, mechanics, and aſtronomy. Reading, writing, arithmetic, natural hiſtory, and ſome ſimple ex-periments in natural philoſophy, might fill up the day; but theſe purſuits ſhould never en-croach on gymnaſtic plays in the open air. The elements of religion, hiſtory, the hiſtory of man, and politics, might alſo be taught, by converſa-tions, in the ſocratic form.

After the age of nine, girls and boys, intended for domeſtic employments, or mechanical trades,

ought

ought to be removed to other schools, and receive instruction, in some measure appropriated to the destination of each individual, the two sexes being still together in the morning ; but in the afternoon, the girls should attend a school, where plain-work, mantua-making, millinery, &c. would be their employment.

The young people of superiour abilities, or fortune, might now be taught in another school, the dead and living languages, the elements of science, and continue the study of history and politics, on a more extensive scale, which would not exclude polite literature.

Girls and boys still together ? I hear some readers ask : yes. And I should not fear any other consequence than that some early attachment might take place ; which, whilst it had the best effect on the moral character of the young people, might not perfectly agree with the views of the parents, for it will be a long time, I fear, before the world is so enlightened that parents, only anxious to render their children virtuous, will let them choose companions for life themselves.

Besides, this would be a sure way to promote early marriages, and from early marriages the most salutary physical and moral effects naturally flow. What a different character does a married citizen assume from the selfish coxcomb, who lives, but for himself, and who is often afraid to marry lest he should not be able to live in a certain style. Great emergencies excepted, which would rarely occur in a society of which equality was the basis, a man could only be prepared to discharge the duties of public life, by the habitu-

al

al practice of those inferiour ones which form
the man.

In this plan of education the constitution of
boys would not be ruined by the early debauche-
ries, which now makes men so selfish, nor girls
rendered weak and vain, by indolence, and frivolous pursuits. But, I presuppose, that such a
degree of equality should be established between
the sexes as would shut out gallantry and coquetry, yet allow friendship and love to temper
the heart for the discharge of higher duties.

These would be schools of morality—and the
happiness of man, allowed to flow from the pure
springs of duty and affection, what advances might
not the human mind make ? Society can only be
happy and free in proportion as it is virtuous ;
but the present distinctions, established in society,
corrode all private, and blast all public virtue.

I have already inveighed against the custom of
confining girls to their needle, and shutting them
out from all political and civil employments ;
for by thus narrowing their minds they are rendered unfit to fulfil the peculiar duties which
nature has assigned them,

Only employed about the little incidents of
the day, they necessarily grow up cunning. My
very soul has often sickened at observing the sly
tricks practised by women to gain some foolish
thing on which their silly hearts were set. Not
allowed to dispose of money, or call any thing
their own, they learn to turn the market penny ;
or, should a husband offend, by staying from
home, or give rise to some emotions of jealousy—
a new gown, or any pretty bawble, smooths Ju-
no's angry brow.   But

But thefe *littleneffes* would not degrade their character, if women were led to refpect themfelves, if political and moral fubjects were opened to them ; and, I will venture to affirm, that this is the only way to make them properly attentive to their domeftic duties.—An active mind embraces the whole circle of its duties, and finds time enough for all. It is not, I affert, a bold attempt to emulate mafculine virtues ; it is not the enchantment of literary purfuits, or the fteady inveftigation of fcientific fubjects, that lead women aftray from duty. No, it is indolence and vanity—the love of pleafure and the love of fway, that will rain paramount in an empty mind. I fay empty emphatically, becaufe the education which women now receive fcarcely deferves the name. For the little knowledge that they are led to acquire, during the important years of youth, is merely relative to accomplifhments ; and accomplifhments without a bottom, for unlefs the underftanding be cultivated, fuperficial and monotonous is every grace. Like the charms of a made up face, they only ftrike the fenfes in a crowd ; but at home, wanting mind, they want variety. The confequence is obvious ; in gay fcenes of diffipation we meet the artificial mind and face, for thofe who fly from folitude dread, next to folitude, the domeftic circle ; not having it in their power to amufe or intereft, they feel their own infignificance, or find nothing to amufe or intereft themfelves.

Befides, what can be more indelicate than a girl's *coming out* in the fafhionable world? Which, in other words, is to bring to market a marriageble

ble mifs, whofe perfon is taken from one public place to another, richly caparifoned. Yet, mixing in the giddy circle under reftraint, thefe butterflies long to flutter at large, for the firft affection of their fouls is their own perfons, to which their attention has been called with the moft fedulous care whilft they were preparing for the period that decides their fate for life. Inftead of purfuing this idle routine, fighing for taftelefs fhew, and heartlefs ftate, with what dignity would the youths of both fexes form attachments in the fchools that I have curforily pointed out ; in which, as life advanced, dancing, mufic, and drawing, might be admitted as relaxations, for at thefe fchools young people of fortune ought to remain, more or lefs, till they were of age. Thofe, who were defigned for particular profeffions, might attend, three or four mornings in the week, the fchools appropriated for their immediate inftruction.

I only drop thefe obfervations at prefent, as hints ; rather, indeed, as an outline of the plan I mean, than a digefted one ; but I muft add, that I highly approve of one regulation mentioned in the pamphlet * already alluded to, that of making the children and youths independent of the mafters refpecting punifhments. They fhould be tried by their peers, which would be an admirable method of fixing found principles of juftice in the mind, and might have the happieft effect on the temper, which is very early foured or irritated by tyranny, till it becomes peevifhly cunning, or ferocioufly overbearing.

My

* The Bifhop of Autun's.

My imagination darts forward with benevolent fervour to greet thefe amiable and refpectable groups, in fpite of the fneering of cold hearts, who are at liberty to utter, with frigid felf-importance, the damning epithet—romantic ; the force of which I fhall endeavour to blunt by repeating the words of an eloquent moralift.—' I ' know not whether the allufions of a truly hu-' mane heart, whofe zeal renders every thing eafy, ' is not preferable to that rough and repulfing ' reafon, which always finds in indifference for ' the public good, the firft obftacle to whatever ' would promote it.'

I know that libertines will alfo exclaim, that woman would be unfexed by acquiring ftrength of body and mind, and that beauty, foft bewitching beauty! would no longer adorn the daughters of men ! I am of a very different opinion, for I think that, on the contrary, we fhould then fee dignified beauty, and true grace ; to produce which, many powerful phyfical and moral caufes would concur.—Not relaxed beauty, it is true, nor the graces of helpleffnefs ; but fuch as appears to make us refpect the human body as a majeftic pile fit to receive a noble inhabitant, in the relics of antiquity.

I do not forget the popular opinion that the Grecian ftatues were not modelled after nature. I mean, not according to the proportions of a particular man ; but that beautiful limbs and features were felected from various bodies to form an harmonious whole. This might, in fome degree, be true. The fine ideal picture of an exalted imagination might be fuperiour to the mate-

rials

rials which the painter found in nature, and thus it might with propriety be termed rather the model of mankind than of a man. It was not, however, the mechanical selection of limbs and features ; but the ebullition of an heated fancy that burst forth, and the fine senses and enlarged understanding of the artist selected the solid matter, which he drew into this glowing focus.

I observed that it was not mechanical, because a whole was produced—a model of that grand simplicity, of those concurring energies, which arrest our attention and command our reverence. For only insipid lifeless beauty is produced by a servile copy of even beautiful nature. Yet, independent of these observations, I believe that the human form must have been far more beautiful than it is at present, because extreme indolence, barbarous ligatures, and many causes, which forcibly act on it, in our luxurious state of society, did not retard its expansion, or render it deformed. Exercise and cleanliness appear to be not only the surest means of preserving health, but of promoting beauty, the physical causes only considered ; yet, this is not sufficient, moral ones must concur, or beauty will be merely of that rustic kind which blooms on the innocent, wholesome, countenances of some country people, whose minds have not been exercised. To render the person perfect, physical and moral beauty ought to be attained at the same time ; each lending and receiving force by the combination. Judgment must reside on the brow, affection and fancy beam in the eye, and humanity curve the cheek, or vain is the sparkling of the

finest

fineſt eye or the elegantly turned finiſh of the faireſt features : whilſt in every motion that diſplays the active limbs and well-knit joints, grace and modeſty ſhould appear.   But this fair aſſemblage is not to be brought together by chance ; it is the reward of exertions met to ſupport each other ; for judgment can only be acquired by reflection, affection by the diſcharge of duties, and humanity by the exerciſe of compaſſion to every living creature.

Humanity to animals ſhould be particularly inculcated as a part of national education, for it is not at preſent one of our national virtues. Tenderneſs for their humble dumb domeſtics, amongſt the lower claſs, is oftener to be found in a ſavage than a civilized ſtate.   For civilization prevents that intercourſe which creates affection in the rude hut, or mud cabin, and leads uncultivated minds who are only depraved by the refinements which prevail in the ſociety, where they are trodden under foot by the rich, to domineer over them to revenge the inſults that they are obliged to bear from their ſuperiours.

This habitual cruelty is firſt caught at ſchool, where it is one of the rare ſports of the boys to torment the miſerable brutes that fall in their way. The tranſition, as they grow up, from barbarity to brutes to domeſtic tyranny over wives, children, and ſervants, is very eaſy.   Juſtice, or even benevolence, will not be a powerful ſpring of action unleſs it be extended to the whole creation ; nay, I believe that it may be delivered as an axiom, that thoſe who can ſee pain, unmoved, will ſoon learn to inflict it.

The

The vulgar are swayed by present feelings, and the habits which they have accidentally acquired; but on partial feelings much dependence cannot be placed, though they be just; for, when they are not invigorated by reflection, custom weakens them, till they are scarcely felt. The sympathies of our nature are strengthened by pondering cogitations, and deadened by thoughtless use. Mackbeth's heart smote him more for one murder, the first, than for a hundred subsequent ones, which were necessary to back it. But, when I used the epithet vulgar, I did not mean to confine my remark to the poor, for partial humanity, founded on present sensations, or whim, is quite as conspicuous, if not more so, amongst the rich.

The lady who sheds tears for the bird starved in a snare, and execrates the devils in the shape of men, who goad to madness the poor ox, or whip the patient ass, tottering under a burden above its strength, will, nevertheless, keep her coachman and horses whole hours waiting for her, when the sharp frost bites, or the rain beats against the well-closed windows which do not admit a breath of air to tell her how roughly the wind blows without. And she who takes her dogs to bed, and nurses them, with a parade of sensibility, when sick, will suffer her babes to grow up crooked in a nursery. This illustration of my argument is drawn from a matter of fact. The woman whom I allude to was handsome, reckoned very handsome, by those who do not miss the mind when the face is plump and fair; but her understanding had not been led from female duties by literature, nor her innocence debauched by knowledge.

knowledge. No, she was quite feminine, according to the masculine acceptation of the word; and, so far from loving these spoiled brutes that filled the place which her children ought to have occupied, she only lisped out a pretty mixture of French and English nonsense, to please the men who flocked round her. The wife, mother, and human creature, were all swallowed up by the factitious character which an improper education and the selfish vanity of beauty had produced.

I do not like to make a distinction without a difference, and I own that I have been as much disgusted by the fine lady who took her lap-dog to her bosom instead of her child; as by the ferocity of a man, who, beating his horse, declared, that he knew as well when he did wrong, as a Christian.

This brood of folly shews how mistaken they are who, if they allow women to leave their harams, do not cultivate their understandings, in order to plant virtues in their hearts. For had they sense, they might acquire that domestic taste which would lead them to love with reasonable subordination their whole family, from their husband to the house-dog; nor would they ever insult humanity in the person of the most menial servant by paying more attention to the comfort of a brute, than to that of a fellow-creature.

My observations on national education are obviously hints; but I principally wish to enforce the necessity of educating the sexes together to perfect both, and of making children sleep at home that they may learn to love home; yet to make private support, instead of smothering, pub-

lic

lic affections, they should be sent to school to mix with a number of equals, for only by the jostlings of equality can we form a just opinion of ourselves.

To render mankind more virtuous, and happier of course, both sexes must act from the same principle; but how can that be expected when only one is allowed to see the reasonableness of it? To render also the social compact truly equitable, and in order to spread those enlightening principles, which alone can meliorate the fate of man, women must be allowed to found their virtue on knowledge, which is scarcely possible unless they are educated by the same pursuits as men. For they are now made so inferiour by ignorance and low desires, as not to deserve to be ranked with them; or, by the serpentine wrigglings of cunning they mount the tree of knowledge, and only acquire sufficient to lead men astray.

It is plain from the history of all nations, that women cannot be confined to merely domestic pursuits, for they will not fulfil family duties, unless their minds take a wider range, and whilst they are kept in ignorance they become in the same proportion the slaves of pleasure as they are the slaves of man. Nor can they be shut out of great enterprises, though the narrowness of their minds often make them mar, what they are unable to comprehend.

The libertinism, and even the virtues of superiour men, will always give women, of some description, great power over them; and these weak women, under the influence of childish passions,

paſſions and ſelfiſh vanity, will throw a falſe light over the objects which the very men view with their eyes, who ought to enlighten their judgment. Men of fancy, and thoſe ſanguine characters who moſtly hold the helm of human affairs, in general, relax in the ſociety of women ; and ſurely I need not cite to the moſt ſuperficial reader of hiſtory the numerous examples of vice and oppreſſion which the private intrigues of female favourites have produced ; not to dwell on the miſchief that naturally ariſes from the blundering interpoſition of well-meaning folly. For in the tranſactions of buſineſs it is much better to have to deal with a knave than a fool, becauſe a knave adheres to ſome plan ; and any plan of reaſon may be ſeen through much ſooner than a ſudden flight of folly. The power which vile and fooliſh women have had over wiſe men, who poſſeſſed ſenſibility, is notorious ; I ſhall only mention one inſtance.

Who ever drew a more exalted female character than Rouſſeau ? though in the lump he conſtantly endeavoured to degrade the ſex. And why was he thus anxious ? Truly to juſtify to himſelf the affection which weakneſs and virtue had made him cheriſh for that fool Thereſa. He could not raiſe her to the common level of her ſex ; and therefore he laboured to bring woman down to her's. He found her a convenient humble companion, and pride made him determine to find ſome ſuperiour virtues in the being whom he choſe to live with ; but did not her conduct during his life, and after his death, clearly ſhew how groſsly he was miſtaken who called her a

U celeſtial

celestial innocent. Nay, in the bitterness of his heart, he himself laments, that when his bodily infirmities made him no longer treat her like a woman, she ceased to have an affection for him. And it was very natural that she should, for having so few sentiments in common, when the sexual tie was broken, what was to hold her? To hold her affection whose sensibility was confined to one sex; nay, to one man, it requires sense to turn sensibility into the broad channel of humanity; many women have not mind enough to have an affection for a woman, or a friendship for a man. But the sexual weakness that makes woman depend on man for a subsistence, produces a kind of cattish affection which leads a wife to purr about her husband as she would about any man who fed and caressed her.

Men are, however, often gratified by this kind of fondness, which is confined in a beastly manner to themselves; but should they ever become more virtuous, they will wish to converse at their fire-side with a friend, after they cease to play with a mistress.

Besides, understanding is necessary to give variety and interest to sensual enjoyments, for low, indeed, in the intellectual scale, is the mind that can continue to love when neither virtue nor sense give a human appearance to an animal appetite. But sense will always preponderate; and if women are not, in general, brought more on a level with men, some superiour women, like the Greek courtezans, will assemble the men of abilities around them, and draw from their families many citizens, who would have stayed at home

had

had their wives had more fenfe, or the graces which refult from the exercife of the underftanding and fancy, the legitimate parents of tafte. A woman of talents, if fhe be not abfolutely ugly, will always obtain great power, raifed by the weaknefs of her fex ; and in proportion as men acquire virtue and delicacy, by the exertion of reafon, they will look for both in women, but they can only acquire them in the fame way that men do.

In France or Italy, have the women confined themfelves to domeftic life ? though they have not hitherto had a political exiftence, yet, have they not illicitly had great fway ? corrupting themfelves and the men with whofe paffions they played. In fhort, in whatever light I view the fubject, reafon and experience convince me that the only method of leading women to fulfil their peculiar duties, is to free them from all reftraint by allowing them to participate the inherent rights of mankind.

Make them free, and they will quickly become wife and virtuous, as men become more fo; for the improvement muft be mutual, or the injuftice which one half of the human race are obliged to fubmit to, retorting on their oppreffors, the virtue of man will be worm-eaten by the infect whom he keeps under his feet.

Let men take their choice, man and woman were made for each other, though not to become one being ; and if they will not improve women, they will deprave them !

I fpeak of the improvement and emancipation of the whole fex, for I know that the behaviour

of

of a few women, who, by accident, or following
a ftrong bent of nature, have acquired a portion
of knowledge fuperiour to that of the reft of their
fex, has often been overbearing ; but there have
been inftances of women who, attaining knowledge, have not difcarded modefty, nor have they
always pedantically appeared to defpife the ignorance which they laboured to difperfe in their own
minds. The exclamations then which any advice refpecting female learning, commonly produces, efpecially from pretty women, often arife
from envy. When they chance to fee that even
the luftre of their eyes, and the flippant fportivenefs of refined coquetry will not always fecure
them attention, during a whole evening, fhould a
woman of a more cultivated underftanding endeavour to give a rational turn to the converfation, the common fource of confolation is, that
fuch women feldom get hufbands. What arts
have I not feen filly women ufe to interrupt by
flirtation, a very fignificant word to defcribe fuch
a manœuvre, a rational converfation which made
the men forget that they were pretty women.

But, allowing what is very natural to man,
that the poffeffion of rare abilities is really calculated to excite over-weening pride, difgufting in
both men and women—in what a ftate of inferiority muft the female faculties have rufted when
fuch a fmall portion of knowledge as thofe women attained, who have fneeringly been termed
learned women, could be fingular ?—Sufficiently
fo to puff up the poffeffor, and excite envy in her
contemporaries, and fome of the other fex. Nay,
has not a little rationality expofed many women

to the feverest censure ? I advert to well known facts, for I have frequently heard women ridiculed, and every little weakness exposed, only because they adopted the advice of some medical men, and deviated from the beaten track in their mode of treating their infants. I have actually heard this barbarous aversion to innovation carried still further, and a sensible woman stigmatized as an unnatural mother, who has thus been wisely solicitous to preserve the health of her children, when in the midst of her care she has lost one by some of the casualties of infancy, which no prudence can ward off. Her acquaintance have observed, that this was the consequence of new-fangled notions—the new-fangled notions of ease and cleanliness. And those who pretending to experience, though they have long adhered to prejudices that have, according to the opinion of the most sagacious physicians, thinned the human race, almost rejoiced at the disaster that gave a kind of sanction to prescription.

Indeed, if it were only on this account, the national education of women is of the utmost consequence, for what a number of human sacrifices are made to that moloch prejudice ! And in how many ways are children destroyed by the lasciviousness of man ? The want of natural affection, in many women, who are drawn from their duty by the admiration of men, and the ignorance of others, render the infancy of man a much more perilous state than that of brutes ; yet men are unwilling to place women in situations proper to enable them to acquire sufficient understanding to know how even to nurse their babes.

So

So forcibly does this truth strike me, that I would rest the whole tendency of my reasoning upon it, for whatever tends to incapacitate the maternal character, takes woman out of her sphere.

But it is vain to expect the present race of weak mothers either to take that reasonable care of a child's body, which is necessary to lay the foundation of a good constitution, supposing that it do not suffer for the sins of its father; or, to manage its temper so judiciously that the child will not have, as it grows up, to throw off all that its mother, its first instructor, directly or indirectly taught; and unless the mind has uncommon vigour, womanish follies will stick to the character throughout life. The weakness of the mother will be visited on the children! And whilst women are educated to rely on their husbands for judgment, this must ever be the consequence, for there is no improving an understanding by halves, nor can any being act wisely from imitation, because in every circumstance of life there is a kind of individuality, which requires an exertion of judgment to modify general rules. The being who can think justly in one track, will soon extend its intellectual empire; and she who has sufficient judgment to manage her children, will not submit, right or wrong, to her husband, or patiently to the social laws which make a nonentity of a wife.

In public schools women, to guard against the errors of ignorance, should be taught the elements of anatomy and medicine, not only to enable them to take proper care of their own health, but to make them rational nurses of their infants, parents,

ents, and hufbands ; for the bills of mortality are fwelled by the blunders of felf-willed old women, who give noftrums of their own without knowing any thing of the human frame. It is likewife proper, only in a domeftic view, to make women acquainted with the anatomy of the mind, by allowing the fexes to affociate together in every purfuit ; and by leading them to obferve the progrefs of the human underftanding in the improvement of the fciences and arts ; never forgetting the fcience of morality, nor the ftudy of the political hiftory of mankind.

A man has been termed a microcofm ; and every family might alfo be called a ftate. States, it is true, have moftly been governed by arts that difgrace the character of man ; and the want of a juft conftitution, and equal laws, have fo perplexed the notions of the worldly wife, that they more than queftion the reafonablenefs of contending for the rights of humanity. Thus morality, polluted in the national refervoir, fends off ftreams of vice to corrupt the conftituent parts of the body politic ; but fhould more noble, or rather, more juft principles regulate the laws, which ought to be the government of fociety, and not thofe who execute them, duty might become the rule of private conduct.

Befides, by the exercife of their bodies and minds women would acquire that mental activity fo neceffary in the maternal character, united with the fortitude that diftinguifhes fteadinefs of conduct from the obftinate perverfenefs of weaknefs. For it is dangerous to advife the indolent to be fteady, becaufe they inftantly become rigor-

ous,

ous, and to save themselves trouble, punish with severity faults that the patient fortitude of reason might have prevented.

But fortitude presupposes strength of mind ; and is strength of mind to be acquired by indolent acquiescence ? by asking advice instead of exerting the judgment ? by obeying through fear, instead of practising the forbearance, which we all stand in need of ourselves ?—The conclusion which I wish to draw, is obvious ; make women rational creatures, and free citizens, and they will quickly become good wives, and mothers ; that is—if men do not neglect the duties of husbands and fathers.

Discussing the advantages which a public and private education combined, as I have sketched, might rationally be expected to produce, I have dwelt most on such as are particularly relative to the female world, because I think the female world oppressed ; yet the gangrene, which the vices engendered by oppression have produced, is not confined to the morbid part, but pervades society at large : so that when I wish to see my sex become more like moral agents, my heart bounds with the anticipation of the general diffusion of that sublime contentment which only morality can diffuse.

C H A P.

C H A P. XIII.

SOME INSTANCES OF THE FOLLY WHICH
THE IGNORANCE OF WOMEN GENE-
RATES ; WITH CONCLUDING REFLEC-
TIONS ON THE MORAL IMPROVEMENT
THAT A REVOLUTION IN FEMALE MAN-
NERS MIGHT NATURALLY BE EXPECTED
TO PRODUCE.

THERE are many follies, in some degree,
peculiar to women : sins against reason of com-
mission as well as of omission ; but all flowing
from ignorance or prejudice, I shall only point
out such as appear to be particularly injurious to
their moral character.   And in animadverting on
them, I wish especially to prove, that the weakness of mind and body, which men have endeavoured, impelled by various motives, to perpetuate, prevents their discharging the peculiar duty
of their sex : for when weakness of body will not
permit them to suckle their children, and weakness of mind makes them spoil their tempers—is
woman in a natural state ?

S E C T. I.

ONE glaring instance of the weakness which
proceeds from ignorance, first claims attention,
and calls for severe reproof.

In this metropolis a number of lurking leeches
infamously gain a subsistence by practising on the
credulity

credulity of women, pretending to caft nativities, to ufe the technical word; and many females who, proud of their rank and fortune, look down on the vulgar with fovereign contempt, fhew by this credulity, that the diftinction is arbitrary, and that they have not fufficiently cultivated their minds to rife above vulgar prejudices. Women, becaufe they have not been led to confider the knowledge of their duty as the one thing necef-fary to know, or, to live in the prefent moment by the difcharge of it, are very anxious to peep into futurity, to learn what they have to expect to render life interefting, and to break the vacuum of ignorance.

I muft be allowed to expoftulate ferioufly with the ladies who follow thefe idle inventions; for ladies, miftreffes of families, are not afhamed to drive in their own carriages to the door of the cunning man*. And if any of them fhould pe-rufe this work, I entreat them to anfwer to their own hearts the following queftions, not forget-ting that they are in the prefence of God.

Do you believe that there is but one God, and that he is powerful, wife, and good?

Do you believe that all things were created by him, and that all beings are dependent on him?

Do you rely on his wifdom, fo confpicuous in his works, and in your own frame, and are you con-vinced that he has ordered all things which do not come under the cognizance of your fenfes, in the fame perfect harmony, to fulfil his defigns?

Do

---

* I once lived in the neighbourhood of one of thefe men, a *handfome* man, and faw with furprife and indignation, women, whofe appearance and attendance befpoke that rank in which females are fuppofed to receive a fuperiour education, flock to his door.

Do you acknowledge that the power of looking into futurity, and feeing things that are not,
as if they were, is an attribute of the Creator ?
And fhould he, by an impreffion on the minds of
his creatures, think fit to impart to them fome
event hid in the fhades of time yet unborn, to
whom would the fecret be revealed by immediate
infpiration ? The opinion of ages will anfwer this
queftion—to reverend old men, to people diftinguifhed for eminent piety.

The oracles of old were thus delivered by priefts
dedicated to the fervice of the God who was fuppofed to infpire them. The glare of worldly
pomp which furrounded thefe impoftors, and
the refpect paid to them by artful politicians, who
knew how to avail themfelves of this ufeful en-
gine to bend the necks of the ftrong under the
dominion of the cunning, fpread a facred myfterious veil of fanctity over their lies and abomi-
nations. Impreffed by fuch folemn devotional
parade, a Greek, or Roman lady might be ex-
cufed, if fhe enquired of the oracle, when fhe was
anxious to pry into futurity, or enquire about
fome dubious event : and her enquiries, however
contrary to reafon, could not be reckoned impious.—But, can the profeffors of Chriftianity ward
off that imputation ? Can a Chriftian fuppofe that
the favourites of the moft High, the highly fa-
voured, would be obliged to lurk in difguife, and
practife the moft difhoneft tricks to cheat filly
women out of the money—which the poor cry
for in vain ?

Say not that fuch queftions are an infult to
common fenfe—for it is your own conduct, O ye
foolifh

foolish women! which throws an odium on your sex! And these reflections should make you shudder at your thoughtlessness, and irrational devotion.—For I do not suppose that all of you laid aside your religion, such as it is, when you entered those mysterious dwellings. Yet, as I have throughout supposed myself talking to ignorant women, for ignorant ye are in the most emphatical sense of the word, it would be absurd to reason with you on the egregious folly of desiring to know what the Supreme Wisdom has concealed.

Probably you would not understand me, were I to attempt to shew you that it would be absolutely inconsistent with the grand purpose of life, that of rendering human creatures wise and virtuous : and that, were it sanctioned by God, it would disturb the order established in creation ; and if it be not sanctioned by God, do you expect to hear truth ? Can events be foretold, events which have not yet assumed a body to become subject to mortal inspection, can they be foreseen by a vicious worldling, who pampers his appetites by preying on the foolish ones ?

Perhaps, however, you devoutly believe in the devil, and imagine, to shift the question, that he may assist his votaries ; but, if really respecting the power of such a being, an enemy to goodness and to God, can you go to church after having been under such an obligation to him ?

From these delusions to those still more fashionable deceptions, practised by the whole tribe of magnetisers, the transition is very natural. With respect to them, it is equally proper to ask women a few questions.

Do

Do you know any thing of the conſtruction of the human frame ? If not, it is proper that you ſhould be told what every child ought to know, that when its admirable economy has been diſturbed by intemperance or indolence, I ſpeak not of violent diſorders, but of chronical diſeaſes, it muſt be brought into a healthy ſtate again, by ſlow degrees, and if the functions of life have not been materially injured, regimen, another word for temperance, air, exerciſe, and a few medicines preſcribed by perſons who have ſtudied the human body, are the only human means, yet diſcovered, of recovering that ineſtimable bleſſing, health, that will bear inveſtigation.

Do you then believe that theſe magnetiſers, who, by hocus pocus tricks, pretend to work a miracle, are delegated by God, or aſſiſted by the ſolver of all theſe kinds of difficulties—the devil.

Do they, when they put to flight, as it is ſaid, diſorders that have baffled the powers of medicine, work in conformity to the light of reaſon ? or, do they effect theſe wonderful cures by ſupernatural aid ?

By a communication, an adept may anſwer, with the world of ſpirits. A noble privilege, it muſt be allowed. Some of the ancients mention familiar dæmons, who guarded them from danger by kindly intimating, we cannot gueſs in what manner, when any danger was nigh ; or, pointed out what they ought to undertake. Yet the men who laid claim to this privilege, out of the order of nature, inſiſted that it was the reward, or conſequence, of ſuperiour temperance and piety. But the preſent workers of wonders

are

are not raifed above their fellows by fuperiour temperance or fanctity.   They do not cure for the love of God, but money.   Thefe are the priefts of quackery, though it be true they have not the convenient expedient of felling maffes for fouls in purgatory, nor churches where they can difplay crutches, and models of limbs made found by a touch or a word.

I am not converfant with the technical terms, nor initiated into the arcana, therefore, I may fpeak improperly ; but it is clear that men who will not conform to the law of reafon, and earn a fubfiftence in an honeft way, by degrees, are very fortunate in becoming acquainted with fuch obliging fpirits.   We cannot, indeed, give them credit for either great fagacity or goodnefs, elfe they would have chofen more noble inftruments, when they wifhed to fhew themfelves the benevolent friends of man.

It is, however, little fhort of blafphemy to pretend to fuch powers !

From the whole tenor of the difpenfations of Providence, it appears evident to fober reafon, that certain vices produce certain effects ; and can any one fo grofsly infult the wifdom of God, as to fuppofe that a miracle will be allowed to difturb his general laws, to reftore to health the intemperate and vicious, merely to enable them to purfue the fame courfe with impunity? Be whole, and fin no more, faid Jefus.   And, are greater miracles to be performed by thofe who do not follow his footfteps, who healed the body to reach the mind ?

The

The mentioning of the name of Chrift, after
fuch vile impoftors, may difpleafe fome of my
readers—I refpect their warmth ; but let them
not forget that the followers of thefe delufions
bear his name, and profefs to be the difciples of
him, who faid, by their works we fhould know
who were the children of God or the fervants of
fin.   I allow that it is eafier to touch the body of
a faint, or to be magnetifed, than to reftrain our
appetites or govern our paffions ; but health of
body or mind can only be recovered by thefe
means, or we make the Supreme Judge partial
and revengeful.

Is he a man that he fhould change, or punifh
out of refentment ? He—the common father,
wounds but to heal, fays reafon, and our irregularities producing certain confequences, we are
forcibly fhewn the nature of vice; that thus learning to know good from evil, by experience, we
may hate one and love the other, in proportion
to the wifdom which we attain.   The poifon
contains the antidote ; and we either reform our
evil habits and ceafe to fin againft our own bodies, to ufe the forcible language of fcripture, or
a premature death, the punifhment of fin, fnaps
the thread of life.

Here an awful ftop is put to our enquiries.—
But, why fhould I conceal my fentiments ? Confidering the attributes of God, I believe that
whatever punifhment may follow, will tend,
like the anguifh of difeafe, to fhew the malignity
of vice, for the purpofe of reformation.   Pofi-
tive punifhment appears fo contrary to the nature
of God, difcoverable in all his works, and in our

own

own reafon, that I could fooner believe that the Deity paid no attention to the conduct of men, than that he punifhed without the benevolent defign of reforming.

To fuppofe only that an all-wife and powerful Being, as good as he is great, fhould create a being forefeeing, that after fifty or fixty years of feverifh exiftence, it would be plunged into never ending woe—is blafphemy. On what will the worm feed that is never to die ?—On folly, on ignorance, fay ye—I fhould blufh indignantly at drawing the natural conclufion, could I infert it, and wifh to withdraw myfelf from the wing of my God !—On fuch a fuppofition, I fpeak with reverence, he would be a confuming fire. We fhould wifh, though vainly, to fly from his prefence when fear abforbed love, and darknefs involved all his counfels !

I know that many devout people boaft of fubmitting to the Will of God blindly, as to an arbitrary fceptre or rod, on the fame principle as the Indians worfhip the devil. In other words, like people in the common concerns of life, they do homage to power, and cringe under the foot that can crufh them. Rational religion, on the contrary, is a fubmiffion to the will of a being fo perfectly wife, that all he wills muft be directed by the proper motive—muft be reafonable.

And, if thus we refpect God, can we give credit to the myfterious infinuations, which infult his laws ? can we believe, though it fhould ftare us in the face, that he would work a miracle to authorife confufion by fanctioning an error ? Yet we muft either allow thefe impious conclufions, or,

or treat with contempt every promise to restore
health to a diseased body by supernatural means,
or to foretell the incidents that can only be foreseen by God.

SECT. II.

ANOTHER instance of that feminine weakness
of character, often produced by a confined education, is a romantic twist of the mind, which has
been very properly termed *sentimental*.

Women subjected by ignorance to their sensations, and only taught to look for happiness in
love, refine on sensual feelings, and adopt meta-
physical notions respecting that passion, which
lead them shamefully to neglect the duties of
life, and frequently in the midst of these sublime
refinements they plump into actual vice.

These are the women who are amused by the
reveries of the stupid novelists, who, knowing little
of human nature, work up stale tales, and describe
meretricious scenes, all retailed in a sentimental
jargon, which equally tend to corrupt the taste,
and draw the heart aside from its daily duties. I
do not mention the understanding, because never
having been exercised, its slumbering energies rest
inactive, like the lurking particles of fire which
are supposed universally to pervade matter.

Females, in fact, denied all political privileges,
and not allowed, as married women, excepting in
criminal cases, a civil existence, have their attention naturally drawn from the interest of the whole
community to that of the minute parts, though
the private duty of any member of society must

be very imperfectly performed when not connected with the general good.   The mighty bufinefs of female life is to pleafe, and reftrained from
entering into more important concerns by political and civil oppreffion, fentiments become
events, and reflection deepens what it fhould, and
would have effaced, if the underftanding had been
allowed to take a wider range.

But, confined to trifling employments, they
naturally imbibe opinions which the only kind
of reading calculated to intereft an innocent frivolous mind, infpires. Unable to grafp any thing
great, is it furprifing that they find the reading
of hiftory a very dry tafk, and difquifitions addreffed to the underftanding intollerably tedious,
and almoft unintelligible ? Thus are they neceffarily dependent on the novelift for amufement.
Yet, when I exclaim againft novels, I mean when
contrafted with thofe works which exercife the
underftanding and regulate the imagination.——
For any kind of reading I think better than leaving a blank ftill a blank, becaufe the mind muft
receive a degree of enlargement and obtain a little ftrength by a flight exertion of its thinking
powers ; befides even the productions that are
only addreffed to the imagination, raife the reader a little above the grofs gratification of appetites, to which the mind has not given a fhade of
delicacy.

This obfervation is the refult of experience ;
for I have known feveral notable women, and one
in particular, who was a very good woman——as
good as fuch a narrow mind would allow her to
be, who took care that her daughters (three in
                                               number)

number) fhould never fee a novel. As fhe was a woman of fortune and fafhion, they had various mafters to attend them, and a fort of menial governefs to watch their footfteps. From their mafters they learned how tables, chairs, &c. were called in French and Italian; but as the few books thrown in their way were far above their capacities, or devotional, they neither acquired ideas nor fentiments, and paffed their time when not compelled to repeat *words*, in dreffing, quarrelling with each other, or converfing with their maids by ftealth, till they were brought into company as marriageable.

Their mother, a widow, was bufy in the mean time in keeping up her connections, as fhe termed a numerous acquaintance, left her girls fhould want a proper introduction into the great world. And thefe young ladies, with minds vulgar in every fenfe of the word, and fpoiled tempers, entered life puffed up with notions of their own confequence, and looking down with contempt on thofe who could not vie with them in drefs and parade.

With refpect to love, nature, or their nurfes, had taken care to teach them the phyfical meaning of the word; and, as they had few topics of converfation, and fewer refinements of fentiment, they expreffed their grofs wifhes not in very delicate phrafes, when they fpoke freely, talking of matrimony.

Could thefe girls have been injured by the perufal of novels? I almoft forgot a fhade in the character of one of them; fhe affected a fimplicity bordering on folly, and with a fimper would

W 2 utter

utter the moſt immodeſt remarks and queſtions, the full meaning of which ſhe had learned whilſt ſecluded from the world, and afraid to ſpeak in her mother's preſence, who governed with a high hand : they were all educated, as ſhe prided herſelf, in a moſt exemplary manner ; and read their chapters and pſalms before breakfaſt, never touching a ſilly novel.

This is only one inſtance ; but I recollect many other women who, not led by degrees to proper ſtudies, and not permitted to chooſe for themſelves, have indeed been overgrown children ; or have obtained, by mixing in the world, a little of what is termed common ſenſe ; that is a diſtinct manner of ſeeing common occurrences, as they ſtand detached : but what deſerves the name of intellect, the power of gaining general or abſtract ideas, or even intermediate ones, was out of the queſtion. Their minds were quieſcent, and when they were not rouſed by ſenſible objects and employments of that kind, they were low-ſpirited, would cry, or go to ſleep.

When, therefore, I adviſe my ſex not to read ſuch flimſy works, it is to induce them to read ſomething ſuperiour ; for I coincide in opinion with a ſagacious man, who, having a daughter and niece under his care, purſued a very different plan with each.

The niece, who had conſiderable abilities, had, before ſhe was left to his guardianſhip, been indulged in deſultory reading. Her he endeavoured to lead, and did lead to hiſtory and moral eſſays ; but his daughter, whom a fond, weak mother had indulged, and who conſequently was

averſe

averfe to every thing like application, he allowed to read novels : and ufed to juftify his conduct by faying, that if fhe ever attained a relifh for reading them, he fhould have fome foundation to work upon ; and that erroneous opinions were better than none at all.

In fact the female mind has been fo totally neglected, that knowledge was only to be acquired from this muddy fource, till from reading novels fome women of fuperiour talents learned to defpife them.

The beft method, I believe, that can be adopted to correct a fondnefs for novels is to ridicule them ; not indifcriminately, for then it would have little effect ; but, if a judicious perfon, with fome turn for humour, would read feveral to a young girl, and point out both by tones, and apt comparifons with pathetic incidents and heroic characters in hiftory, how foolifhly and ridiculoufly they caricatured human nature, juft opinions might be fubftituted inftead of romantic fentiments.

In one refpect, however, the majority of both fexes refemble, and equally fhew a want of tafte and modefty. Ignorant women, forced to be chafte to preferve their reputation, allow their imagination to revel in the unnatural and meretricious fcenes fketched by the novel writers of the day, flighting as infipid the fober dignity and matronly graces of hiftory*, whilft men carry

W 3

the

---

* I am not now alluding to that fuperiority of mind which leads to the creation of ideal beauty, when life, furveyed with a penetrating eye, appears a tragi-comedy, in which little can be feen to fatisfy the heart without the help of fancy.

the fame vitiated tafte into life, and fly for amufement to the wanton, from the unfophifticated
charms of virtue, and the grave refpectability of
fenfe.

Befides, the reading of novels makes women,
and particularly ladies of fafhion, very fond of
ufing ftrong expreffions and furperlatives in converfation; and though the diffipated artificial
life which they lead prevents their cherifhing any
ftrong legitimate paffion, the language of paffion
in affected tones flips forever from their glib
tongues, and every trifle produces thofe phofpho-
ric burfts which only mimick in the dark the
flame of paffion.

S E C T. III.

IGNORANCE and the miftaken cunning that
nature fharpens in weak heads as a principle of
felf-prefervation, render women very fond of
drefs, and produce all the vanity which fuch a
fondnefs may naturally be expected to generate,
to the exclufion of emulation and magnanimity.

I agree with Rouffeau that the phyfical part of
the art of pleafing confifts in ornaments, and for
that very reafon I fhould guard girls againft the
contagious fondnefs for drefs fo common to
weak women, that they may not reft in the phyfical part. Yet, weak are the women who imagine that they can long pleafe without the aid of
the mind, or, in other words, without the moral
art of pleafing. But the moral art, if it be not a
profanation to ufe the word art, when alluding to
the grace which is an effect of virtue, and not
the

the motive of action, is never to be found with ignorance ; the fportivenefs of innocence, fo pleafing to refined libertines of both fexes, is widely different in its effence from this fuperiour gracefulnefs.

A ftrong inclination for external ornaments ever appears in barbarous ftates, only the men not the women adorn themfelves ; for where women are allowed to be fo far on a level with men, fociety has advanced, at leaft, one ftep in civilization.

The attention to drefs, therefore, which has been thought a fexual propenfity, I think natural to mankind. But I ought to exprefs myfelf with more precifion. When the mind is not fufficiently opened to take pleafure in reflection, the body will be adorned with fedulous care ; and ambition will appear in tattooing or painting it.

So far is the firft inclination carried, that even the hellifh yoke of flavery cannot ftifle the favage defire of admiration which the black heroes inherit from both their parents, for all the hardly earned favings of a flave are commonly expended in a little tawdry finery. And I have feldom known a good male or female fervant that was not particularly fond of drefs. Their clothes were their riches ; and, I argue from analogy, that the fondnefs for drefs, fo extravagant in females, arifes from the fame caufe—want of cultivation of mind. When men meet they converfe about bufinefs, politics, or literature ; but, fays Swift, ' how naturally do women apply their ' hands to each others lappets and ruffles.' And very natural is it—for they have not any bufinefs

to

to intereſt them, have not a taſte for literature, and they find politics dry, becauſe they have not acquired a love for mankind by turning their thoughts to the grand purſuits that exalt the human race, and promote general happineſs.

Beſides, various are the paths to power and fame which by accident or choice men purſue, and though they joſtle againſt each other, for men of the ſame profeſſion are ſeldom friends, yet there is a much greater number of their fellow-crea-tures with whom they never claſh. But women are very differently ſituated with reſpect to each other—for they are all rivals.

Before marriage it is their buſineſs to pleaſe men ; and after, with a few exceptions, they fol-low the ſame ſcent with all the perſevering per-tinacity of inſtinct. Even virtuous women never forget their ſex in company, for they are forever try-ing to make themſelves *agreeable*. A female beau-ty, and a male wit appear to be equally anxious to draw the attention of the company to themſelves ; and the animoſity of contemporary wits is pro-verbial.

Is it then ſurpriſing that when the ſole ambition of woman centres in beauty, and intereſt gives vanity additional force, perpetual rivalſhips ſhould enſue ? They are all running the ſame race, and would riſe above the virtue of mortals, if they did not view each other with a ſuſpicious and even en-vious eye.

An immoderate fondneſs for dreſs, for pleaſure, and for ſway, are the paſſions of ſavages ; the paſ-ſions that occupy thoſe uncivilized beings who have not yet extended the dominion of the mind, or even learned to think with the energy neceſſary

to

to concatenate that abstract train of thought which produces principles. And that women from their education and the present state of civilized life, are in the same condition, cannot, I think, be controverted. To laugh at them then, or satirize the follies of a being who is never to be allowed to act freely from the light of her own reason, is as absurd as cruel ; for, that they who are taught blindly to obey authority, will endeavour cunningly to elude it, is most natural and certain.

Yet let it be proved that they ought to obey man implicitly, and I shall immediately agree that it is woman's duty to cultivate a fondness for dress, and in order to please, and a propensity to cunning for her own preservation.

The virtues, however, which are supported by ignorance, must ever be wavering—the house built on sand could not endure a storm. It is almost unnecessary to draw the inference.—If women are to be made virtuous by authority, which is a contradiction in terms, let them be immured in seraglios and watched with a jealous eye.—Fear not that the iron will enter into their souls—for the souls that can bear such treatment are made of yielding materials, just animated enough to give life to the body.

> ' Matter too soft a lasting mark to bear,
> ' And best distinguish'd by black, brown, or fair.'

The most cruel wounds will of course soon heal, and they may still people the world, and dress to please man—all the purposes which certain celebrated writers have allowed that they were created to fulfil.

SECT.

SECT. IV.

WOMEN are supposed to possess more sensibility, and even humanity, than men, and their strong attachments and instantaneous emotions of compassion are given as proofs ; but the clinging affection of ignorance has seldom any thing noble in it, and may mostly be resolved into selfishness, as well as the affection of children and brutes. I have known many weak women whose sensibility was entirely engrossed by their husbands ; and as for their humanity, it was very faint indeed, or rather it was only a transient emotion of compassion. Humanity does not consist ' in a squeam-' ish ear,' says an eminent orator. ' It belongs ' to the mind as well as the nerves.'

But this kind of exclusive affection, though it degrades the individual, should not be brought forward as a proof of the inferiority of the sex, because it is the natural consequence of confined views : for even women of superiour sense, having their attention turned to little employments, and private plans, rarely rise to heroism, unless when spurred on by love ; and love, as an heroic passion, like genius, appears but once in an age. I therefore agree with the moralist who asserts, ' that women have seldom so much generosity as ' men ;' and that their narrow affections, to which justice and humanity are often sacrificed, render the sex apparently inferiour, especially, as they are commonly inspired by men ; but I contend that the heart would expand as the understanding gained strength, if women were not depressed from their cradles.

I

I know that a little fenfibility, and great weaknefs, will produce a ftrong fexual attachment, and that reafon muft cement friendfhip ; confequently, I allow that more friendfhip is to be found in the male than the female world, and that men have a higher fenfe of juftice. The exclufive affections of women feem indeed to refemble Cato's moft unjuft love for his country. He wifhed to crufh Carthage, not to fave Rome, but to promote its vain-glory ; and, in general, it is to fimilar principles that humanity is facrificed, for genuine duties fupport each other.

Befides, how can women be juft or generous, when they are the flaves of injuftice ?

SECT. V.

As the rearing of children, that is, the laying a foundation of found health both of body and mind in the rifing generation, has juftly been infifted on as the peculiar deftination of woman, the ignorance that incapacites them muft be contrary to the order of things. And I contend that their minds can take in much more, and ought to do fo, or they will never become fenfible mothers. Many men attend to the breeding of horfes, and overlook the management of the ftable, who would, ftrange want of fenfe and feeling ! think themfelves degraded by paying any attention to the nurfery ; yet, how many children are abfolutely murdered by the ignorance of women ! But when they efcape, and are neither deftroyed by unnatural negligence nor blind fondnefs, how few are managed properly with refpect to the in-

fant

fant mind ! So that to break the spirit, allowed to become vicious at home, a child is sent to school ; and the methods taken there, which must be taken to keep a number of children in order, scatter the seeds of almost every vice in the soil thus forcibly torn up.

I have sometimes compared the struggles of these poor children who ought never to have felt restraint, nor would, had they been always held in with an even hand, to the despairing plunges of a spirited filly, which I have seen breaking on a strand : its feet sinking deeper and deeper in the sand every time it endeavoured to throw its rider, till at last it sullenly submitted.

I have always found horses, an animal I am attached to, very tractable when treated with humanity and steadiness, so that I doubt whether the violent methods taken to break them, do not essentially injure them ; I am, however, certain that a child should never be thus forcibly tamed after it has injudiciously been allowed to run wild ; for every violation of justice and reason, in the treatment of children, weakens their reason. And, so early do they catch a character, that the base of the moral character, experience leads me to infer, is fixed before their seventh year, the period during which women are allowed the sole management of children. Afterwards it too often happens that half the business of education is to correct, and very imperfectly is it done, if done hastily, the faults, which they would never have acquired if their mothers had had more understanding.

One

One striking instance of the folly of women must not be omitted.—The manner in which they treat servants in the presence of children, permitting them to suppose that they ought to wait on them, and bear their humours. A child should always be made to receive assistance from a man or woman as a favour ; and, as the first lesson of independence, they should practically be taught, by the example of their mother, not to require that personal attendance, which it is an insult to humanity to require, when in health ; and instead of being led to assume airs of consequence, a sense of their own weakness should first make them feel the natural equality of man. Yet, how frequently have I indignantly heard servants imperiously called to put children to bed, and sent away again and again, because master or miss hung about mamma, to stay a little longer. Thus made slavishly to attend the little idol, all those most disgusting humours were exhibited which characterize a spoiled child.

In short, speaking of the majority of mothers, they leave their children entirely to the care of servants ; or, because they are their children treat them as if they were little demi-gods, though I have always observed, that the women who thus idolize their children, seldom shew common humanity to servants, or feel the least tenderness for any children but their own.

It is, however, these exclusive affections, and an individual manner of seeing things produced by ignorance, which keep women for ever at a stand, with respect to improvement, and make many of them dedicate their lives to their chil-

dren

dren only to weaken their bodies and spoil their tempers, fruftrating alfo any plan of education that a more rational father may adopt ; for unlefs a mother concurs, the father who reftrains will ever be confidered as a tyrant.

But, fulfilling the duties of a mother, a woman with a found conftitution, may ftill keep her perfon fcrupuloufly neat, and affift to maintain her family, if neceffary, or by reading and converfations with both fexes, indifcriminately, improve her mind. For nature has fo wifely ordered things, that did women fuckle their children, they would preferve their own health, and there would be fuch an interval between the birth of each child, that we fhould feldom fee a houfeful of babes. And did they purfue a plan of conduct, and not wafte their time in following the fafhionable vagaries of drefs, the management of their houfehold and children need not fhut them out from literature, nor prevent their attaching themfelves to a fcience with that fteady eye which ftrengthens the mind, or practifing one of the fine arts that cultivate the tafte.

But, vifiting to difplay finery, card-playing, and balls, not to mention the idle buftle of morning trifling, draw women from their duty to render them infignificant, to render them pleafing, according to the prefent acceptation of the word, to every man, but their hufband. For a round of pleafures in which the affections are not exercifed, cannot be faid to improve the underftanding, though it be erroneoully called feeing the world ; yet the heart is rendered cold and averfe to duty, by fuch a fenfelefs intercourfe, which becomes

neceffary

neceſſary from habit even when it has ceaſed to
amuſe.

But, till more equality be eſtabliſhed in ſociety,
till ranks are confounded and women freed, we
ſhall not ſee that dignified domeſtic happineſs,
the ſimple grandeur of which cannot be reliſhed
by ignorant or vitiated minds ; nor will the important taſk of education ever be properly begun
till the perſon of a woman is no longer preferred
to her mind. For it would be as wiſe to expect
corn from tares, or figs from thiſtles, as that a
fooliſh ignorant woman ſhould be a good mother.

S E C T. VI.

IT is not neceſſary to inform the ſagacious
reader, now I enter on my concluding reflections,
that the diſcuſſion of this ſubject merely conſiſts
in opening a few ſimple principles, and clearing
away the rubbiſh which obſcured them. But, as
all readers are not ſagacious, I muſt be allowed to
add ſome explanatory remarks to bring the ſubject
home to reaſon—to that ſluggiſh reaſon, which
ſupinely takes opinions on truſt, and obſtinately
ſupports them to ſpare itſelf the labour of thinking.

Moraliſts have unanimouſly agreed, that unleſs virtue be nurſed by liberty, it will never attain due ſtrength—and what they ſay of man I
extend to mankind, inſiſting that in all caſes morals muſt be fixed on immutable principles ; and,
that the being cannot be termed rational or virtuous, who obeys any authority, but that of reaſon. To

To render women truly useful members of society, I argue that they should be led, by having their understandings cultivated on a large scale, to acquire a rational affection for their country, founded on knowledge, because it is obvious that we are little interested about what we do not understand. And to render this general knowledge of due importance, I have endeavoured to shew that private duties are never properly fulfilled unless the understanding enlarges the heart; and that public virtue is only an aggregate of private. But, the distinctions established in society undermine both, by beating out the solid gold of virtue, till it becomes only the tinsel-covering of vice; for whilst wealth renders a man more respectable than virtue, wealth will be sought before virtue; and whilst women's persons are caressed, when a childish simper shews an absence of mind—the mind will lie fallow. Yet, true voluptuousness must proceed from the mind—for what can equal the sensations produced by mutual affection, supported by mutual respect? What are the cold, or feverish caresses of appetite, but sin embracing death, compared with the modest overflowings of a pure heart and exalted imagination? Yes, let me tell the libertine of fancy when he despises understanding in woman—that the mind, which he disregards, gives life to the enthusiastic affection from which rapture, short-lived as it is, alone can flow! And, that, without virtue, a sexual attachment must expire, like a tallow candle in the socket, creating intolerable disgust. To prove this, I need only observe, that men who have wasted great part of their lives

lives with women, and with whom they have
fought for pleasure with eager thirst, entertain the
meaneft opinion of the fex.—Virtue, true refiner
of joy !—if foolifh men were to fright thee from
earth, in order to give loofe to all their appetites
without a check—fome fenfual wight of tafte
would fcale the heavens to invite thee back, to
give a zeft to pleafure !

That women at prefent are by ignorance rendered foolifh or vicious, is, I think, not to be
difputed ; and, that the moft falutary effects tend-
ing to improve mankind might be expected
from a REVOLUTION in female manners, appears, at leaft, with a face of probability, to rife
out of the obfervation. For as marriage has
been termed the parent of thofe endearing charities which draw man from the brutal herd, the corrupting intercourfe that wealth, idlenefs, and folly, produce between the fexes, is more univerfally
injurious to morality than all the other vices of
mankind collectively confidered. To adulterous
luft the moft facred duties are facrificed, becaufe before marriage, men, by a promifcuous
intimacy with women, learned to confider love
as a felfifh gratification—learned to feparate it
not only from efteem but from the affection
merely built on habit, which mixes a little humanity with it. Juftice and friendfhip are alfo
fet at defiance, and that purity of tafte is vitiated
which would naturally lead a man to relifh an art-
lefs difplay of affection rather than affected airs.
But that noble fimplicity of affection, which dares
to appear unadorned, has few attractions for the libertine, though it be the charm, which by cement-

X

ing

ing the matrimonial tie, secures to the pledges of
a warmer paſſion the neceſſary parental attention;
for children will never be properly educated till
friendſhip ſubſiſts between parents. Virtue flies
from a houſe divided againſt itſelf—and a whole
legion of devils take up their reſidence there.

The affection of huſbands and wives cannot
be pure when they have ſo few ſentiments in
common, and when ſo little confidence is eſtabliſhed at home, as muſt be the caſe when their purſuits are ſo different. That intimacy from which
tenderneſs ſhould flow, will not, cannot ſubſiſt
between the vicious.

Contending, therefore, that the ſexual diſtinction which men have ſo warmly inſiſted
upon, is arbitrary, I have dwelt on an obſervation, that ſeveral ſenſible men, with whom I
have converſed on the ſubject, allowed to be well
founded; and it is ſimply this, that the little
chaſtity to be found amongſt men, and conſe-
quent diſregard of modeſty, tend to degrade both
ſexes; and further, that the modeſty of women,
characterized as ſuch, will often be only the artful veil of wantonneſs inſtead of being the natural reflection of purity, till modeſty be univerſally
reſpected.

From the tyranny of man, I firmly believe, the
greater number of female follies proceed; and
the cunning, which I allow makes at preſent a part of their character, I likewiſe have repeatedly endeavoured to prove, is produced by oppreſſion.

Were not diſſenters, for inſtance, a claſs of
people, with ſtrict truth characterized as cunning?

ning ? And may I not lay fome ftrefs on this fact to prove, that when any power but reafon curbs the free fpirit of man, diffimulation is practifed, and the various fhifts of art are naturally called forth ? Great attention to decorum, which was carried to a degree of fcrupulofity, and all that puerile buftle about trifles and confequential folemnity, which Butler's caricature of a diffenter, brings before the imagination, fhaped their perfons as well as their minds in the mould of prim littlenefs. I fpeak collectively, for I know how many ornaments to human nature have been enrolled amongft fectaries ; yet, I affert, that the fame narrow prejudice for their fect, which women have for their families, prevailed in the diffenting part of the community, however worthy in other refpects ; and alfo that the fame timid prudence, or headftrong efforts, often difgraced the exertions of both. Oppreffion thus formed many of the features of their character perfectly to coincide with that of the oppreffed half of mankind ; for is it not notorious that diffenters were, like women, fond of deliberating together, and afking advice of each other, till by a complication of little contrivances, fome little end was brought about ? A fimilar attention to preferve their reputation was confpicuous in the diffenting and female world, and was produced by a fimilar caufe.

Afferting the rights which women in common with men ought to contend for, I have not attempted to extenuate their faults ; but to prove them to be the natural confequence of their education and ftation in fociety. If fo, it is reafonable

able to suppose that they will change their character, and correct their vices and follies, when they are allowed to be free in a physical, moral, and civil sense*.

Let woman share the rights and she will emulate the virtues of man ; for she must grow more perfect when emancipated, or justify the authority that chains such a weak being to her duty.—If the latter, it will be expedient to open a fresh trade with Russia for whips ; a present which a father should always make to his son-in-law on his wedding day, that a husband may keep his whole family in order by the same means ; and without any violation of justice reign, wielding this sceptre, sole master of his house, because he is the only being in it who has reason :—the divine, indefeasible earthly sovereignty breathed into man by the Master of the universe. Allowing this position, women have not any inherent rights to claim, and by the same rule, their duties vanish, for rights and duties are inseparable.

Be just then, O ye men of understanding ! and mark not more severely what women do amiss, than the vicious tricks of the horse or the ass for whom ye provide provender—and allow her the privileges of ignorance, to whom ye deny the rights of reason, or ye will be worse than Egyptian task-masters, expecting virtue where nature has not given understanding !

* I had further enlarged on the advantages which might reasonably be expected to result from an improvement in female manners, towards the general reformation of society ; but it appeared to me that such reflections would more properly close the last volume.